THE RULER OF BARODA

THE RULER OF BARODA

AN ACCOUNT OF THE LIFE AND WORK OF THE MAHARAJA GAEKWAR

PHILIP W. SERGEANT

GYAN

Published by

GYAN

Gyan Publishing House
5, Ansari Road
Daryaganj, New Delhi-110002
Phone: 011-47034999, 9811692060
E-mail: books@gyanbooks.com

Distribution Network
gyanbooks.com
India, USA, Canada, UK, Australia

ISBN: 978-93-7447-062-6 (PB)

First Published, 1928

2nd Impression 2025

Printed at: Gyan Press, Delhi.

THE RULER OF BARODA
Author: PHILIP W. SERGEANT

H.H. Sayajirao Gaekwar III.
Maharaja of Baroda.

From a picture by Solomon J. Solomon R.A.

THE RULER OF BARODA

AN ACCOUNT OF THE LIFE AND WORK OF THE MAHARAJA GAEKWAR

BY PHILIP W. SERGEANT, B.A.

LONDON
JOHN MURRAY, ALBEMARLE STREET, W. 1
1928

RAILWAY WORKSHOPS, GOYA GATE, JANUARY 1ST, 1922.

PREFACE

GIFTED by Nature with a remarkable power of brain and a very strong will; deprived by circumstances of education of any kind up to his twelfth year; lifted, entirely beyond expectation, from the life of a peasant boy to a throne and great riches; thereafter subjected to a course of intensive culture which would have given most boys a profound distaste for study, but which left him with a sense of his deficiencies and a determination to make them good; invested with full powers, within the limits imposed by his position as a native ruler in India, at the age of eighteen, and called upon, without the aid of anyone on whom he might look as a friend and companion, to exercise those powers—His Highness Maharaja Sayajirao III. was marked out for a human experiment of the highest interest.

Apart from the question of what his personality might effect, the odds were that the experiment would fail. Tradition was against success; the traditions of a parvenu, the traditions of Baroda. Wealth and an autocratic position, coupled with freedom from outside dangers, offered the young Prince the opportunity to pass a life of ease, extravagance and dissipation, like so many of the distant kinsmen who had preceded him on the throne of Baroda, like so many more of the Indian Rajas his neighbours.

But Sayajirao III. flouted tradition. He put aside resolutely the temptation to follow the easy road, and from the beginning of his actual rule kept his steps, undeviating, to the path of duty toward his State. From this path he has never since strayed. Handicapped by attacks of ill-health and many domestic sorrows, he has fixed his eyes on the goal for forty-five years, overcoming obstacles by steady persistency and ever searching for new ideas which will help him to the attainment of his desire. His illnesses he has even turned to profit; for, compelled to look for the remedy in foreign travel, he has made foreign travel the means of his own higher education. He has proved, indeed, his favourite contention that travel is the highest form of education; and characteristically he has given the opportunity to others to prove it, with a view to fitting them for the task of helping him in the administration of Baroda.

He has his reward in the affection of his subjects, the admiration of educated and discerning Indians, and even some measure of appreciation from the rest of the world, not apt to give much attention to the rulers of Indian States. He has not lacked detractors; a sure sign that a man has tried to accomplish something in his life. He has passed through storms at home and abroad. But injustice has left him, if not untouched, at least unfaltering. A will like his does not bow to accidents. He has lived down the unfair criticisms, the unwarranted interpretations, the ill-informed condemnations, and the intentional malice, and now perhaps, after fifty years of reign, will be permitted to enjoy the prize which he has so deserved.

An obvious comment on his achievement is that it is on a very small scale, that he is only the ruler of a territory of 8,000 square miles, of a people 2,000,000 in number, of a puppet State. How would he have done if he had a large kingdom, many millions of subjects, an absolutely independent authority? But such belittlement of what he has done would be absurd. The value of an experiment does not depend on its size. Great tests can be made even under the microscope. His Highness has taken the material which was to hand, and within its bounds has striven to prove his understanding of the duties of the governor to the governed. He has felt himself that his sphere is small; but feels also that on a larger scale his opportunities would have been greater, not less. The testimony of history is on his side.

If, however, the limits of Baroda have cramped its Maharaja's scope, they have not prevented him from setting an example worthy to be followed far beyond the frontiers of his State.

"Whatsoever the noble man do, that same the other folk do; whatever he make his standard, that the world obeys."*

But, alas! Shri Krishna's words are too seldom illustrated in the life of today.

* *Bhagavad-Gita* (L. D. Barnett's translation).

ACKNOWLEDGMENTS

I DESIRE to express my thanks for assistance in the preparation of this book, in the first place, to His Highness the Maharaja Saheb himself, who not only gave orders that all material which I might want should be placed at my disposal, but also invited me to spend the winter of 1925–6 with him in Baroda. There, as well as on the two voyages between Marseilles and Bombay, and subsequently in London and in Paris, he submitted with the utmost patience to my questions as to his actions and motives, and answered all with a frankness for which I had scarcely dared to hope.

Secondly, I would thank for their always ready help Sir Manubhai Mehta, at the time of my visit Dewan of Baroda; Mr. C. N. Seddon, a former Dewan; Mr. N. K. Dikshit, Educational Commissioner; Mr. M. B. Nanavati, Director of Commerce and Industries; Mr. S. V. Mukerjea, Subha of Baroda District; Mr. S. G. Burrow, Principal of Baroda College; Mr. C. H. Vora, Principal of the Kalabhavan; Mr. N. M. Dutt, Curator of the Central Library; Mr. A. T. Houldcroft, Engineer-in-Chief of the Railway Department; and Messrs. G. A. Lele and V. Wakaskar, both of whom did me the greatest service by abridged translations from Marathi documents.*

* The "Huzur Orders" and the "Life of His Highness," from which numerous quotations appear in the following pages.

There are many other names which I might, indeed ought to, mention; but, if I included all who endeavoured to make my task easier, my list would extend to the proportions of a chapter. I can only thank them collectively and ask them to pardon my omission of a specific reference to each of them.

In conclusion, I am well aware that I may not have made the best use of the information which has been so generously imparted to me, and I have been compelled, by the limitations of space, to leave out much which my informants may think should have been put in. For such shortcomings I beg indulgence.

PHILIP W. SERGEANT.

ST. JOHN'S WOOD,
1927.

CONTENTS

PAGE

PREFACE v

ACKNOWLEDGEMENTS ix

PART I

CHAPTER

I. GOPALRAO GAEKWAR 1

II. HIS PREDECESSORS IN BARODA . . . 6

III. FROM PEASANT BOY TO PRINCE . . . 22

IV. THE EDUCATION OF A MAHARAJA . . 26

V. MARRIAGE; AND A FINISHING EDUCATION . 39

VI. PERSONAL RULE BEGINS . . . 50

VII. THE MAN AND THE MACHINE . . . 57

VIII. DISTRICT TOURS 66

IX. DOMESTIC AFFAIRS; AND A VICEREGAL VISIT . 75

X. FOREIGN TRAVEL 82

XI. TROUBLES OF STATE 94

XII. THE CURZON CIRCULAR; AND THE 1903 DURBAR. 104

XIII. THE CALM BEFORE A STORM . . . 115

XIV. THE STORM 127

XV. THE WAR YEARS 143

XVI. TRAVEL AGAIN; AND TWO BEREAVEMENTS . 156

XVII. THE FIFTEENTH EUROPEAN TRIP . . . 165

XVIII. THE GOLDEN JUBILEE 171

PART II

CHAPTER PAGE

XIX. THE REFORMER 188

XX. THE EDUCATIONALIST 197

XXI. RELIGIOUS VIEWS 210

XXII. THE RAILWAY BUILDER 222

XXIII. DEVELOPMENT: AGRICULTURAL AND INDUSTRIAL 238

XXIV. CONSTITUTIONALISM AND ITS PRICE . . 252

XXV. GOVERNMENT AND THE PRIMITIVE TRIBES . 266

XXVI. JUSTICE 273

APPENDIX I: SOME DIFFICULTIES OF INDIAN PRINCES 278

APPENDIX II: EDUCATION IN BARODA . . 286

INDEX 309

LIST OF ILLUSTRATIONS

H.H. SAYAJIRAO GAEKWAR III., MAHARAJA OF BARODA
From a painting by the late Solomon J. Solomon, R.A. *Frontispiece*

FACING PAGE

MAKARPURA PALACE 10

THE MAHARAJA AT THE AGE OF TWELVE . . 22

F. A. H. ELLIOT 32

LAXMI VILAS PALACE 44

A VIEW OF BARODA CITY 58

SAYAJI SAROVAR (AJWA LAKE) 72

H.H. THE MAHARANI CHIMNABAI II. . . . 76

THE OLD PALACE AND MANDVI 90

THE MAHARAJA 104
From a picture by S. R. Samuel

PRINCE PRATAPSINGHRAO 122

H.H. THE MAHARANI OF COOCH BEHAR . . . 144

THE MAHARAJA AND HIS FAMILY . . . 154

THE GOLDEN JUBILEE PROCESSION . . . 176

THE PIER AT ADATARA (PORT OKHA) . . . 184

BARODA COLLEGE 202

THE MAHARAJA IN 1925 220

RAILWAY WORKSHOPS, GOYA GATE . . . 236

THE MAHARAJA AND HIS DEWANS, 1875-1925 . . 252

THE LAW COURTS AND SURSAGAR TANK . . 274

THE MAHARAJA INSPECTING THE BOY SCOUTS . . 306

THE RULER OF BARODA

PART I

CHAPTER I

GOPALRAO GAEKWAR

THE Maratha boy who was so unexpectedly to become the Maharaja of a leading Indian State and a pattern to all Indian rulers was born on March 17th, 1863, in the little village of Kavlana, about eighteen miles distant from Manmad, an important railway-junction in the Nasik district of Bombay Presidency. He was the second of the three sons of Kashirao Gaekwar, one of five brothers descended from Prataprao, younger brother of the famous Damajirao Gaekwar,* who

* The second of the name, and grand-nephew of the first Damaji. The family name Gaekwar (also transliterated Gaikvad, Gaikwad, and Gaekwad) is explained thus by C. A. Kincaid in the *History of the Maratha People*, which he wrote in collaboration with D. B. Parasnis: Nandaji, the grandfather of Damaji I., was a Maratha officer in charge of a fort in the Bhor State. One day he saw a Mohammedan butcher driving a herd of cattle past the fort, and, as a good Hindu, felt impelled to rush out and rescue the cows, letting them in by a side-door of the fort. He then took the name of Gaikvad (*gai* =cow, *kavad* =a small door).

The sound, intermediate between D and R, with which the name terminates, is somewhat puzzling to the European tongue.

in the middle of the eighteenth century carried on a successful struggle against the Peshwa, the great Maratha Minister at Poona, and carved out for himself the kingdom which later got the name of Baroda.

Prataprao is reputed to have been introduced to Khandesh by his brother Damaji on one of his periodical raids from his fortress of Songadh (the remains of which are still to be seen by the modern visitors to Baroda State), and to have been left in control of forty-seven villages. After Prataprao's death, however, the Peshwa made a forcible exchange of these villages for a district of Naosari; and, though Prataprao's descendants remained in Khandesh, they sank to so poor an estate that their very existence seems to have been forgotten in Baroda. The Kavlana Gaekwars lived, as did the rest of the villagers, by farming. Kashirao shared with his brothers a family house of the type common in Indian villages—that is to say, of the utmost simplicity. Here they all dwelt with their wives and children. Kashirao was a noted athlete, and, like his distant kinsman, Maharaja Khanderao of Baroda, achieved considerable fame as a wrestler. Education, in those days, was hardly within reach of an Indian villager.

Gopalrao, as the future Maharaja Sayajirao Gaekwar was originally named, was the second of his father's three sons, Anandrao being his senior by five years and Sampatrao two years his junior. Naturally, there is no history of the boy's early days, an attack of smallpox at the age of five being the only event recorded; and his own recollections are now dimmed by the lapse of years. When in February, 1926, His Highness paid his first visit to his birthplace since he left it for Baroda in 1875, his chief impression was that everything was very small compared with what he remembered of it—the bridge which to his childish eyes looked so big; the river in which he used to wade with his brothers and a cousin, now utilised chiefly for irrigation purposes; the high-road from Manmad, which is only a stone's-throw from Kavlana, but had once seemed a good distance away. He compares this "small" effect with that produced on him when he returned to England after a visit to America in 1906.

In one respect His Highness found Kavlana greatly changed in 1926. Where formerly had been a wide open space there are now the houses of the various members of the Gaekwar family, built on a very different scale from that in which Kashirao and his brothers had lived when Gopalrao was born. He has himself had a house built, in the Indian style, on the site of his birthplace; but it is rather a memorial than a dwelling-place, for only sentiment can suggest a reason for a visit to this obscure village of about two hundred houses, eighteen miles distant from the nearest railway-station.

Kashirao Gaekwar was the third in age of the Kavlana brothers. The two youngest, Okhajirao and Sakharam, discontented with the low level of the family fortunes, determined at last to make an effort to raise it by getting in touch with the rich and powerful Maharaja of Baroda, their relative, however remote the relationship might be. Khanderao was then on the throne of Baroda.

Okhaji managed to get access to him, and was favourably received, but very shortly afterwards the Maharaja died, without having done anything of practical assistance to his needy kinsmen.

Some time later Okhaji succeeded in attracting the notice of the new Maharaja, Malharrao, who proposed to acknowledge their relationship by bestowing on him a *poshak*, or robe of honour. Okhaji, however, explained that he had an elder brother to whom the honour should rather go.* Malharrao sent for Kashirao, and bestowed on him the *poshak* and a small pension, with which he returned to Kavlana.

Here the matter ended for the present. But suddenly, in the early May of 1875, a police party appeared at Kavlana, collected all the males of the village, and made enquiries about the Gaekwar family, subsequently taking Kashirao and his three sons to Nasik, where Colonel Etheridge enlightened the father as to the meaning of this rather alarming experience, which was that Mararaja Malharrao had been deposed, and that a suitable heir to the throne of Baroda was being sought. The claims of the Kavlana branch of the Gaekwar family were to be examined by Etheridge, in conjunction with the Collector of Nasik.

It is uncertain who first suggested to the British authorities that the humble Kavlana brothers might provide the solution of a difficult question. A Mr. Prescott, of the Nasik Police,

* The two still older brothers, Gabajirao and Baburao, had no male issue, it seems, which was the reason for passing them over.

is said to have urged that the Brahman records at that place should be consulted. Anyhow, evidence was forthcoming of the genuineness of the connection between the Kavlana and the Baroda Gaekwars; and Kashirao and his sons were at once taken to Baroda, where already were Okhaji and his young son Dada. The choice of successor to the throne was narrowed down to the four members of the younger generation. Finally—to anticipate the order of events—the twelve-year-old Gopalrao was selected; and on May 27th, 1875, after adoption into the reigning family, he was installed upon the throne, being given the name of Sayajirao, already famous in the annals of the Gaekwars.

We must now go back a considerable number of years, in order to see how this extraordinary, and for Baroda so lucky, elevation of a poor country boy to the proud rank of Maharaja suggested itself to those in control of the destinies of the State.

CHAPTER II

HIS PREDECESSORS IN BARODA

H.H. Sayajirao III. came to the throne at a very critical moment for Baroda. His four immediate predecessors, of the elder branch of the Gaekwar family, Sayajirao II. and his sons, had between them in various ways reduced the State's credit and prosperity to a low level. The four were certainly not equally blameworthy, but they all contributed something to their country's ill condition.

Sayajirao II. was neither an immoral liver nor a tyrannical ruler toward the general body of his subjects. Greedy for money and impatient of opposition, to the point of relentless persecution of those who would not fall in with his wishes, he was yet not unpopular in Baroda. But his foreign relations—that is to say, his dealings with the Government of Bombay—were marked by a countless succession of intrigues and disputes, and by several temporary sequestrations of Baroda territory by Bombay. The weapon on which he relied in diplomacy was corruption, and he did not hesitate to try it on the Governor and others of the highest officials. He evidently held, like Jugurtha, that every man had his price; but found British officials different from what the Numidian chieftain found the Romans. With the lower clerical staff, however, both at the Bombay Secretariat and at the Baroda Residency, he was more successful, and by bribes he secured the theft of many important secrets. Bombay treated him with alternate severity and leniency. But to the end of his twenty-eight years of reign cordiality of relationship between Baroda and the Paramount Power remained impossible.

The succession went to the eldest son, Ganpatrao, a Prince of feeble character and destitute of education. He was not incapable of listening to good advice, and some very useful reforms and public works were carried out in his reign. To check the intrigue rampant in his State, however, he showed himself utterly incompetent. At last, in 1854, the Government of India stepped in and took over from Bombay the guardianship of Baroda, which it did not restore until six years later.

Meanwhile, in 1856, Ganpatrao had died. He was succeeded by his brother Khanderao, a much stronger character in every way, of whom his first Resident, Colonel C. Davidson, wrote that he "was a man of bodily and mental energy, sometimes self-willed, was very shrewd and observant and took a large share in the administration, had a mind open to kindly impressions, and was actuated by generous impulses." A later Resident, Colonel J. T. Barr, spoke of his rule as being one of reform and real progress. Other critics do not entirely confirm this favourable impression. F. A. H. Elliot, for instance, while allowing Khanderao's mental energy, his shrewdness and power of observation, his retentive memory and other good qualities, finds two things wanting to make his reign a beneficial one: "His ministers and advisers were incompetent men, and some of them were bad men; and his own aspirations were for display rather than for the attainment of solid advantage to his people." His generous impulses not seldom led to lavish expenditure, and the permanent results of his actions were exceedingly small. Reforms were attempted, Elliot allows; "but there was an absence of skill and thoroughness in them which went far to deprive them of any solid value."*

Undoubtedly Khanderao was personally popular in his State, and his memory persists in Baroda today as a kind of "bluff King Hal"—without the vices, crimes, and cruelty of Henry VIII. He was passionately addicted to manly sports, and, of a very powerful physique, was a noted wrestler, willing to take on champions from other parts of India, the legend being that he never lost a contest, which, in the circumstances, is not improbable. Hunting was another of his passions. In a manuscript note in his own copy of *The Rulers of Baroda*, Elliot quotes a British officer's description of the Prince, when heir-apparent, at a boar-hunt: "He rode with a native sword, and was neck-and-neck with an officer who was trying for first blood with a keen *salem* of ordinary length. Seeing the boar failing, he gave his horse his heel and, withdrawing his left foot from the stirrup, wound the stirrup-

* *The Gazetteer of Baroda*, ii., 8 *ff*., shows that Khanderao made a good start to reform the iniquitous revenue-farming system, but failed fully to achieve his aim. Some critic of this Maharaja has said of him that "he could pull down, but was not good at reconstruction."

leather round his left wrist, and, leaning out of the saddle to the right and only held to the horse by the strained stirrup-leather, he drew his sword across the boar, and, cutting through the backbone of the animal, he won the tusks."

Khanderao's love of the chase led him to build what is now the old portion of the Makarpura Palace, south of Baroda City, and to maintain the great deer-preserves in its neighbourhood. This was a costly undertaking, and the story of how he found the money for it is characteristic of the man. Being anxious to provide the city with good drinking-water, which it then almost entirely lacked, he took up a scheme for a waterway to be constructed from the Narbada River all the way to Baroda at the expense of R. 3,600,000. Next year, finding the scheme impracticable, he diverted the money he had intended for it to Makarpura Palace, to the purchase of new jewelry, to the casting of two silver guns, and to the giving of magnificent arena sports for the people.

His jewelry cost this Maharaja very large sums, to the draining of the resources available for the improvement of his State. Two of the most remarkable objects to be seen in the Nazar Bag Palace, where the Baroda Crown jewels are kept, date from the reign of Khanderao. The 125-carat diamond, the "Star of the South," which is part of the principal necklace of state for the Gaekwars, was bought by Khanderao for £80,000, having been discovered in 1853 at Minas Geraes, Brazil. The carpet embroidered with seed-pearls and small precious stones, hanging on a wall of the Nazar Bag, and valued at R. 125,000, was intended by

Khanderao (always ready, like a prudent Hindu ruler, to conciliate his Mohammedan subjects) as a present to the Prophet's tomb at Mecca; but he died before the carpet was completed, and his successor did not make the present.

To meet the demands made on his treasury by his extravagant tastes, Khanderao was reduced to piling a heavy burden of taxation on his subjects. Fortunately for him, the American Civil War, causing a sensational rise in cotton prices, brought great prosperity to cotton-growing Gujarat, and led to a great increase in the area under cotton throughout Baroda. While prices remained high, the high land-assessment based upon them was not objected to; but, when prices began to fall, the excessive nature of the taxation was more and more felt. In other ways, too, the latter part of Khanderao's reign exhibited him in a less favourable light. While his appetite for pleasure grew, his energy of character declined, and such enthusiasm as he had for reforms evaporated, while he chose as his ministers men of decreasingly high ability and honesty. It was as well for his reputation that his reign was cut short by sudden illness after fourteen years.

In one respect, however, Maharaja Khanderao put his country under a great obligation to him. By his unswerving loyalty to the British connection he won for Baroda a claim to considerate treatment, which stood her in good stead during the misrule of his successor, and perhaps even saved her from loss of independence. This loyalty was most marked at the time of the Mutiny, for it was found possible to withdraw the British troops from

MAKARPURA PALACE.

10]

Gujarat and leave Khanderao to keep order, with his army in "a state of thorough efficiency," as the Resident, Sir Richmond Shakespeare, gratefully acknowledged.

The Government of India, when the Mutiny was over, passed a resolution in which it was stated that, but for the Maharaja's loyalty, its hold on the whole of Western India would have been most seriously compromised, and as a reward remitted the fine imposed in 1839 on Sayajirao II. to pay for the maintenance of the Gujarat Irregular Horse. The remission of this fine, amounting to three lakhs of rupees levied annually on the revenues of Kathiawar, was very gratifying to Khanderao, as also were the grants of the insignia of royalty, and of the right of adopting an heir. In the *sanad* granting the latter there appears for the first time the title of "His Highness the Maharaja Gaekwar of Baroda."

Khanderao's death, on November 28th, 1870, left the succession to the throne in an ambiguous position. There was no legitimate son alive, and Khanderao had not exercised his right of adoption. Normally, therefore, his younger brother, Malharrao, would succeed him. But his widow, the young Maharani Jamnabai, declared herself pregnant, and the Bombay Government directed that the child's birth should be awaited, the regency to be in Malharrao's hands until it should be seen whether a boy or a girl arrived.

Malharrao's credentials were far from good. Sir Richmond Shakespeare in 1857 had summed him up as too weak in intellect to be dangerous, though already, at the age of twenty-eight, he had been mixed up in a criminal plot against his brother and the British supremacy. In 1863 he was involved in a second conspiracy against his brother, who thereupon threw him into prison. Here, at Padra, near Baroda, he was when Khanderao's death set him free.

The Maharani Jamnabai, a girl of noble Maratha family from near Satara, was, at the age of thirteen, taken by Khanderao as his second wife. She was still little more than seventeen, and was obviously, from her conduct in a very difficult situation, already a woman of some force of character. Malharrao was a dangerous opponent. While he attempted, with some show of goodwill, to conciliate the British, he made every effort to prevent the possibility of a child of Khanderao ousting him from the throne he coveted. He questioned the genuineness of his sister-in-law's pregnancy, and then, when that was proved, the legitimacy of the coming child. Being intensely superstitious, he tried witchcraft; and the Maharani believed that he was trying poison also, which from Malharrao's general character is not unlikely. She refused to touch any food in the Palace, unless cooked by her own servants. Finally she persuaded the Resident, Colonel Barr, to allow her to come to the Residency for her confinement. As an extra precaution, a special guard was sent from Bombay to protect her. In these circumstances, on July 5th, 1871, she gave birth to the Princess Tarabai.

Malharrao, now securely Maharaja, was exultant. Mounted on a triumphal elephant, he rode through the streets of Baroda, scattering largesse to the crowds. He lost no time before wreaking his vengeance on Khanderao's advisers and supporters, including Bhau Shinde, the former notorious Dewan, to whose credit, however, stands the fact that he had persuaded his master to put Malharrao in prison in 1863. Now Bhau Shinde himself went to prison, dying there next year, probably by poison. In place of his brother's ministers, whom he swept away, Malharrao put in power his own creatures, men of even more worthless character than Khanderao's advisers towards the end of his reign.

With regard to his sister-in-law, the Maharaja had suggested that she should return to the Palace. Since she was no longer dangerous to him as the possible mother of an heir to the throne, he may have desired to get hold of her for other reasons. The Maharani Jamnabai would have nothing to do with him, and retired with her little daughter to Poona, where Malharrao was later reluctantly induced to make her an allowance out of his revenues.

Khanderao's heavy taxation and his extravagant expenditure have been described. His younger brother continued the taxation, adding to it the exaction of enormous sums for the benefit of himself and the disreputable crowd of men and women with whom he surrounded himself. When the state of the Baroda revenues was examined in January, 1875, it was found that in the previous year Malharrao had received 94 lakhs and had expended 171 lakhs, of which about four-fifths went in presents to favourites. He spent lavishly on jewelry, and, to outdo his brother's two silver guns, had two gold ones made.* He began the building of a new palace, the Nazar Bag behind the old Sarkarwada; though, in view of the decayed and insanitary condition of the latter, this cannot be condemned as an entirely unnecessary extravagance. Financial corruption was rife throughout Baroda. But Malharrao's tyranny was exhibited in other more objectionable ways. His amours, abductions of respectable women, tortures and murders of innocent people, are still a tradition in Baroda City, where even the conversion of the Sarkarwada into the Central Library and various offices, etc., has not succeeded in dispelling the ghosts.

The Bombay Government could not ignore the serious reports reaching it concerning the misrule in Baroda, particularly as the Maharani Jamnabai had her partisans in the city stirring up complaints to the Residency. It was decided to send Colonel Robert Phayre, C.B., as Resident, in the hope that he would be strong enough to tackle the situation. With his arrival on March 18th, 1873, a crisis was soon reached. He had been only four days in Baroda when he heard that eight men had been flogged in the streets, some of them to death, for the alleged poisoning of one of the Maharaja's servants. Stimulated by this and other reports, Phayre urged that an enquiry should be held. A Commission of four was appointed by the Government of India, with Colonel Richard Meade as

* H.H. the present Maharaja has had one each of the silver and gold guns melted down and converted into money, retaining the others as part of the pageantry on high State occasions.

president, which in due course brought in a studiously moderate verdict, finding, however, that Baroda was generally misgoverned.

Lord Northbrook, the Governor-General, thereupon wrote a letter to Malharrao, in which he said:

"Misrule on the part of a government which is upheld by the British power is misrule in the responsibility for which the British Government becomes in a measure involved. It becomes, therefore, not only the right, but the positive duty of the British Government to see that the administration of a State in such a condition is reformed, and that gross abuses are removed. . . . If substantial justice be not done to the subjects of the Baroda State, if life and property be not protected, if the general welfare of the country and the people be persistently neglected, the British Government will assuredly intervene in the manner which, in its judgment, may be best calculated to remove the evils and to secure good government."

The date December 31st, 1875, was fixed as the time-limit within which Malharrao must carry out the reform of his administration; and in particular he was asked to get rid of his evil counsellors and appoint as his chief minister someone acceptable to the Government.

The Maharaja made some show of listening to the serious warning which he had received. He dismissed his Dewan, Nana Khanvelkar, who was also his brother-in-law and was high in his favour. This step he could not avoid taking, as Khanvelkar was one of the officials most obnoxious to Bombay.

But in removing him from the Dewanship he conferred upon him the honourable title of *pratinidhi*, which stirred the wrath of Colonel Phayre. Nor did the Resident approve of the substitute whom Malharrao selected. This was Dadabhai Naoroji, the Parsi gentleman who afterwards represented Central Finsbury in the British House of Commons. Malharrao had asked permission from Bombay to utilise the services of Naoroji, and on August 4th, 1874, he took up office, bringing with him several members of his own race to assist him in setting matters right in Baroda. This appointment had every appearance of being a sincere attempt at reform. Phayre, however, was not satisfied. To him it was a mere parade, and he would not believe that the new Dewan would be able to do anything. He was right in so far as there was much opposition from the Baroda officials to their Parsi chief. But the Resident's attitude certainly made the situation worse.

So strained became the relations between the Residency and the Palace, and so schoolmasterly was Colonel Phayre's handling of the Maharaja, that on November 2nd Malharrao, on the advice of his Dewan, addressed a letter to the Government of India, petitioning that Phayre should be withdrawn from Baroda. That there was felt to be some ground for complaint was evident; for the reply was to instruct the Resident to leave the Residency, and in his place to send Colonel Sir Lewis Pelly, K.C.S.I., with the title of Special Commissioner and Agent to the Governor-General.

Before the Resident was withdrawn, however,

a great sensation convulsed Baroda. On November 9th he fell ill from drinking some sherbet, and looking at the glass found a sediment in it, which the Residency doctor analysed and found to be mixed arsenic and diamond-dust. Someone had tried to poison Colonel Phayre; but for the moment there was no clue to the instigator of the crime, and he handed over affairs to Sir Lewis Pelly and left Baroda at the end of the month without the mystery being solved.

Sir Lewis Pelly's first relations with Malharrao were "on an excellent footing," according to a report in *The Times of India*, and the Maharaja was "quite docile." But very soon an awkward situation arose. Sir Lewis was obliged, on instructions from above, to refuse to call at the Palace and pay the customary honours on the birth of an heir to the throne. The story of this affair began before he came to Baroda. In the previous March a man, a British subject, complained at the Residency that his wife had been taken from him and was living with Malharrao as his mistress. In May Malharrao, who had no offspring by his first wife, Mahalsabai, married the woman, Laxmibai, an invitation to attend the wedding being declined by Colonel Phayre. Now on December 16th a boy was born, whom Malharrao acknowledged as his son and called Jayajirao. Many questioned the paternity, and Sir Lewis Pelly, as has been said, was instructed not to pay the honorary call at the Palace.

But a far more serious matter occupied the Special Commissioner's attention within a few days. Detectives had been sent to Baroda by the

Government of India; and they extracted confessions from two of the Residency servants that they had been given poison by Malharrao and bribed to administer it to Colonel Phayre. After this it was obviously necessary to take action. On January 14th, 1875, the Government of India announced the arrest of Malharrao and its assumption of control of Baroda, pending an enquiry.

Malharrao made no attempt to resist, allowing himself to be taken to the house of the Residency doctor, where he was put under a guard of British troops. Sir Lewis Pelly on the same day assembled the leading men of Baroda and explained matters to them, assuring them that no annexation of the State was intended. With this they expressed themselves satisfied. General Devine, the Commander of the State Army, was told that he would be held responsible for the conduct of his troops. who, however, showed no signs of resentment at what had happened. (A speedy payment of about R. 80,000 arrears of pay, no doubt, soothed their feelings.) Reports had reached Bombay that Baroda was swarming with an armed rabble, and reinforcements in consequence had been hurried to the British garrison in the camp outside the city walls. But all remained perfectly peaceful for the present. The arrest of Nana Khanvelkar and of Damodar Pant, Malharrao's favourite and private secretary, were easily effected.

To investigate the question of Malharrao's complicity in the attempt on Colonel Phayre, a Commission of six was appointed. The president of this was Sir Richard Couch, Chief Justice of Bengal, who was assisted by Sir Richard Meade,

Mr. P. S. Melville, the Maharajas of Gwalior and Jaipur, and Sir Dinkar Rao, who had been Dewan in Gwalior during the Mutiny, and had done his utmost to keep the State troops from joining in the rising. Malharrao's solicitors were allowed £7,500 for the expenses of his defence, and the services of Serjeant Ballantine were engaged.

The evidence brought before the Commission was most contradictory and unsatisfactory, and although the sittings were continued into the second half of March no unanimous decision was reached. The three British Commissioners held that Malharrao had instigated an attempt at poison, while the Indian Commissioners could not agree that the charge was proved.

In spite of the unsatisfactory nature of the Commission's finding, the Government of India advised the Secretary of State that Malharrao should be deposed, and that an heir to the throne should be chosen from among the Gaekwar family, who should be adopted as son by the Maharani Jamnabai, widow of Khanderao. This latter step had been constantly urged by the Maharani in her exile at Poona. She had pointed out that the right of adoption had been conferred on her husband as a special favour, though he was prevented by death from exercising it, and suggested that it might be transferred to her, which would make the succession of a new Maharaja right in Hindu eyes.

The British Government, while not accepting Malharrao's guilt as proved, decided to depose him, and to appoint a new heir as suggested. Accordingly, on April 19th a proclamation announced the

3

Maharaja's deposition because of his notorious misconduct and gross misgovernment of his State; and three days later he was taken away under escort to Madras, in spite of his indignant protests. His request that the infant Jayajirao should succeed him was refused.

The deposition was carried out by Sir Richard Meade, who had succeeded Sir Lewis Pelly at the Residency on April 18th, and, having safely despatched Malharrao on his way, Sir Richard met a gathering of the chief people of Baroda, whom he had summoned to the Residency, and informed them of the intentions of the Government, assuring them that there was no design against the independence of the State.

All passed off quietly at first. But Malharrao, like many another bad ruler, was not without friends and supporters, attached to him by motives of self-interest. On April 28th these made a demonstration in his favour. In Baroda City the shops had been closed, on the legitimate pretext that this was the custom when the *gadi* (throne) was vacant; but also crowds paraded the streets with sticks and stones in their hands, and made violent attacks upon any British officer they met. Captain Jackson, the Assistant-Resident, was severely handled, but escaped after shooting one man dead. General Devine was also assaulted. The rioters, joined by some Palace guards, proceeded to install Laxmibai's son upon the *gadi*, and to proclaim the elder Maharani, Mahalsabai, Regent.

Sir Richard Meade acted promptly. He marched a body of troops, supported by artillery, from the

Camp to the walled city, which was entered by the Leheripuraj or Western Gate, and reduced to order without any loss of life, though one hundred and fifty arrests were made. He then called the merchants to the Residency, severely reprimanded them, and ordered them to reopen their shops under penalty of a fine. He gave another assurance, however, that it was not intended to annex Baroda, the fear of which was what induced a number of people not particularly attached to Malharrao* to join his adherents in the outbreak. The two Maharanis, Mahalsabai, who was suspected of being the chief instigator of the trouble, and Laxmibai, with the latter's infant son, were sent off next day to Bombay, on their way to share Malharrao's exile.

Baroda City continued for a brief while in the occupation of a mixed British and Indian force; but no further rioting required their intervention. Outside the city there had been very little disturbance beyond an attempt to damage the railway-line.

* The fact that there was a divergence of feeling among the rioters was shown by the looting of the house of Damodar Pant, Malharrao's favourite, and the throwing of his family into the street.

CHAPTER III

FROM PEASANT BOY TO PRINCE

THE way was now clear for the elevation of a new heir to the throne of Baroda. The legitimacy of Jayajirao was not recognised. There were in Baroda four other possible claimants, members of the Gaekwar family: Sadashivrao, Murarrao, Ganpatrao, and Khanderao. All these were over twenty-four years of age, which was against them, as it was felt that the successor to Malharrao must be young enough to be trained up into a very different kind of ruler from that Maharaja. The two first named, moreover, were barred from the succession by the fact that when their father, Govindrao (a descendant of the first Damaji's younger brother Jhingoji), was adopted by the widow of Fatesingrao the Regent, in 1818, it was expressly stipulated that the adoption should not carry with it any right to the succession. Nevertheless, both Sadashivrao and Murarrao cherished hopes of becoming Maharaja Gaekwar, with disastrous results to themselves.

Preparations for the settlement of the succession proceeded apace after the quelling of the trouble in Baroda City. The Maharani Jamnabai arrived in Baroda on May 2nd, and entered the Moti Bag Palace next day, when also came the person who had been chosen to conduct the administration

THE MAHARAJA AT THE AGE OF TWELVE.

of the State. This was Madhavrao Tanjorkar, generally known in Baroda history as Sir T. Madhavrao. A Maratha Brahman, born in Tanjore in 1828, educated and for some time a professor at Madras University, he had served fourteen years as Dewan of Travancore, in which post his father and his uncle had preceded him. From Travancore he went to Indore and there served two years as Dewan. He had already, when the Commission was sitting to consider the charges against Malharrao, been invited by the Government of India to make an unofficial report on Baroda affairs. The suggestions in his report were considered too advanced to be safely adopted at present; but the Government of India looked on him as a fit man to be Dewan, and so recommended him to the Secretary of State. The recommendation was accepted. Now he arrived, destined to be a very important figure in the histories of both Baroda State and its new Maharaja.

The first duty which devolved on the restored Maharani Jamnabai was, with the advice of Sir T. Madhavrao and the approval of the Paramount Power, to choose whom she would adopt as her son, and consequently as heir to the throne. We have heard how attention was drawn to the Kavlana branch of the Gaekwars. Their age was against Kashirao Gaekwar and any of his brothers. Kashirao's eldest son, Anandrao, being already over seventeen, was also unlikely to meet with the Indian Government's approval, as someone of malleable age was wanted, who might be shaped according to the right ideas. Of the two younger boys, Gopalrao took the Maharani's fancy,* and no objection was made to her choice, which was therefore ratified.

On hearing of the selection of one of the Kavlana branch, the senior Baroda Gaekwar, Sadashivrao, attempted to stir up a revolt in his own favour. He was easily dealt with, being arrested and sent to Benares, where he lived in safe keeping until his death fifteen years later. His brother Murarrao, who was weak in intellect, committed suicide through disappointment. The other two Baroda Gaekwars accepted the situation calmly, and had the satisfaction of seeing their heavily accumulated debts paid off and pensions allowed them. Sadashivrao was also liberally treated in money matters, though punished for his rebellion.

All dispute being now at an end, Sir Richard Meade on May 25th proclaimed the Maharani's choice of an heir, who would be adopted and formally installed two days later. Early on the morning of the 27th the boy was awakened in his temporary residence in the Camp, and, with the appropriate Hindu ritual, was handed over by his father and adopted by the Maharani Jamnabai as

* The story is an old one, and has often been repeated, though of its authenticity there is no proof, that one reason for the selection of Gopalrao was that, when the three brothers were asked why they had been brought to Baroda, the eldest and youngest made no satisfactory reply; but Gopalrao bravely said, "To be Maharaja!" Another tale is that, while his brothers were at a loss to know how to behave at the dinner-table, he watched the Maharani eating and imitated her.

It is curious that a positive report reached Bombay that Anandrao, who is described in the papers as "a young Khandesh Prince," was the choice for the next Gaekwar.

her son. He was then dressed in robes provided by his new mother, and conducted to the Palace. After his coronation the Resident and his suite arrived on elephants at the Palace, and Sir Richard, entering the Durbar room, greeted him, placed him upon the *gadi*, and, in the name of the British Government, installed and invested him as Maharaja of Baroda, under the name of Sayajirao III. The royal salute was immediately fired by the artillery of the British garrison and of the State Army. The Resident, having addressed the assembly in Hindustani, and called upon them to give faithful support to the new administration, took His Highness behind the *purdah*, where the Maharani Jamnabai was waiting, and impressed on him the serious nature of the duties of his position. With that he took his leave. The durbar closed with the offering and the acceptance by the Maharaja of the presents, the latter being signified by his touching them with his hand. These presents included not only those from his own people, but also a gift of costly apparel from the Maharaja Holkar of Indore.

On May 29th the young Maharaja paid a visit to all the temples of Baroda City, and made his first official call at the Residency. The ceremonies of his installation had come to an end, and immediately before him lay the years of his minority, the preparation for the happily much longer years of his personal rule.

CHAPTER IV

THE EDUCATION OF A MAHARAJA

THE little Sayajirao's education nominally began on June 7th, 1875, when, after the religious ceremony of initiation and of dedication to Saraswati, the goddess of learning, the two teachers who had been assigned to him took up their duties. These were Keshav Rao Pandit, who remained his responsible Indian tutor during the whole of his minority; and Vyankatesh Joshi, generally known as "Bhau Master." A room on the top floor of the Sarkarwada was made his school-room, and here Pandit and Joshi taught him in turn for about five hours a day.

It is difficult for those who know the stately Laxmi Vilas Palace of modern Baroda to picture the surroundings in which Maharaja Sayajirao's training began, even though the Old Palace buildings still remain in something like their original shape. Visitors to the Central Library, however, can trace certain features of the former royal dwelling in the decorations of the first floor. The steep narrow staircase also, which leads up to that floor, takes the imagination back to the past. Formerly, we know, a narrow doorway gave access to the stair, which in its windings was guarded at intervals by trapdoors, a necessary precaution, no doubt, in the dark ages of Baroda history. On the first floor were the throne-room, where the *gadi* was kept, and the *devghar*, or shrine, with its thousands of little images of gods and goddesses of the Hindu Pantheon. On the floor above was the jewel-chamber, full of the treasures accumulated by the Gaekwars, and above that again the living-rooms, with beds of gold and silver, innumerable mirrors, and pictures of very poor quality.* The roof was flat, and was the haunt of flocks of pigeons, protected from human molestation by the religious sentiments of the people and the special favour of the Gaekwars.

In this abode, primitive in its sanitation and always lacking in fresh air, the boy, just come from the freedom of village life, must have felt at first a prisoner, whatever the compensations of his new grandeur. Nor did he find the first steps in education easy. He began the study of reading and writing Marathi, which hitherto he had only spoken. On August 26th Sir Richard Meade reported that his progress so far was limited. He described him at this early period as "a quiet, self-possessed boy, with a thoughtful expression of face, of an extremely amiable disposition," not robust, but anxious to practise native gymnastics, riding, etc.

Sir Richard was not satisfied that the boy had the right environment in the Sarkarwada, where, apart from the society of the Maharani, he lived among Palace females and menials. Obviously, too, he considered his education, under his two

* "Cheap German prints of ladies representing the seasons," says the *Gazetteer* (iv. 470), "and, in Malharrao's time, other subjects which necessitated their destruction when the Palace was purified."

Indian tutors, and in the company of his younger brother Sampatrao and his cousin Dadasaheb Gaekwar, unlikely to produce the desired result. He urged on the Bombay Government the desirability of establishing a " Raja's school," open to the sons of nobles and officials, who should be of approximately equal age to the young Prince, and that neither in school nor in playground should there be any distinction made between him and the other boys. The school should have "a qualified English gentleman" as principal, who should also act as his companion as much as possible out of school-hours.

For the present there was no change, except that lessons in Marathi were supplemented by lessons in Gujarati, the language of the bulk of the Baroda people, and Urdu, that of the Mohammedan subjects.

The first break in the course of studies was occasioned by the visit to India of the Prince of Wales, the future King Edward VII., in November, 1875. It was thought fitting that the boy who was to be the ruler of Baroda should have the opportunity of meeting the heir to the Imperial throne. Accordingly, in the company of the Maharani Jamnabai, Sir Richard Meade, and a large suite, the young Maharaja went to Bombay on October 25th, being officially received at the station, and conducted to the bungalow at Lall Bag, which had been taken and fitted up for him by the authorities. His first duty in Bombay was the exchange of visits with the Governor, Sir Philip Wodehouse, after which he was at leisure to see, for the first time in his life, the sights of Bombay.

There already, at the end of October, about forty Indian Princes and chiefs gathered together to await the Prince of Wales's arrival. The display made by Baroda was as imposing as any of the others. A portion of the State Army, to the number of 1,500, had come to Bombay, including Malharrao's favourite regiment, the Gaekwar's, or Baroda, Highlanders,* and the gold and silver guns. The latter were mounted in front of the bungalow at Lall Bag, and excited much wonder.

The Viceroy, Lord Northbrook, arrived in Bombay on November 2nd, all the Princes being at the station to meet him. The exchange of ceremonial calls followed. The Prince of Wales reached Bombay Harbour in the *Serapis* six days later, the Viceroy going on board to conduct him ashore, while the Governor, the Commander-in-Chief, a great assembly of European officials and others, and the Indian Princes and chiefs, now increased in number to seventy, awaited his landing. A reception was held at Government House on November 9th, where the Prince spoke to the boy Maharaja, telling him, it is recorded, that he should watch his career with interest, and urging him to continue his studies in English and horsemanship. Next day the Prince called at Lall Bag, and presented the Maharaja with a whip, a sword, a jewelled snuffbox, a ring, and two albums. On the 12th he inspected the Baroda troops, and expressed his admiration for the gold and silver guns.

* Malharrao's army in 1874 had cost him R. 3,800,000, and these Highlanders, in full Highland costume, with pink tights to conceal the colour of their knees, were his great pride.

It had not originally been intended that the Prince should include Baroda in his tour of India. But a surprise was in store, for on the 17th, after his return from a visit to Poona, it was suddenly announced that he wished to go to Baroda on a short sporting excursion and to see the arena games. Maharaja Sayajirao left Bombay hastily to prepare for his reception. On the morning of the 19th the Prince arrived, and was escorted by the Maharaja, Sir T. Madhavrao, and the newly appointed Agent, Mr. P. S. Melville, to the Residency, the Prince riding with his little host in the golden *ambari* upon the best of the royal elephants. At the Residency the customary offerings of flowers and *pan-supari* were made to the Prince before the Maharaja took his leave. In the afternoon the Prince paid official visits to the Maharaja and the Maharani Jamnabai at the Moti Bag, and then went to see the wrestling, and the elephant, rhinoceros, buffalo, and ram fights. At night the city was illuminated.

The early part of November 20th was devoted by the Prince to sport, including the hunting of black buck by cheetahs. In the evening he visited the Moti Bag again, and was shown the Crown jewels. A dinner was served in a pavilion in the grounds, the Maharaja coming in at dessert-time and sitting in a chair beside the Prince. Sir T. Madhavrao gave the toasts of the Queen and of the Prince of Wales, who, in responding for himself, spoke of the pleasure his visit to Baroda had given him, and predicted that the Maharaja, who had a great career before him, would devote himself to promoting the welfare of his people and developing the resources of his country—a prophecy which has singularly been fulfilled. He proposed the toast of the Maharaja and the Maharani, Sir T. Madhavrao responding on their behalf, and the evening closed with music and fireworks.

This was the first entertainment of its kind in which His Highness had taken part, and, as may be seen, his youth and lack of experience of European ways did not allow him to play a very prominent part. But the visit of the Prince of Wales was certainly an important incident in his training. The remainder of the Prince's stay in Baroda was given up chiefly to sport, including pig-sticking at Dabka, Maharaja Khanderao's hunting-box eighteen miles west of Baroda City. On the evening of November 23rd he left Baroda, being escorted to the station by the Maharaja and the Dewan.

It has been mentioned that the new Agent to the Governor-General, during the Prince of Wales's visit to Baroda, was Mr. P. S. Melville, who had sat on the Commission to enquire into the subject of Maharaja Malharrao's guilt. To Melville fell the duty of carrying out his predecessor's suggestions as to a change in the young Maharaja's regimen, which the Bombay Government had sanctioned.

The most important point was the selection of an English tutor. Melville sought the advice of H. M. Birdwood, District Judge at Ratnagiri. Judge Birdwood recommended F. A. H. Elliot, son of a former Acting-Governor of Madras, and himself an Indian Civil Servant, who, when Assistant-Collector at Ragnagiri, had married the

Judge's sister-in-law. At the moment he was Director of the Public Instruction in Berar.

Events fully justified Judge Birdwood's recommendation of his brother-in-law; and, as in the case of Sir T. Madhavrao, Baroda and its Maharaja were most lucky in the appointment now made by the British. Naturally, there have not been wanting critics of swarajist views, who complain that the head of an Indian State should rather have had an Indian as his governor.

Elliot arrived in Baroda on December 10th, 1875. Soon a small house, near the Moti Bag building in the present Laxmi Vilas Palace grounds, was prepared as a temporary school, pending the erection of a permanent building, the Princes' School of today, where His Highness's sons received, and his grandsons still receive, their education.

Under Elliot's direction study began in earnest, the Maharaja and his selected schoolmates, his brother, his cousin, and a few sons of leading men in Baroda, attending daily from 10 a.m. to sunset. The introduction of English into his curriculum gave the Maharaja four languages to acquire, but down to the end of 1876 instruction was of a primary character. This, indeed, could not be otherwise, seeing that, as Elliot wrote later, "the beginning was an absolute beginning." The very foundation had to be laid after the boy came to Baroda. Writing later still (in 1880), Elliot stated that at the start his pupil was "apparently and actually dull," and spent some time in shaking this off.

In his favour, however, were his strong natural

F. A. H. ELLIOT.

intelligence, a good constitution, and a liking for physical exercise, which has remained with him throughout life. Another favourable factor in his training was that his adoptive mother was a woman of great sense, who, though she had speedily become attached to him, put no obstacle in the way of his separation from her for the greater part of the day, while in his home life she kept a watchful eye over the development of his character.

The course of his new studies was temporarily broken at the end of 1876, when he made his first Indian tour, which extended to nearly 3,500 miles in all. The principal object of the journey was to attend, at the Viceroy's invitation, the great Durbar at Delhi, where Queen Victoria was proclaimed Empress of India. Starting from Baroda on December 7th in the company of the Maharani Jamnabai, her daughter Tarabai, Melville, Elliot, and a large suite, he travelled by way of Naosari and Allahabad, and reached Delhi on the 14th. It was not until Christmas Day that the new Viceroy, Lord Lytton, arrived, being welcomed at the railway-station by a full gathering of Indian Princes, including the boy Maharaja of Baroda.

On the following day the Viceroy received him in the Durbar pavilion, and presented him with a special banner of the Baroda colours and an Imperial gold medal bearing Queen Victoria's image. Nor were these the sole marks of favour. On the 29th Lord Lytton, returning his call, informed him that the Queen had been pleased to bestow on him the title of *Farzand-i-Khas-i-Daulat-i-Inglishia* ("Own favoured son of the British Empire"). Then, on January 1st, 1877, came the Imperial Assemblage, at which the newspapers recorded how " the young Gaekwar, resplendent in velvet and diamonds," was led across the arena by Mr. Melville. The public announcement of his new title was made that day.

On January 9th Maharaja Sayajirao started on his return journey to Baroda, visiting Agra, Lucknow, Benares, and for the second time Allahabad, and reaching home finally on February 5th, after a trip of the most instructive nature. He had, during it, performed the duty of a pious Hindu, bathing in the Narbada, the Jumna, and the Ganges. He had made himself acquainted with the other leading rulers.* He had brought back with him most flattering tokens of esteem by the Paramount Power. But, above all, he had begun his career as a *traveller*, and perhaps, even at the tender age which he had then reached, had commenced to see what travel means in the progress of the mind.

The Maharaja's return was marked by a round of festivities in Baroda to celebrate the new title bestowed upon him. There was a durbar at the Nazar Bag Palace, a review of the British troops at the camp, races, athletic sports, a dinner and a ball at Makarpura Palace, etc.

The remainder of the year passed quietly, the only two events to interrupt the school studies being a brief visit from Sir Richard Temple,

* " In his person," says the *Gazetteer* (i. 609), " a Gaekwad met Sindia and Holkar at Delhi for the first time since the memorable struggle at Panipat. He met also and conversed with such Princes as His Highness the Nizam and His Highness of Mysore."

Governor of Bombay, in May, and the death on July 26th of Shrimant Kashirao Babasaheb Gaekwar, as His Highness's father was now called. Kashirao had been living in Baroda since his arrival four years before.

Writing of the Maharaja's progress in this year (1877), when he was still under fifteen, Melville reports that he is " rapidly developing into a strong, wiry young man," " most industrious," and at the same time " addicted to manly sports and exercises."

The school curriculum was now enlarging, and with English, Marathi, and Gujarati as his main languages, the boy devoted special attention to English and Indian history. A difficulty which his tutor found in the conduct of the school as a whole was that, while his chief pupil, conscious of his own deficiencies, worked hard to make them up, the others were quite unable to keep pace with him. Fresh pupils were introduced, but they also failed to emulate him, in consequence of which it was necessary to give him much individual teaching.

In 1878 Elliot's report notes the addition of chemistry to the Maharaja's other studies. His worst subject is arithmetic. He reads and understands both Marathi and Gujarati fairly, but neither speaks nor writes them fluently. He has daily translation work, and frequent essays to improve his English style. History occupies considerable time, while geography, the elements of political economy, and conversations on given subjects fill up his remaining school-hours.

The general course of his day now seems to

have been as follows, if we may reduce it to tabular form:*

Rise at 6 a.m.

Riding (or other exercise) until 8 a.m.

An hour's study.

Breakfast with the Maharani.

Drive from the Palace to the school, accompanied by a military escort.

Work from 10.30 a.m. to 5 p.m., with an hour's interval for lunch.

Exercise on the *maidan* adjoining the school.

Return to the Palace at nightfall.

Preparation for next day's lessons.

Supper.

To bed at 10 p.m.

By this time the school had been erected about two miles away from the Old Palace, and the *maidan* mentioned above is now part of the Laxmi Vilas grounds. The exercises on the *maidan* were various Indian games, squadron drill, and sword exercise. Swimming was also practised after school, and in the school-house was a billiard-table, on which the Maharaja laid the foundations of his future proficiency at the game. Once a fortnight there were hunting excursions.

G. S. Sardesai, in his *Account of the Education of His Highness*, says that the style of his life was essentially Indian, with plain Indian food, and a regular observance of fasts and ceremonies. Both at school and at the Palace he was under strict surveillance; but we are assured that he never found this irksome, owing to the tact of the Maharani and of Mr. Elliot.

* There are several accounts, not entirely consistent.

It is not surprising to learn from the same work that, with so many subjects crowded into the curriculum, His Highness had hardly time to assimilate the vast amount of knowledge poured into him. It would be interesting to know who was primarily responsible for this intensive "cramming." One rather suspects that it was Sir T. Madhavrao, a man himself capable of a tremendous amount of hard work.

However, the Maharaja did not break down under the strain. His steady progress continued, and won the admiration of both Melville and Elliot, to whom fell the duty of reporting on it. Melville, in the 1879-80 *Administration Report*, states that "by great good fortune the young Gaekwar has developed a thoroughly healthy moral nature, and has proved that he possesses mental qualities which, if not brilliant, are solid and adequate to the position he will soon have to assume."

Elliot is still more enthusiastic. "Fortunately," he says, writing of him just before his attainment of his seventeenth birthday, "though at the outset His Highness was slow at acquiring information, he has refused to forget much of anything which he has once learnt." He also asserts, at the end of an association with him of four years and a half: "I have not had occasion once to find fault with him. A better or more affectionate pupil could not be found."

With the year 1880 a very important change came into the Maharaja's life. It had been decided that he should get married—early marriages are, of course, the rule all over India—as soon as a suitable bride could be found, and the year was to be the last of his second period of education, which was equivalent to a High School course.

Before we come to this change in his life, however, it is interesting to note his personal impressions of his boyhood. It was, he says, a very solitary one, in which he had no friends or companions of his own age. He was never permitted to forget the fact that he was "the Maharaja."* Those about him were mostly subservient, ill-educated, and ill-paid. The Indian tutors were conscientious men, according to their lights, but were scarcely capable of influencing him. Elliot, on the other hand, was a genuine influence. His school curriculum was very wide indeed, and left him far too little leisure for the simpler tasks, such as mastering the reading and writing of the various scripts which it was necessary for him to learn. He was compelled to work overtime in the mornings to make up his deficiencies in the elementary subjects, and would often send for a tutor at an early hour to help him in the practice of writing, etc. His handwriting, owing to previous neglect, was a great handicap to him. It remained, indeed, in later years a complaint of his that so much time had to be "wasted" on writing. It was a distress to him that the hand could not keep pace with the brain.

* From the moment of his installation down to today, as he remarks, he had never been allowed to be anything else. Whether in public life or in private—if one can speak of such a thing as "private life" in his case (see p. 77)—he always has been and is Maharaja Saheb. Only in Europe can he escape a little from the burden of his rank.

CHAPTER V

MARRIAGE; AND A FINISHING EDUCATION

THE matter of Maharaja Sayajirao's marriage was one which greatly exercised his adoptive mother and Sir T. Madhavrao. The latter* amusingly describes the labour of choosing a wife.

"Trusted emissaries started from Baroda," he says, "and went to divers countries, some travelling in disguise, and others with pomp and circumstance. In a short time descriptive letters, illustrated photographs, and complete horoscopes, wonderfully showing all the planets in their best behaviour, poured in upon the Maharani in almost embarrassing abundance. The blessing of the tutelary deities was devoutly invoked, the goodwill of the priests was propitiated, and astrologers in solemn conclave were bidden to unerringly interpret the mystic influences of the zodiac. But the Maharani was also desirous of fulfilling more prosaic conditions, and she had to satisfy in her choice such worldly persons as the Governor-General's Agent and the Dewan of the State."

The Dewan (that is to say, Madhavrao himself) was sent in person to Poona to inspect certain Maratha ladies; for the field was limited to the Maratha race. Several reported eligible happened, "by pure accident," writes the Dewan with merry pen, to be present in Poona when he arrived. "We

* *Administration Report*, 1878–9.

saw them, but we could not decidedly approve of any of them." The perplexed Maharani, therefore, asked Sir T. Madhavrao to "extend the politico-æsthetic exploration" beyond Bombay Presidency, and "the predestined sharer of the young Gaekwar's fortunes was at last found on the banks of the Cauvery."

It was, in fact, in distant Tanjore that the Dewan of Baroda discovered a suitable bride. She was a Princess Laxmibai of the Mohite clan of the Marathas, niece to the husband of the Maharani of Tanjore. In age she was a year and a half younger than Sayajirao. The alliance seemed all that could be desired, as the Tanjore family was well known; and the announcement of the choice was welcomed in Baroda. The Bombay Government also signified its approval.

At the same time, but with less difficulty, a bridegroom was chosen for the young Princess Tarabai, whom it had been decided to marry almost simultaneously with her adoptive brother. For her Raja Saheb Ragunathrao, of Savantvadi, a small Maratha State in the south of Bombay Presidency, was selected. As will be seen, the two unions turned out very differently.

It remained now to fix an auspicious date for the Maharaja's wedding. Sir T. Madhavrao describes* the difficulties which arose. "The astrological advisers of both sides were at first seriously divided in their views as to which days the planets most favoured. Those on the side of the bride desired to fix the days most propitious to the bride, and similarly those on the side of the

* *Administration Report*, 1879–80.

bridegroom were anxious to give preference to the day most propitious to the bridegroom. The controversy waxed warm, feelings of jealousy or rivalry were excited, proud challenges were uttered, and laymen were in perplexity as to how to bring about a compromise. However, after allowing the combatants a fair opportunity to display their learning, an agreement was happily effected."

It is a curious picture, in view of the subsequent great reputation for enlightenment of the Prince whose wedding-day was in question, this scene of wrangling astrologers; and Sir T. Madhavrao's quaint style does not detract from the curiosity of it.

The festivities had begun before the decision of the date—as early, indeed, as December 12th, 1879—and the Princess Tarabai's marriage took place on December 21st. The Maharaja's bride, however, did not arrive until the end of the month, and then the astrological battle took place. Finally, January 6th having been agreed upon, and all the preliminary religious and social ceremonies having been performed, everything was ready for the great occasion. Baroda City was decorated with triumphal arches, its streets overflowing with processions, in which elephants, camels, and horses took their part, while music, both Indian and European, filled the air. Along the route which the Maharaja's elephant was to pass were lined the State troops and the police. Starting from the Old Palace at 3 p.m., and visiting first the temple of Raj Rajeshwar to receive the homage of the bride's uncle and guardian, he then was joined by the Agent to the Governor-General, in whose company he proceeded to the Nazar Bag Palace, which was to be the scene of the wedding.

We leave the description of the actual ceremony to Sir T. Madhavrao:

"The Palace itself was the scene of many interesting ceremonies. The tutelary deities were being constantly propitiated. Prayers were constantly offered to the planets to shed their benign influences. The priests were repeating ancient hymns in praise of the Almighty or offering abundant blessings to the bride and bridegroom. . . . The actual marriage ceremony itself was extremely interesting. The bride and bridegroom stood facing each other, taking their stand on heaps of consecrated corn, but with a thick curtain held up between them. Both wore rich clothes and ornaments of ancient style, but the bride was covered with a veil to protect her from the public gaze. In this position the family priests solemnly recited ancient texts and went through mystic ceremonies. Just when the propitious hour struck the curtain dropped, and then it was that, really or conventionally, the bride and bridegroom first saw each other. Showers of coloured rice were discharged upon the happy pair from all around, accompanied by fervent benedictions. The bride is given away by her father or guardian, and the gift is made by pouring water mixed with rice into the hand of the bridegroom, followed by placing the hand of the one on that of the other. During a subsequent ceremony the father or guardian of the bride says to the bridegroom and to all his party: 'This child, heretofore affectionately brought up by me, has now been given to you. Do you hereafter tenderly take care of her as your own. . . .' The bride and bridegroom make solemn promises of fidelity to each other. The bridegroom conducts the bride to a block of stone near the altar of fire, and makes her stand on it, and says: 'Behold this immovable stone on which you are standing. May your constancy to me be as immovable as this stone!' The couple walk seven paces on heaps of corn, at each step the bridegroom offering good wishes to the bride in respect of health, strength, longevity, constancy, abundance, progeny, and prosperity. A long succession of picturesque and primitive ceremonies of this sort were gone through at the Palace, in accordance with a ritual of unknown antiquity. The earth has changed, races have altered in their distribution and destinies, empires have risen and fallen, yet that ritual remains the same."

The rejoicings in connection with the two weddings continued until January 16th, thus lasting a whole month. One of the most notable events was the laying of the foundation-stone of a new Palace, the Laxmi Vilas, "the house of the pleasures of Laxmi," so named with an allusion to the young Maharani, although her name was changed on marriage to Chimnabai. Sir Richard Temple came from Bombay with the Commander-in-Chief, General Warre, to be present on the occasion. The day chosen was January 12th, and the stone was laid by Mr. Melville in the presence of the Maharaja and his guests. Both the Agent and Sir Richard made speeches in which they expressed the best wishes for the future welfare of the royal tenants of the Laxmi Vilas Palace.

The building was not completed until 1890, and by that time, alas ! Her Highness was dead.

Now, therefore, Maharaja Sayajirao was a married man. A description given of him a few months later by W. W. Locke, who during the months from May to October relieved Elliot of his duties as tutor, represents him as " very much like an English schoolboy, with good health and high spirits." Melville about the same time describes him as " thoughtful, good-tempered, and determined."

Elliot, on his return, was able to state that the marriage ceremonies had not seriously interfered with his pupil's work. It was planned, however, to make his education more intensive than ever, in view of an early termination of his minority. The Viceroy, Lord Ripon, was in favour of this, and, in spite of some opposition, finally had his way, fixing the date for December 28th, 1881, when the Maharaja would be well over eighteen.

Sir T. Madhavrao's attitude, on the suggestion of an early majority, was that His Highness's early education must be hurried on. In his opinion he had much to learn, especially in reference to his future work. " In Native States," he urged, " much (probably too much) depends on the personal character and capacity of the ruler." The science and art of ruling such a State today was " quite beyond the dreams of Hyder Ali, Ranjit Singh, and Damajirao." Accordingly, in August, 1880, he drew up a long memorandum on the principles on which the Maharaja should govern, such as that he should be taught that he was

LAXMI VILAS PALACE.

made for the people of Baroda, not they for him; that everything should be subordinated to their welfare, etc.

This memorandum the Dewan passed to Elliot, who thereupon proposed a change of curriculum. The young Gaekwar should remain at the Raja's School, but his instruction should be carried on entirely alone. The emulation with which it had been desired to furnish him had scarcely been successful. When his earlier Maratha school-fellows had failed to keep pace with him, a Brahman boy, Godbole, had been introduced to give him stimulus in his work and mental companionship. Even his presence would only be a hindrance in the last stage of His Highness's education, so he should be sent to the High School.

It had originally been intended that the period of the finishing education should be spread over several years, and that it should include a tour of inspection of Baroda's public offices and institutions, and of the country districts. But if the assumption of power by the Maharaja was to take place in December, 1881, a much shorter programme was necessary. Accordingly, it was decided that in March a nine month's course of lectures on the principles and practice of good government should begin, while the tour of inspection must be left over until after the assumption of power.

It was, indeed, a heavy task which the Maharaja was called upon to face in the last nine months of his minority. It is true that most of his ordinary studies hitherto, with the exception of Gujarati, Urdu, and arithmetic, were dropped to make time for the lectures. But, even so, the list of lectures has a most formidable look:

Twenty-three by the Dewan on general government principles, with some minor ones on the behaviour of a Prince.

Twenty-seven by Kazi Shahabuddin, *Sar Subha* (equivalent to Revenue Commissioner) of Baroda, on revenue matters.

Eighteen by Cursetji Rustonji, Chief Justice, on the law of the land.

Seven by J. S. Gadgil, Judge of the High Court, on Hindu law.

Six by V. J. Kirtane, *Naib* (Assistant) *Dewan*, on police matters.

Nine by Pestonji Jehangir, Settlement Officer and Military Secretary, on the affairs of his two departments; and

Certain other lectures by A. H. Tahmane on accounts, and by C. R. Thanawalla on law.

These lectures were delivered in English, and we are assured by Elliot that His Highness devoted to them all the powers of mind which he possessed. One must suppose that it was very necessary for him to do so, as he was not at that time proficient in English.

Elliot bears witness to the excellence of the matter and the charm of the delivery of the Dewan's lectures, the results of the varied experience of a long life spent at Indian Courts. Their text is preserved in a privately printed work entitled *Minor Hints*, and they certainly contain much sound advice on all sorts of matters connected with government, varying from the elementary, almost the trivial, to the very subtle.

"A Maharaja," says Sir T. Madhavrao, for instance, "ought not to overburden himself with work. He ought not to undertake so much work that his health would suffer thereby, that his recreations would be cut off or reduced, and that the work itself could not be done with that knowledge and deliberation which are necessary for it proper performance."

Again, "The demand for the best Ministers is especially imperative in Baroda, because of its situation and circumstances. There is probably no other Native State in all India which has to deal with interests more involved, more intricate, and more trying to the intellect. And there is probably no other Native State which is more exposed to public observation and criticism."

Sir T. Madhavrao is very staunch in his support of the Paramount Power, whose might, reason, and justice he emphasises. The best way to conciliate the British Government, he says, is to govern the State well. Treaties must be scrupulously observed. Secret emissaries of foreign Powers must be kept away, and all disputes with Native States must be referred to the British Government. Advice given by that Government must always be listened to—the advice, that is to say, of the Viceroy in Council, not necessarily that of a local subordinate, to which the treaties do not bind His Highness to listen. But the Resident must always be treated with respect, and freely consulted. And so on.

Against some of the other lecturers it has been objected that their deliverances were more calculated to show off their own erudition than to educate the Maharaja, that they have the effect of an attempt to impress a boy of eighteen with the idea of his backwardness and incapacity for personal administration. Whether this criticism is quite just it is difficult to say, even after reading some of the lectures. It must be remembered that to the lecturers, as to their hearer, English was a foreign tongue; and translation of thought plays many tricks. Moreover, excellent officials often have little capacity for oral instruction.

* * * * *

With the arrival of December the third and last stage in the young Maharaja's education came to an end. He had listened assiduously to the lectures, making notes as they proceeded, and asking any questions he might like to put. In the intervals between them he was given such books to read as were thought of service. Now, in the opinion of his guardians, he might be permitted to exercise the powers of his position, though, as we shall see, there were some people who thought that he still required leading-strings.

Speaking at the present day, His Highness regrets that he attained his official majority so young. Three more years of education, he feels, would have done him good,* and taught him many of the smaller things which he was forced to neglect,

* In an article contributed to *The Nineteenth Century* in February, 1901, he wrote to the same effect, adding: "For instance, I might have been brought more in contact with the people and the chiefs, and might have travelled more about the State and India." As we have seen, it had originally been intended that he should spend some time in a tour of his State.

and had to study later, when he had leisure for them. It was fortunate, however, seeing that time was so limited, that he had the wisdom to devote himself particularly to the more important subjects connected with the art of government, and that, having a logical and argumentative mind, he was able to grasp them sufficiently well to thresh them out with his ministers later.

CHAPTER VI

PERSONAL RULE BEGINS

THE investiture of Sayajirao III. with the full powers of government took place in December, 1881. The festivities in connection with it began on the 24th, and continued for eight days. The actual ceremony was performed on the morning of the 28th in a durbar tent in the grounds of the Nazar Bag Palace. The Viceroy of India, being unable to come to Baroda himself, was represented by Sir James Fergusson, Governor of Bombay, who, on his behalf, presented the Maharaja with the robes of State, placed him on the *gadi*, and made the speech declaring him a ruler in his own right.

Everything, Sir James declared, promised His Highness a prosperous and happy life, but the duration of that happiness would greatly depend on his appreciation of its conditions and uses. The time had gone when territories and populations would be regarded by sovereigns as the instruments of their personal glory and pleasure. Thrones and dynasties existed for higher ends. Happily, there were rewards for the faithful discharge of duty; but to gain them there must ever be kept in view an aim above self-gratification, or even human praise, a denial to self of that which would injure others or impede one's own usefulness. If, however, the Prince would subordinate his own desires to the good of his subjects, then he would be loved by them, and would ever enjoy the Imperial favour.

The Maharaja read a reply in English, in which he expressed his gratitude for all that the British Government had done for his State and himself, and made special acknowledgment of the services of Mr. Melville, of his predecessor, Sir Richard Meade, and of Sir T. Madhavrao. He promised, as his future policy, to be sincerely loyal to the Empress of India, and to strive for the good of his people.

Speeches on occasions like this will always seem, when read in the cold light of later days, a trifle inflated. But it must be admitted that Sir James Fergusson's words on the conduct necessary to obtain the rewards that are to be obtained by the faithful discharge of duty were an unconscious prophecy. They became, as it were, an inspiration to the Prince whom he was addressing.

* * * * *

The Maharaja of eighteen was now ruler in fact, instead of only in name. But that he was not even now an absolute ruler he was speedily made aware. His presence was desired at the Residency, where the Agent to the Governor-General informed him that there were certain matters connected with Baroda with which he would be expected to refrain from interfering for another two years. Being as yet, as he says himself, only a schoolboy, with less than six years of education behind him, he was in no position to argue with the representative of the Government of India, and gave the promise required of him. At the end of the two years he was to find that he was still expected to leave these matters alone. To the present day it has remained galling to him that the question of the equipment of the Baroda State Army is one which he may not be allowed to decide. To be asked to keep his forces efficient without being permitted actually to make them so does not seem to him reasonable.

This, however, is anticipating; for no such discussion occurred at the beginning of the reign. What occupied the Maharaja's attention at present was the putting into practice of the theories of good government which he had assiduously been trying to learn during the last period of his minority.

Had His Highness been obliged to take over the government of Baroda in the condition in which his predecessor had left it, he would have been faced with an almost superhuman task. Baroda in 1875 was on the very verge of bankruptcy. Malharrao had showered gifts upon his friends out of the public funds, leaving unpaid the *sardars*, or military class, the bankers, the jewellers, and anyone, indeed, whom he could leave unpaid. The State records were in "dire confusion," as Melville wrote in his introduction to the first *Administration Report* of the new reign, and there was not even a list of the Palace jewels, estimated to be worth £4,000,000. The people were grievously overtaxed and ground down by the revenue-farmers. In the towns—as, of course, in the country—sanitation was non-existent. In the same *Administration Report* Sir T. Madhavrao writes that the number of victims of cholera must continue unless the drainage and water-supply are improved. In Baroda City itself, "in many ill-ventilated houses, men, women, and children live together with horses, bullocks, and goats in a dim dungeon light."

The Dewan and his assistants had set themselves to work hard after the removal of Malharrao. In the first place a Central Government was erected, presided over by the Dewan, and comprising seventeen principal departments. Civil and criminal justice was reorganised; for, though adequate civil and criminal codes had been prepared in Khanderao's reign, it required men of good character to administer them, who so far had been lacking. The iniquitous revenue-farming system was abolished, and "ryotwary" established in its place, each ryot to pay a fixed assessment. The land assessment generally, one of the main grievances of the last two reigns, was considerably lowered. With the reform of the customs duties, another great grievance, it was found impossible to proceed at once, owing to the immense complexity and extraordinary inequalities of the prevailing system. A beginning was made with the cleansing and improvement of Baroda City, but not much could be done until the water-supply could be increased. A scheme for medical aid all over the State was considered, and the services of a medical officer was asked for from the Government of India.

For these and numerous other reforms it was necessary to find money, and the chief way to find money was to save it. Here, in Baroda, there was a wide field for economy. The Palace expenses had been enormous, and some of the debts which Malharrao left behind him had, in justice, to be paid. But it was possible to effect an immediate retrenchment by cutting off the allowances to the late Maharaja's favourites and dependents. Something could be done, too, though less easily, to make these people disgorge their plunder from the public funds in the past. The great staff of singers, dancers, musicians, and athletes attached to the Palace was not dismissed, but no new appointments were made.

A more difficult problem was to deal with the profuse waste of money on "charity" and supposedly pious objects. Baroda had long had the reputation of being a *Dharm Raj*, or kingdom of charity, and this reputation had not been lessened under Malharrao. Melville tells of the daily feeding of 7,000 Hindus and 3,000 Mohammedans, at a cost to the State of £200,000 a year. This could not at once be done away with, except at the cost of popularity for the new régime, but in the *Administration Report* of 1878-9 there is recorded a permanent reduction of R. 10,000 in Palace expenses, which had been devoted to free meals for Mohammedans.

In the previous *Report* Melville had written: "I believe that, if the truth were known, it would be found that not much short of a quarter of the whole revenues of the State are devoted to religious and charitable purposes." With all the badness of his character, Malharrao had been "pious," and a horde of undeserving holy men had flourished in his reign. It was an invidious task to check expenditure of this kind, nor did the attempt enjoy the sympathy of the Maharani and other Palace ladies. "The Royal ladies," writes

Sir T. Madhavrao,* "prompted by the Shastras to incessant benevolence, make new vows and undertake new rites, the merit of the large usual charities being too much regarded by these ladies as belonging to those who originally instituted them. Yet the ladies are unwilling to allow reductions in these usual charities initiated by their predecessors. In the course of my experience of Native States I have come across pious Brahmans being still employed in fervently praying for the long life of Maharajas long since demised."

However, retrenchment was gradually effected, and unnecessary expenditure avoided in all directions, so that, while just claims, of no light nature, against the late Maharaja were met, and great sums of money were spent on public works, when Sayajirao III. took up the reins of government he found no less than a crore and a half of rupees in reserve in his treasury.

Many allusions will be made hereafter to the innumerable useful activities of the Madhavrao administration of Baroda, and it is unnecessary here to give a complete history of reforms in the State between May, 1875, and December, 1881. It may suffice to say that under Sir T. Madhavrao, in addition to the reforms already mentioned, a Settlement Department was instituted, which at least began to tackle the thorny question of alienation of land; some, if rather cautious, steps were taken to free the people from vexatious taxation; arrears which were obviously beyond the means of the agriculturalists to pay were written off; assessments were reduced; the Public

* *Administration Report*, 1876–7.

Works Department was changed from a hopelessly incompetent to an efficient organisation; Baroda City was provided with a Public Park and the nucleus of a State Library; a Vernacular Education Department was formed, and Baroda College was opened; a Medical Department was created, and a beginning made of systematic medical relief in the district headquarters.

The question of communications also had serious attention. The Dewan, from his past experience in India, was an enthusiast for good roads; but the terrible cost of road-metalling in Baroda " has made us pause," he wrote in his first *Administration Report*. The main streets of the city were put in good order. For the districts, Sir T. Madhavrao gave consideration to the possibilities of cheap light railways. As we shall see in the chapter on railways, however, not very much progress was made until the Maharaja attained his majority.

Altogether it must be admitted that Sir T. Madhavrao, by what he did as Dewan of Baroda, showed that he fully deserved the honorary title of Raja which was bestowed on him at the Imperial Assemblage of January, 1877.

CHAPTER VII

THE MAN AND THE MACHINE

THE great difficulty which Maharaja Sayajirao felt when he became the actual ruler of Baroda was still the lack of friends and companions. It was even more a handicap now than in his boyhood, for his great need was sympathetic advice. F. A. H. Elliot, his work as tutor being ended, retired from his post on January 1st, 1882, though he remained another month in Baroda to complete the volume on the State for the official *Gazetteer* of the Bombay Presidency. The Maharaja was loth to part with him, and obtained from Bombay the loan of his further services, which were, however, employed chiefly in the very important Settlement Department.

The Marathi *Life* of His Highness makes it clear that it was a popular idea that Elliot had a complete hold over the mind and opinions of his former pupil, who, it was suspected, would in time become a *nastik* (unbeliever)! Such jealousy is, perhaps, inevitable where a British official exercises influence in an Indian State. But it undoubtedly made the Maharaja's task the harder.

The same Marathi *Life* speaks of the lack of sympathy for the Maharaja at the beginning of his reign, shown alike by his officers and by the public, whereby, however anxious he might be to initiate reforms, he was unable to make any immediate changes in the working of the administration. He says himself that he was conscious of being very much alone in the world, and found his Ministers only too willing to throw the decision of every matter, great or small, upon him. They did not say to him, "You decide upon more important affairs, while we look after the minor ones." He must take the responsibility for all decisions. At the same time they had their own ideas of what he ought to do, and expected him to do it.

Maharaja Sayajirao was never a man who could not brook opposition. In fact, he is, perhaps, unique among Indian Princes in his toleration of expressions of opinion contrary to his own. He has liked, and still likes, to hear the honest views of other men. What he has always demanded is that he shall be convinced before he gives way; and being, in his own words, "logical and argumentative," he can only be convinced by the exertion of his opponent's full reasoning powers. He insists on getting down to the bottom of things.

Nothing can give a better idea of the variety and complexity of the questions brought up for decision in the early part of his rule than a study of the "Huzur Orders."* When he began

* These Huzur, or Royal, Orders, of which there have been 49,472 in the course of forty-four years, embody an instructive diary of His Highness's opinions during the period of his personal administration; for it has been his practice, in giving the orders, to point out the general principles on which he acts, to be circulated afterwards for the guidance of his affairs. A two-volume compendium has been prepared and printed in the Marathi language, abbreviating and classifying the Maharaja's observations as set out in his orders. As an example of this guide for officers, we may take the following

A VIEW OF BARODA CITY.

to govern in person, the powers of the various officers were not fixed, no general principles had been laid down, nor was there a body of precedents for guidance. He had himself to go into everything before him. How trivial were some of the matters brought up for his decision can be easily illustrated.

In 1882 he was asked to sanction the expenditure of less than eight annas for candles when he rode one night to the Residency on an elephant, the expenditure of one rupee eight annas on the purchase of gunny-sacks, and the transfer of one acre from waste to arable land. In 1883 he was asked to agree to the grant of a quarter acre of land for sinking a public well. In 1885 the question of a monthly rent of four rupees for a house to be used as a village school required his consent. Some years later he noted in an order that he had spent time and energy in disposing of cases asking for sanctions for a door-handle and a mat!

---

extract, referring to the subject, just mentioned, of divergences of opinion:

"In some cases where His Highness has certain inclinations or convictions of his own, he yields to the pressing recommendations of the higher officials, either out of deference to their position, or in order to test their capacities and to allow them to show results in their own way, so that they may not be discouraged for want of sufficient latitude. He never fails, however, to express his own views, even when giving sanction against those views."

This may seem inconsistent with the statement above, that he insists on being convinced before giving way. But obviously there is a distinction between giving way on a matter of principle and giving way to test the theories of the opposition.

Maharaja Sayajirao, while appreciating that he learnt the petty details of administration and acquired a fund of general information by this laborious training, was speedily convinced of the necessity of organising the powers of departmental heads and their subordinates. This, again, entailed strenuous work, though more worthy of his mental exertions than sanctions for door-handles and mats. There was no settled procedure for the presentation of cases to him, no proper preparation by the minister who should have been responsible for it, no clear recording of departmental opinion as to the issues involved. Sir T. Madhavrao, when conducting the administration, must, of course, have had some method, or he would never have been able to accomplish what he did in Baroda. But all seems to have been forgotten in the dislocation caused by the handing over of the reins of government, so that what came before His Highness were multitudes of files, or even loose correspondence, from which he was asked to form his opinion on the merits of a case. The waste of time was enormous.

Fortunately, if there is one thing to which the Maharaja attaches especial importance in life, it is system. He has even been accused, though in no unfriendly spirit, of over-systematising his government, so that he leaves small scope for the ministers to use their abilities. This is by no means his view, which is well set out in a letter written to his nephew Ganpatrao on taking up some official work in 1895. "Do not attempt," he writes, "to centralise everything in your own hands, like our old people; but try to decentralise, and teach every subordinate of yours to do his work and use his brain and authority."

Similarly, in a Huzur Order he writes: "Heads of departments should not concentrate all their powers in themselves, but should decentralise, dividing them among their subordinates, and allowing them to assume due responsibility with regard to those powers."

We shall revert to this matter later, when the system will appear more in working order; for it will not be imagined, of course, that the young Maharaja in his early reign either had a system planned out or was able readily to impose his ideas upon his officers. For over thirteen years—1895 seems to mark an epoch in the reign—he was still learning the business of a ruler, while his ministers, unwilling to believe that he was ripening into a skilled administrator, were still fighting for supremacy.

To learn his business the Maharaja devoted all his energy, almost all his hours. His life was regulated by the clock, as in the days when he was still Elliot's pupil. He was up at sunrise, took light refreshment, walked or rode, worked till lunch-time, then after a brief rest worked again until tea. A little recreation, reading or talking, followed, then an evening walk. After dinner came reading until eleven o'clock, when he retired to bed. Such, indeed, has been his general programme in Baroda for fifty years, nor has he varied it, more than he can help, when away from his capital. The amount of physical exercise has diminished, but its regularity never. The attention to work is undiminished.

It will have been gathered, moreover, that when he worked there was no pretence at working. In his determination to introduce method into the departments of State he insisted on dealing with them personally, setting aside one day a week for each of the principal ones. In the end he had all their essential details at his finger-tips.

"There has been no room in my life for relaxation," observed His Highness one day on the voyage out to India in November, 1925. "That is a mistake which I would rectify if I could live my life again." Characteristically, what was at the back of his mind was that by some relaxation from the daily round of work in youth his health today would have been better, and he might have been able to spend more months of the year in Baroda—working on the spot. He made himself too much of a machine, he remarked on another occasion; and now the machine will not carry on its functions as well as he would wish it to. Still, it was his natural temperament, as well as his training, which caused him to lay down for himself so exacting a rule of life.

There is no doubt, however, that his insistence on regular exercise has enabled him to carry out the rest of his heavy daily programme in comparatively good health, even down to the present day. He has been a notable rider. The best of horses, says the Marathi *Life,* could not maintain their stamina under His Highness's long and strenuous rides. Twenty miles every day used to be his custom. The royal stables in Baroda are fine buildings, though now, in the age of the motor-car, the number of horses in them is reduced.

As a hunter His Highness has made his mark. Eleven tigers have fallen to his rifle, and as regards black buck, duck, and other lesser game, his reputation as a shot is high. As far as possible, with the development of Baroda State, the royal preserves have been maintained, especially beyond Makarpura, so dear to Maharaja Khanderao's heart. Today, however, these preserves see little of their master, though the sport which they provide is always to be had by visitors to the State.

Walking, as has been mentioned, has always been a favourite exercise with His Highness. Even in hilly country, such as Mahableshwar and the Nilgiris, he would not forgo it, and in such walks his companions used to find it difficult to keep pace with him. In his capital itself he still contrives to get about two hours' walking in the early morning and the evening. On board ship, too, during his many voyages, he has been an indefatigable promenader; nor is his rapid pace appreciably diminished by such obstacles as deck-chairs and perambulators, as anyone who has accompanied him can testify.

Among athletic sports, his chief game since boyhood has been lawn tennis, which he was still playing in 1926, after his sixty-third birthday. Of cricket he writes in 1904 to J. M. F. Patel, a well-known performer in India: "I have not myself played the game, but I have had it taught to all my sons by professonial Parsi cricketers."*

* His Highness's third son, Prince Shivajirao, showed promising cricketing form at Oxford. In the Freshmen's match of 1911 he scored 10 and 51, and in a subsequent trial 4 and 61, which secured him a place in four of the University

"It has always been my desire," he continues, "to see open-air pastimes in my territory, and I have myself tried to develop some of them. . . . The need for recreation seems to grow greater and greater, and indeed indispensable, as the race of life gets keener and the pace swifter."

Maharaja Sayajirao's patronage of athletics is well shown by the fact that the seventh annual Hind Vijaya Gymkhana was held in Baroda on December 23rd to 26th, 1925, when nearly 2,200 entries were received from various parts of Western India, as well as Baroda itself, and a long programme was carried out of running, jumping, wrestling, gymnastics, etc., and of Indian games, such as *atya-patya*, *khokho*, *hututu*, and *farigatka*. Even women and girls took part in this Gymkhana, though not in public. The Maharaja and Maharani, with the junior members of the royal family, were all present on the last day, when a crowd of about 10,000 people witnessed the final events and the prize-giving. It is His Highness's ambition to turn this Gymkhana into the Olympic Games of India, and a handsome subvention is paid to it annually from the Baroda Treasury.

---

fixtures. In seven completed innings he made 97 (including 51 not out *v.* Kent), with an average of 16·16. Next year, after 92 in the Senior's match and 31 in the Trial, he played against both the South Africans and the Australians (it was the year of the Triangular Tournament), making 62 and 0 *v.* the former and 17 and 12 *v.* the latter. Wisden's *Cricketers' Annual* for 1913 says: "Early in the season the Gaekwad of Baroda batted in such good style that he seemed almost certain of a 'blue,' but a serious accident—sustained away from the field—cut short his cricket."

It may be added that the name of the Maharaja Gaekwar of Baroda figures among those of the Vice-Presidents of the new Indian Gymkhana Club at Osterley.

As the late Dewan of Baroda, Sir Manubhai Mehta, puts it, His Highnesss is a firm believer in the motto *mens sana in corpore sano.*

CHAPTER VIII

DISTRICT TOURS

One of Maharaja Sayajirao's earliest acts after his assumption of control was the visitation of the whole of his kingdom, a part of his education which, through the curtailment of the period of his minority, had hitherto been neglected. It is, perhaps, noteworthy that the first district tour, the journey to Kadi, began in November, 1882, and that the 29th of the previous month had seen the retirement from the office of Dewan of Sir T. Madhavrao, who was succeeded by Kazi Shahabuddin, the former Revenue Commissioner.

The conflict of wills between a young ruler and an old minister is a frequent occurrence in history. His Highness, thirteen years later, in a confidential letter to V. M. Samarth, then Subha of Baroda, speaking of the frequency of changes of ministers, says that Sir T. Madhavrao left "not expecting, I suppose, to be always entirely satisfied with the course things would take. It is not easy," he goes on, "for a man who has ruled a State with supreme authority, and stood, in fact, almost in the position of a Raja, to step down to a less commanding level, where his will would not be so entirely absolute."

Though Sir T. Madhavrao may have felt, after his more than seven years in the dewanship of Baroda, that he was no longer required for the government of the State, he left with a proud record of work accomplished. He had done for Baroda what he had previously done for "the priest-ridden, debt-burdened State of Travancore," as Elliot called it; and on the foundations which he laid the modern progressive Baroda has been built.

With the change of Dewan accomplished and a more docile Minister installed in office, Maharaja Sayajirao set out on his trip. He recalls that it was on his way to Kadi, at Ahmedabad railway-station, that he first partook of European food—a startling innovation for a Hindu ruler, as it appeared then. His tour lasted for two months, during which he visited every town and every considerable village of the largest of the four *prants* which composed his kingdom, and made himself generally acquainted with every available detail concerning it.

This visitation he extended to Naosari in 1883-4, to Baroda *prant* in 1884-5, and to Amreli, the Kathiawar section of his State, in 1886-7, so that he was able to write to his younger brother Sampatrao in January, 1887, of "the last of my first tours in the kingdom." He had now acquired that first-hand knowledge of his realm which had rightly been held a most important part of his training as a ruler. He had seen every *taluka* (sub-district*) of every *prant*, examined the local records, even down to those of many of the villages, inspected the offices, schools, and other buildings, and reviewed the police.

This practice of district-touring His Highness

* There is actually another unit, the *vibhag*, intermediate between the *prant* and the *taluka* ; but it is difficult to find exact English equivalents for these terms.

6

has never dropped, in spite of his numerous visits to Europe. In the winter of 1925-6 he journeyed to Dabhoi, and various other parts of Baroda *prant*, to South and West Kadi, to Dwarka (Okhamandal), and to the main division of Amreli; and, had there been time, he would have seen more of Naosari than was allowed by his few railway journeys through it.

The routine of a *swari* (tour) has been very completely organised by him. On the first visit to Kadi a most elaborate bullock-train was required to move his camp, employing, it is said, two thousand animals. Now everything has been worked out on a thorough system, so as to be ready automatically when needed, tents and all, according to the size and character of the places visited. No great staff is required to do the work, which is in keeping with the love of simplicity that has increasingly marked His Highness through his reign. His travel-wardrobe has been similarly cut down. He tells how in the old days he used to be accompanied by a staff of thirty valets, who would bring with them all his clothes, from the age of sixteen upwards. Now he is content, on tour, with the services of one valet, and a few changes of dress.

The vast railway progress in Baroda has, of course, made for simplicity, as every town in the State can today be reached by light railway. Again, adequate rest-houses have been built in every considerable place, lessening the number of tents required. When the decision has been made to visit a spot, the necessary tents are erected in advance, the whole party travels by train, and only the State elephants make the journey on foot.

The procedure on *swari* is much the same everywhere. As soon as possible after arrival at his destination, Maharaja Sayajirao receives the town or the rural leaders at a durbar, sometimes two durbars, accepts the gifts of flowers, fruit, vegetables, etc., and listens to any complaints which they have to put forward, such as lack of roads or of water, over-taxation, and so on. He has always made a point also, from the time of his first trip to Kadi, of having presented to him the prominent local representatives of the arts, sciences, and crafts. After the durbar he has, ready prepared for him, the local reports, with which he quickly makes himself acquainted. On the next day he likes to visit, almost unattended, some of the neighbouring villages, and to look personally into the causes of complaint without ceremony or official interference. He may go on his round on horse, on elephant, in a carriage, or even in a bullock-cart, as may be most convenient, motoring being so often out of the question, owing to Baroda's paucity of metalled roads.

It is his custom to question casual people, even of the sweeper caste, it may be, and to get from them suggestions as to how things can be improved. Such suggestions are noted down for him, and afterwards considered.

First-hand information is a passion with him. He wishes to keep in direct touch with his people, and prides himself on his accessibility to all. His theory is that he should be always open to receive complaints and criticism. With regard to the airing of grievances, he says that he has during his reign provided the proper channels by which they can be redressed. But he does not want too much of the "middleman" system, which would lead his people to look on their Maharaja as unapproachable, and at the same time give the middleman too great a sense of his own importance. There must be no wall built up between ruler and ruled.*

Generally speaking, there is little pomp about His Highness's provincial tours. The long ceremonies of the durbars are inevitable. ("One must make a response to the people," he remarked once, after a specially protracted morning in durbar.) And in the tours of the winter of 1925-6 the rejoicings over the Jubilee called for some extra display. But simplicity is the rule.

Nor is this the case only on *swari*. In the capital itself undue elaboration has been abolished. Although, fresh from boyhood, Maharaja Sayajirao started perhaps with some liking for ceremonial, he soon grew out of it. At the beginning of his personal rule it was the custom, inherited from many past reigns, to have a regular army of servants in the Palace, from which the Maharaja could not stir without a whole crowd following him. This became irksome to him, and also he found that,

* A passage in Huzur Orders seems at first sight to contradict this: "When His Highness is touring the district, he keenly notes all points connected with his subjects' welfare and also critically observes his officers' methods. If applicants avoid the intermediate steps and approach him direct, he is deprived of the opportunity of testing the officers' capacity; and, besides, he has not all the facilities and information at his disposal in the districts."

This passage, however, refers to the *legal* redress of grievances, and aims at inculcating the use of the proper channels for obtaining justice.

the more the servants, the worse he was served. If he wanted a glass of water, says the Marathi *Life*, a hunt had to be made for the proper attendant to bring it to him. He therefore gradually cut down the staff, until, whereas about 1883 the number of Palace servants was two hundred, today it is only forty.

He has similarly dealt with his suite of honour. When he began his rule he found that all the *mankaris*—relatives and other courtiers—did personal service to him. This custom was not so easily broken. In 1900, however, he dispensed with the *mankaris*, and substituted, for the performance of their duties, a limited number of *aides-de-camp*, which four years later he reduced to three, working in rotation and under definite regulations, drawn up under his personal supervision. Of these officers a high standard of efficiency is demanded.

Between his first tours in Kadi and Naosari, Maharaja Sayajirao received an invitation from Lord Ripon to pay a visit to him in Calcutta. Accordingly, in February, 1883, he crossed India, arriving in Calcutta on the 18th, and exchanging calls with the Viceroy next day. While in Calcutta he took the opportunity to make himself acquainted with the principal objects of interest in the great city, which he was now seeing for the first time.

On his way back to Baroda His Highness paid visits to Benares, Allahabad, and Agra, and spent four days in Gwalior, with the Maharaja Sindia, with whom he was now on terms of intimate friendship, and on whose advice on the government of a kingdom he set great value. The Gwalior

Prince died in July, 1886. But the bonds between these two leading Maratha States have continued unbroken to the present day. In 1912 His Highness was anxious to draw them still closer by a marriage between his daughter, Indira Raja, and the then Maharaja Sindia, the son of his old friend; but the Princess willed otherwise, and became instead Maharani of Cooch Behar.

The visitation of the central portion of his kingdom, the Baroda *prant*, was spread by the Maharaja over the years 1884-5, that of his Kathiawar territory, Amreli, being left until the year-end, 1886-7, by which time he had put himself in direct touch with every division of the State.

It was inevitable that a personal knowledge of the conditions of life among his subjects should impress upon the Maharaja's mind the supreme importance to Baroda of a better water-supply, and the beginning of 1885 was marked by an event which was destined to bring vast changes in the health records of the capital. Under the rule of Khanderao, and again during the administration of Sir T. Madhavrao, the efforts of the engineers called in to suggest how water could be obtained to fill a reservoir sufficient for the needs of the city were in vain. The cost was prohibitive of any scheme which promised an adequate supply. At last, however, it was decided that the plans of an Indian engineer, Mr. Jagannath Sadashiv, should be adopted, to dam the Surya River, a tributary of the Vishvamitri, and a neighbouring watercourse, and so form a lake from which the water could be led through settling-tanks, filter-beds, and a service reservoir to Baroda City.

SAYAJI SAROVAR (AJWA LAKE).

The first sod in connection with this great scheme was cut on January 8th, 1885. The work was completed five years later, when the Sayaji Sarovar, or Ajwa Lake, began to supply Baroda with the long-prayed-for supply of pure water. Situated about thirteen miles east of the Pani Gate of the city, the lake had at first a catchment area of thirty-six square miles, which was subsequently increased to fifty square miles. Its actual water-spread is five and a half square miles, with an average depth of eleven feet, and, when full, its available yield is over 10,500,000 gallons.* This is calculated as sufficient to supply the City and the Camp for two years and a half, even in the absence of rainfall. When the present writer saw the Sayaji Sarovar in the winter of 1925-6 the water was low, and only about one year's supply was left; but a good monsoon in 1926 greatly improved the situation.

The cost of these waterworks was great, R. 3,400,000 in all. But apart from the fact that there is an annual revenue therefrom of about R. 70,000, the boon to Baroda is inestimable. Encouraged by the success of the scheme, the Maharaja was led to take an unceasing interest in the supply of water to other parts of his State. Suggestions of his on the subject are frequent in Huzur Orders. In 1900 he set up a permanent Irrigation Department, on the basis of a temporary existing division of the Public Works Department. In 1901, and again in 1906, he called for the submission of possible irrigation schemes for all districts in need of water. Much of the necessary

* See *Gazetteer*, ii., 334-5, for full details.

work has now been done; but His Highness's concern with the water question in Baroda continues lively. In the winter of 1925-6 he devoted attention to it in the course of his district tours, especially when visiting Savli, Sankheda, Kadi, and Bechraji, where, as always, he would take no evidence except that of his own eyes.

CHAPTER IX

DOMESTIC AFFAIRS; AND A VICEREGAL VISIT

In the year 1885 Maharaja Sayajirao suffered a great domestic affliction, which had also a considerable effect on his public life. He was strongly attached to his wife, the Maharani Chimnabai, who had borne him first a daughter and then a son, Fatesinghrao. Unhappily, on May 7th, soon after the Prince's birth, she died. For long the Maharaja was inconsolable. He went through a nervous crisis, and suffered severely from insomnia. His ministers and the Palace doctors failed to understand his case. The former, as he recalls with amusement today, when they found him not sleeping, remarked admiringly that "Maharaja is vigilant !" The doctors thought that a few weeks' rest and a second marriage would be enough to cure him.

The memory of his young first wife was not to be so easily effaced as this.* He consented to take a rest, but without appreciable benefit. Before the end of the year he agreed to contract a second marriage, and on December 28th he took to wife the Princess Gajrabai, one of the numerous

* When laying the foundation-stone of the "Chimnabai" NyayaMandir (Temple of Justice, *i.e.*, Law Courts) on May 28th, His Highness said : "I wish to commemorate the virtues of her late Highness, and the admiration I entertained for her—the mild, charitable, amiable woman, the devoted mother, and the loving wife."

daughters of Bajirao Amritrao Ghatge, member of a well-known Maratha family in Dewas State.* This accomplished lady, who took on her marriage the name of Chimnabai II., is the present Maharani Saheb, the mother of His Highness's sole surviving son and daughter. To her co-operation with her husband in the work of progress in Baroda allusion will be made elsewhere. It will not, of course, be supposed that Her Highness was from the beginning ready to embrace modern ideas. The Marathi *Life* makes it clear that the Maharaja, who had not had the time to educate his first wife to share his passion for reform, including the abolition of the *purdah* system, set himself to imbue the second Maharani Chimnabai with his views. The opposition of their relatives and of the orthodox Hindus had to be faced; but he did not hesitate. It required the help of several European trips and contact with Western society to complete the process. It was not until after the tenth trip, at a prize-giving in the Nyaya Mandir in February, 1914, that by sitting in public on the same sofa their Highnesses gave the sign of the abandonment of *purdah.*

If it took so long to combat one of the most firmly rooted of Indian social prejudices (though not, be it said, an original Hindu idea, but an imposition of Mohammedan origin), there was another restriction which Maharaja Sayajirao, for all his wishing, was unable to remove. It has

* According to the Marathi *Life*, "Bajirao's sister was married to Bapusaheb Maharaj, of the Dewas junior branch (of the Ghatges), which made Bajirao come to stay at Dewas, leaving his ancestral property in the Deccan."

H.H. THE MAHARANI CHIMNABAI II.

already been remarked that he felt most keenly the demand made upon him to maintain his royal rank on every occasion. This demand followed him even into the family circle. "I never had any family life," he told a friend once, "no kissing—to mention a small point—no familiarity, all salaams! This was so when I was a boy. When I married and had children of my own, I did not know *how* to be anything else than Maharaja. My children have said to me, 'You are always the Maharaja.' I have never ceased to look after them; but there has been no intimacy." He would have given very much, he added, to have been able to cut his life in two, to retire, when he pleased, from Palace to "home." His early training in Baroda, however, acting on his natural sensitive reserve, left him without power to break through a barrier which irked him grievously.

This is a curious confession, coming from a man who has had the courage to break through so many barriers. But it is not difficult to understand. With many people who can unflinchingly follow a general principle to its end, undeterred by opposition, where the personal element comes into the question the action of the will seems paralysed.

Soon after the Maharaja's second marriage, Lord Reay, Governor of Bombay, came to Baroda for a three days' visit, leaving on January 14th for Delhi to witness the Army manœuvres. Later in the year a still more important visitor came, Lord Dufferin, who was the first Viceroy thus to favour Baroda. He would have been accompanied by Lady Dufferin, but for the illness of their son. Arriving on November 8th, he was received with great pomp at the station. Visits were then exchanged between him and the Maharaja. The newspapers comment on the fact that, when the latter paid his call, the Viceroy advanced to the edge of the durbar carpet to meet him—an honour accorded only to few of the great ruling Princes of India.

The day was observed as a public holiday in Baroda, while at night there were illuminations and a display of fireworks. The most important ceremonies, however, were reserved for the next day, November 9th. They began with the opening by the Viceroy of the newly finished hospital, designed by the late Major C. Mant, and erected, at the cost of R. 350,000, on the right-hand side of the road leading to the western gate of Baroda City. This building was given the name of the "Countess of Dufferin Hospital." It would bear, said the Maharaja in his opening address on the occasion, "the honoured name of Her Excellency, in order that this auspicious visit may for ever be recorded, and that Lady Dufferin's exertions in the cause of the women of India may be gratefully remembered in Baroda." In his reply the Viceroy paid a tribute to the great progress which Baroda, "thanks to the intelligent energy of its ruler," had made in everything tending to ameliorate the social conditions of the inhabitants.

After the hospital had been opened the Maharaja and his guest drove to see the Baroda jewels, and then to a review of the State Army. It was remarked later in the Bombay Press that nothing interested the Viceroy more in the tour he was then making of India than the manner in which the Gaekwar's army had been reorganised. In place of the former large and badly equipped force, mostly irregulars, Baroda now possessed a compact, smart little army, in which discipline was good and the regiments were able to bear comparison with the best of the Bombay Army.

In the evening there was a State banquet at the Palace. In his speech proposing Lord Dufferin's health the Maharaja expressed his pride at the first Viceregal visit to Baroda. He alluded to the forthcoming Jubilee of Queen Victoria, whom he called " one of the most fortunate, glorious, and beneficent rulers the world has ever seen," and spoke of his meeting, as a little boy, with the Prince of Wales, to whom he asked the Viceroy to present his respects.

Lord Dufferin, in his reply, called attention to the air of universal prosperity which characterised Baroda, and the happy and contented appearance of the people—the marks of a conscientious and intelligent administration. They confirmed him, he said, in the opinion that the Gaekwar was one of the most promising, high-minded, and wise rulers with whom India had ever been blessed, and that in him the Queen-Empress possessed a noble *Arkan-i-Daulat* (Pillar of State).

Another firework display marked the close of the evening. At daybreak the next day Lord Dufferin left Baroda for Bombay, both carrying away with him and leaving behind the impression of the utmost cordiality of relationship between Baroda and the Paramount Power. To the happy circumstances of this visit was partly due, no doubt, the bestowal, among the Jubilee Honours, of the G.C.S.I. upon the Maharaja Gaekwar.*

* * * * *

When speaking at the opening of the Countess of Dufferin Hospital, the Maharaja had made a modest allusion to what had already been accomplished in his reign—the provision of drinking-water for the city, the building of Laxmi Vilas, the construction of Baroda College, the Public Park, the Government Offices, many schools and dispensaries, etc. He had reminded his hearers that in the districts, too, progress had been made with public works, notably with a railway-line in Kadi —" one only, let us hope, of many railway-branches in the future."

There were other progressive measures of this period to which His Highness might have referred, had he not desired to confine himself to actual achievements, more or less complete. In 1885 he had given orders for an important step to be taken in the land settlement of his State; and in 1886 he had directed that a beginning should be made with the task of separating the judicial and executive powers of his officers in the districts. The latter measure is dealt with elsewhere.† With regard to land settlement, he commissioned F. A. H. Elliot to deal with the vexed question of *barkhali* lands, an evil legacy from past rulers of Baroda.

* The honour was not gazetted till February 15th, 1887, but in a letter to Lord Dufferin on the previous January 16th. Maharaja Sayajirao speaks of Queen Victoria's extreme kindness in honouring him with the insignia of the Order.

† See Chapter XXVI.

Barkhali lands were lands wholly or almost free from taxation, representing the reckless grants of earlier Gaekwars for pious purposes or as rewards for real or imaginary services rendered. Moreover, not only the Gaekwars themselves had thus alienated land; so, too, had officials who had no shadow of right to do so. Maharajas Anandrao and Sayajirao II. had endeavoured to stop further alienation. Khanderao went beyond them, and demanded a quit-rent from genuinely alienated land, while refusing to recognise recent sales or mortgages of such land. Malharrao made fresh grants in pious gratitude for a recovery from illness, and the beginning of the present reign found nearly one-tenth of the villages in Baroda practically exempt from taxation. To Elliot now was entrusted the task of remedying this situation. His labours ultimately bore fruit in 1889, when legislation was introduced on the subject.

CHAPTER X

FOREIGN TRAVEL

THE year 1887 marked a very important epoch in the life of Maharaja Sayajirao. His health at the beginning of this year was very unsatisfactory, and in a letter* to his recent visitor, Lord Dufferin, on January 16th he writes of feeling "seedy and unwell," and of contemplating a trip to Ceylon. "I hate the idea of an absent Maharaja," he continues. "Of late, you know, I have not been able to keep such good health as I consider necessary in a man of my position. . . . I will make the best possible arrangements under the circumstances for the safe going of my State. . . . I love my people, and I would not have chosen to be away had it not been imperatively necessary."

There is the same note of uneasiness in a letter to F. A. H. Elliot sixteen days later. "The truth is that the people do not like to see me run about so much," he writes. "They do not know the reasons that compelled me to go. Still, taking all in all, I cannot say that they are wrong."

His Highness only took three weeks for the trip to Ceylon, where he stayed at the Mount Lavinia Hotel—an even more startling innovation for an Indian Prince than his meal at Ahmedabad Station in November, 1882. From Colombo he went to Mahableshwar, to continue his search for health.

* From the end of 1886 we have the inestimable benefit of His Highness's collected letters, 1,800 in number.

But he was not successful, for he writes thence to his brother Sampatrao in England on April 11th that he is suffering from loss of weight and sleepless nights still, and is determined to have a complete rest of six months.

He had, in fact, conceived the revolutionary idea, as it seemed to pious Hindus, of crossing the *Kala Pani* (" Black Water ") and visiting Europe. His sending of Sampatrao as a student to England had been a shock to Hindu tradition. For himself, a Hindu Maharaja, to cross the ocean was a far greater shock still. But his continued nerve trouble and insomnia prompted him to consult Sir William Moore, head of the Bombay Medical Service, who ordered him to Europe; and, in addition, he was bent on seeing the world outside India. How momentous was his resolution is evident from the subsequent history of his administration of Baroda.

Having handed over the reins to his Dewan, Laxman Jagannath (who had succeeded Kazi Shahabuddin in the previous August), on May 31st, 1887, His Highness set sail from Bombay, accompanied by the Maharani, a private physician, and a suite of over fifty people. This royal retinue was very different from the modest staff which accompanied him in later years; but he could not yet dispense with all the ceremony which was expected of a Maharaja. Old customs must not be shattered all at one blow.

In a later brief travel diary (May, 1900) he recalls some of the feelings of his subjects and his relatives on the eve of this first journey to Europe. In Baroda there was a great reluctance to let him go at all. He speaks of the people who saw him off with "expressions of deep sorrow and tears in their eyes." His adoptive mother and aunts were full of dread of the voyage, the unknown country which he was visiting, the strange food and water, the different ways of society. They implored him, however, to think only of his health, and to forget State affairs until it was restored.

The first place visited in Europe was Venice, where the Maharaja and his companions spent three days before proceeding to Aix-les-Bains. At Aix a long stay was made, and it was not until the end of September that he felt sufficiently well to carry out the wish which he cherished of seeing something of England. In particular, he promised himself to pay a visit to Oxford, where not only his brother, but also his cousin, Ganpatrao Gaekwar, was in residence. He was able to gratify his desire, spending part of October and November in the University town; but to the present day he talks of a higher ambition, which he was compelled to leave unsatisfied, to spend at least a year at the University itself, so that he might endeavour to remedy some of the deficiencies of which he was acutely conscious in his education. Not only had he to repress this condition; there was no one even to whom he could confide it. It remained, like so many of his aspirations, "bottled up."

At the end of November the Maharaja was in London, where, in apartments which had been taken for him in Victoria Street, he received a visit from the Secretary of State for India, Viscount Cross, to arrange the details of a call at Windsor Castle for the purpose of being invested with the insignia of the G.C.S.I. On December 2nd, together with the Maharani and Lord and Lady Cross, he travelled by special train from Paddington to Windsor. "In deference to native custom," as the newspapers reported, no males were allowed on Windsor platform except the officials on duty. The Maharani, studiously avoiding attention, walked to the closed carriage waiting for her outside the station with a lady on either side of her, and drove to the Castle behind her husband's open carriage. It was a strange ordeal for a Hindu Princess in those days.

After lunch the Maharaja went for a drive with Lord Cross in Windsor Park, and at six o'clock the ceremony of investiture took place. This was the first occasion on which he had met Queen Victoria. It marked, as we shall see, the beginning of an attitude of mutual esteem which lasted to the end of the Queen's life.

Part of the visit to England was spent at Brighton, and it was not until February, 1888, that the Maharaja started back for Baroda, which he regained after an absence of nearly nine months.

It had been hoped that his health would be set up by his European trip. Unfortunately, this did not prove to be the case. He was still ailing, and decided to go to Ootacamund. The climate here disappointed him; but in May he was able to write to Lord Dufferin (in a letter which mentions the receipt of congratulations from Queen Victoria on the birth of his second son, Jaisinhrao) that he was sleeping soundly and that his digestion was better. Nevertheless, next month, on medical advice, he was again on his way to Switzerland for a short visit. He made St. Moritz his headquarters, and derived considerable benefit from a stay of two months and a half.

It must not be thought that these constant allusions to the bodily condition of the Maharaja are superfluous; for it has been a factor of serious importance through the greater part of his reign, and the failure of long spells of ill-health to check his labours on behalf of his State is a wonderful tribute to his persistence of purpose in the face of a heavy handicap. In the spring of 1889 he was obliged to leave Baroda and seek the better conditions of Mahableshwar. From there he wrote to Elliot in May that he had taken to work again and was "enjoying it." For the next two years, however, his energies were much restricted by physical infirmity, until early in 1892 he resolved to make a third European trip.

In the interval Baroda twice received distinguished visitors, whom, fortunately, the Maharaja was sufficiently well to entertain with due honour. At the end of 1889 Lord Reay paid his second visit to Baroda, this time accompanied by his wife. His term as Governor of Bombay was drawing to an end—he retired in the following April—so that he would have no opportunity of coming to Baroda again. But he had by now formed a friendship with its Maharaja which was to endure, as the latter's many letters to him show.

The other visitor was Prince Albert Victor of Wales, who was on a sporting tour in India in early 1890, and arrived in Baroda on March 13th from the Nepal Terai. The festivities in his honour were much the same as on other visits of

State, except that now the Laxmi Vilas Palace was completed and had become the permanent royal residence, where banquets and durbars were held. The young Prince spent two days at Baroda, and then went on to Kathiawar in search of lion, which, however, proved very scarce.

Two very important events in connection with the public health of Baroda occurred before the Maharaja left for Europe again. In 1891 a Sanitary Department, under a Commissioner, was set up for the whole State, taking over the work hitherto inefficiently performed by the local authorities with their staffs of *bhangis* (sweepers). On Baroda City an even greater boon was bestowed when, on March 29th, 1892, the Ajwa Waterworks began to supply pure water for drinking purposes to the whole population. What this meant can easily be appreciated by anyone who has lived in the East.

Another progressive step was taken in the early months of 1892, when the task of codifying the laws of Baroda was entrusted to two experts, one a Hindu, the other an Englishman.*

On May 7th, 1892, Maharaja Sayajirao for the third time set sail from Bombay to Europe. This time he went first to London, and thence to Norway, which he did not much appreciate; to Dresden and Berlin, which appealed to him much more; and finally to " my tried friend St. Moritz," as in one of his letters he calls it. In December he sailed from Brindisi for Bombay, and on January 1st, 1893, he was once more in Baroda.

Although, as we shall see later, his mind was now

* See Chapter XXVI.

very full of his scheme for the introduction of compulsory education into his State, he was still struggling with ill-health, principally gout, and was advised to make an early return to Europe and try a cure at Carlsbad, travelling to Trieste by the Austrian Lloyd boat. He was not accompanied by the Maharani, and took but a small staff. He writes to one of his ministers from Vienna in May, 1893, of the pleasure of having a small number of well-trained attendants instead of "a large number which mostly consist of useless, idle men."

In Carlsbad he met Lord Lansdowne, to whom he was careful to explain the reason of his being away from his State; and he wrote to Lord Reay in July declaring that he felt more than anybody the evils of his absence. He went straight back to Baroda in October without visiting England, though only to return barely seven weeks later, having being advised to complete his cure by spending the winter in the Riviera.

As it turned out, his fifth trip was His Highness's longest absence to date from Baroda, lasting thirteen months. Before he left Baroda there was some friction with the Agent to the Governor-General; for the Maharaja complained, some time after his return,* that he had been forced to dele-

* Letter of September 24th, 1895, to Dr. Nevins (see p. 96). In his article in the *Nineteenth Century* of February, 1901, His Highness alludes to the powers of the Resident (Agent), and says: "The effects of my absence are determined very much by the personal characteristics of this officer; but it may be generally stated that the result of my being away is to make his intervention more frequent and more felt. The result

gate practically all his powers to the Council and to the Agent to the Governor-General. He doubtless felt the more aggrieved because he had already, by the time of the fifth trip, organised a system of keeping in touch with Baroda affairs, even if it had not reached that thoroughness which all those who come in close contact with him during his visits to Europe must know and admire. When he is away from Baroda, copies of all political correspondence are sent to him, with a précis of the past history of each case. From his ministers he gets weekly letters, and from the heads of departments and the *subhas* monthly letters. Even the agenda of all Council meetings are forwarded to him. Thus it is only a matter of a fortnight's delay before he is fully informed of what is happening in Baroda (provided, of course, that his officers on the spot do their duty), and by the use of the telegraph even this delay can be avoided. In his turn, the Maharaja can convey his precise orders to Baroda with a speed only limited by the question of expense. At the present day, since the introduction of wireless telegraphy, he can, and does, transmit orders on the voyage from or to India.

During his twelve months' continuous absence in Europe His Highness made a considerable addition to his experience of travel; for, in addition to London, Edinburgh and the Scottish Highlands, Paris and Nice, Vienna, Munich, various parts of Switzerland, Florence, and Genoa, he paid a visit to Constantinople.

---

of this external and, I might almost add, needless intervention is that it multiplies and accentuates the slight inconveniences of my absence into serious difficulties."

He returned from his fifth foreign tour in January, 1895; and here we may conveniently break off the story of his travels and return to that of his government of Baroda. As a matter of fact, there was a lapse of more than five years before he again ventured to leave his State, except for retirement to the hills during the hot weather and one brief trip to Egypt. The reason for this was not merely an improvement in his health, but also the very unsatisfactory condition in which he found Baroda. "I am astonished," he writes to Colonel N. C. Martelli, officiating Agent to the Governor-General, soon after his return, "at the change wrought in the people during the last twelve months. . . . *Khatpat** is very rampant. How one is forcibly reminded of old *khatpati* Baroda ! . . . Without a great change, which I am afraid cannot safely be postponed too long, I cannot expect thorough sympathy and honest help. I don't think I am faithfully and rightly served by those from whom I have a right to expect (it)."

What had happened was that professional agitators, taking advantage of his absence from Baroda, had stirred up discontent, and those whom he had left in charge of the administration had proved too weak to "keep up the dignity of the State," as he expresses it in another letter to

* Intrigue. The allusion in "old *khatpati* Baroda" is to the days of Sayajirao II. and Ganpatrao, and to the famous report of Colonel J. Outram of April 30th, 1851, which led to his temporary removal from Baroda by the Bombay Government, stung by his criticisms of their neglect to deal with the situation. They afterwards repented and sent Outram back to the Residency in spite of Ganpatrao's protests.

THE OLD PALACE AND MANDVI.

Martelli. There were other troubles, too, to which we shall come later, which made him determine that for the present he must forgo the further enlightenment of his mind by travels abroad.

* * * * *

Many years afterwards the Maharaja, speaking of travel, maintained that it is the highest form of education. Among the Indians, in particular, it would lead to rapid reform, he said. "If one could get hold of them young, and take them in hand, all would move quickly." But he fully admitted the danger for Indian youth of contact with the West. "Although there is an intense conservation in India, when its people come in contact with European forms of life they are prone to imitate them, without necessarily understanding them. There is the lure of Fashion!"

In his inaugural address to the Industrial Conference at Calcutta nineteen years earlier* he had insisted on the value for Indians of training abroad. "For years, and perhaps generations," he said, "you must send your young men to Europe, America, and Japan for that complete industrial training which they cannot yet receive at home. Make no mistake, and let no time-honoured prejudices deter you from travelling in other parts of the earth, and receiving that new life, that new culture, those new ideas, which even the most gifted and advanced nations always receive by mixing with other people, and which India needs, perhaps, more than any other civilised nation."

At the same time His Highness has always

* December, 1906.

insisted that the example of Japan, in a discriminate borrowing from the West, is the right one for India to imitate. In particular, he regrets the decay of many ancient customs, which were a legacy from India of the past. "It is a great pity," he wrote to his Dewan, Manibhai, in January, 1894, "that with a kind of Western education our old and popular institutions are being deprived of their life and vitality. Baroda is following the example of other British places, and it is to be deplored. It is our right interest to try to preserve our national customs. They have grown by ages, and have history in their favour."

This letter to Manibhai, written in Nice, affords a good instance of the Maharaja's desire to preserve the old features of Indian life, while introducing new ideas. With the aid of F. A. H. Elliot, at the head of the Survey and Settlement Department, he had been doing his utmost to foster the ancient village-community system, which had been much weakened by the introduction of ryotwary and the centralisation of powers in the *taluka* headquarters. In a departmental report for 1893 Elliot wrote of His Highness's "generous wish that the village should once again" be self-ruling. This meant the restoration of the *panchayats* (councils of elders, village boards) under the hereditary officials known as *patels*. Now in January, 1894, His Highness writes to his Dewan that Elliot is to be told he must, before he leaves India, introduce in at least a hundred villages *elective* councils. "I am deeply interested in that measure, and wish it to extend to all my

State. . . . It will be a keystone of what I wish to develop in my State."

It was not until eight years later that the "*Gramya Panchayat* Rules" were issued, establishing a *panchayat*, half nominated and half elected, in every village of a thousand or more inhabitants; and not until another eighteen years that the new "Village *Panchayat* Act" was passed, increasing the elective element to two-thirds. But the germ of the idea was present, we see, in His Highness's mind long before, and occupied his attention while he was far away from his kingdom. As always, foreign travel, while he made it the source of inspiration, was not allowed to distract him from the care of Baroda.

CHAPTER XI

TROUBLES OF STATE

It was with an anxious heart that Maharaja Sayajirao came back to Baroda at the beginning of 1895. We have heard how he found agitation and intrigue rampant. He felt that there were people at the Residency who, instead of helping him, made the position more difficult for him. This is abundantly clear from his letters of the period. "The problems which engage the attention of a Native Ruler," he writes to General Sir John Watson in May, "become yearly more perplexing. Hedged in by difficulties and restrictions, he loses some of his self-respect and a large share of personal influence which was the heritage of his predecessors. . . . It is only bare justice that the Imperial Government should realise these facts, and not depend simply on those smooth and carefully edited official versions they are served with by the Residency."

"The Residency," he tells his brother Sampatrao in July, "is ever on the watch to take advantage of any seeming defects in our native administration." And to Kazi Shahabuddin, the ex-Dewan, he says: "The officers are much more afraid of this Residency now than I have ever seen them. . . . I write this, not as a Prince discontented with the British, but give my impressions to a friend as they strike a person in my difficult position."

He complains to Kazi Shahabuddin of the agitation in the vernacular papers, in which the Dewan Manibhai "is held up as a good man, and it is I who, with the advice of bad men, wish to interrupt the course of justice." The allusion here is to the "Bapat case," which was made by F. A. H. Elliot's enemies the occasion for an attack on him. There were accusations against various subordinates in the Settlement Department, notably one V. S. Bapat, of corruption and extortion. His Highness appointed a commission of enquiry, and a report was presented, which, however, he had not had time to study by July. The Residency asked for certain papers in the case, and the Dewan was of opinion that some of them should be handed over. A prosecution followed of the accused parties by a former British assistant in the Settlement Department. The result was an acquittal; but His Highness decided to dispense with Bapat's further services. In a letter to Elliot, who had now at last left Baroda and reverted to British service as Collector of Bijapur, he wrote (December 13th, 1895) that if there had been any delay in the decision of the Bapat case, it was "merely the result of extreme caution on my part, arising from the fear of the Residency." Had the case been treated in the ordinary judicial way, he added, the State might have been saved two or three lakhs of rupees.

There is no doubt that the Maharaja was hurt by the removal of Elliot from his employment in Baroda, and indignant at the intrigues against him. Other changes in his ministers, however, he considered necessary for the good of the State. He displaced Manibhai in November, his next Dewan being S. R. Iyangar, a native of Madras. Explaining the supersession of Manibhai and other officials in a friendly letter to V. M. Samarth, he says that, through the unsoundness and confusion of the management during his absence from Baroda, the machinery of government had been thrown out of gear. The corruption in the Settlement Department had not been reported to him, the administration of justice had been dilatory, the Accounts Department had disregarded instructions, and generally progress had been suspended.

In a similar letter to Jaisingrao Angre (who acted as Dewan pending the appointment of Iyangar) he complains of almost an upset of the balance of power by recent events in Baroda, and the ruin of his prestige. " It is a serious question how the race feelings and the rampant intrigues will get less. Unless the ruler is respected and bad people punished, no government is possible."

To Sir John Watson about the same time he writes that " one of the results of the recent commotion is that certain classes of people and courtiers are inclined to press their demands in rather an obtrusive manner, and to hint at appeals to the Agent to the Governor-General in case they are not complied with "; and to Dr. J. E. Nevins, who had been some years combined medical adviser and companion to him, that " had not the Residency forced my hand to delegate all my powers to the Council and the Agent to the Governor-General, all the mischief in Baroda would have been avoided."

It is evident that the Maharaja felt a distinct

grievance against the Residency, or, at least, against some person or persons in it, whom he suspected of being behind the trouble in his State.* He had learnt a lesson, however, and did not again leave India without assuring himself that the machinery of government during his absence was in safe charge.

Echoes of the storm of 1895 continue to be heard through His Highness's correspondence for a considerable time. To Lord Reay in January, 1897, he complains that the Agent to the Governor-General has not the independence of character to fight for the views of Baroda against the surrounding political officers and others, and suggests that this is one of the results of the Residency having been reduced to a lower status. (This suggestion bore fruit; for in April, 1899, the designation of Resident was restored, Colonel Martelli being the first to bear it again.) Of the removal of Elliot from his service he has much to say to Lord Northbrook a few weeks later. The officials who wanted to get rid of Elliot had talked of him as his old tutor exercising absolute influence over him. "This sort of report, especially when first started by Residents and other European officers, will always serve to blind people."

Former Residents, he adds, are said to have recorded unfavourable opinions of Elliot; but the

* With Colonel Martelli himself he appears from his letters on excellent terms, mentioning, for instance, to Lord Northbrook his "kindness and sympathy"; but of a certain assistant he writes sarcastically to the Dewan Manibhai in August, 1895: "He thought, I am told, that he was an able Police Officer, having learnt that useful art in the malicious [*sic*] districts of Burma."

truth is that they, and still more the native officials, were jealous of the trust imposed in him. "The manner of his departure and the circumstances under which it was brought about here had a very demoralising influence on the administration. You can no longer get people to do progressive work, which goes against the grain of the people with an honest and unflinching courage."

Elliot retired from work in India in May, 1896. The Maharaja's affectionate regard for him continued unbroken until his death in London on March 18th, 1910. We shall meet with a few references to him in the interval.

Apart from the unsound state of Baroda politics during his thirteen months' absence from the State, there was also to trouble the Maharaja the financial position which had arisen. We have seen his allusion to this in a letter to V. M. Samarth. In a later letter to Jaisingrao Angre in the December of 1895 he complains that Baroda has been spending, on an average, over four lakhs of rupees more than its income. One of the chief faults which he found with Manibhai as Dewan was that he would not keep within the limits of the last budget, and had delayed to present a new one. It was imperative that this state of affairs should be brought to an end.

While with the return of the ruler to the personal control of his State the political and financial troubles which had disturbed his peace of mind abated, two domestic afflictions in successive years caused him great sorrow.* In June, 1897,

* It may be noted that H.H. the Maharani Chimnabai lost her father in September, 1895, and her mother in December, 1898.

he lost his adoptive sister, Tarabai, who succumbed to liver complaint in her twenty-sixth year. Her marriage with the Raja of Savantwadi had not turned out as happily as had been hoped; but the present Raje Saheb of Savantwadi, who has married His Highness's granddaughter, is a welcome guest in Baroda today. The Princess Tarabai's death caused a curtailment of the public ceremonies which would otherwise have marked the celebration in Baroda of Queen Victoria's Diamond Jubilee. In commemoration of that auspicious occasion, however, His Highness ordered the building of a ward of fifteen beds in the Dufferin Hospital, to be known as the "Victoria Ward."

The second bereavement was through the death on November 29th, 1898, of the Maharani Jamnabai, to whose assumption of the duties of mother the young Maharaja had owed so much, and for whose character he had so much esteem and love. Thus both the kinswomen with whom his boyhood's home-life in Baroda had been associated were taken from him.

In the autumn of 1897 His Highness had felt the equilibrium of his State to be sufficiently restored to allow him to make a visit to Egypt, spending two months away from Baroda. He travelled up the Nile to Cairo, and through the region of the Pyramids to Thebes, etc. He was much interested in the irrigation work done for Egypt by Sir William Willcocks (a product of Roorkee College, India), and particularly in the progress of the Assuan Dam. Anything connected with the question of water-supply naturally attracted his close attention, in view of the vital importance of water to Baroda.

He was not destined to find affairs perfectly peaceful on his return home. Following on a scarcity of food-stocks in both Gujarat and Kathiawar, enhanced by the demands from famine-stricken districts of India, there was an outbreak of plague, and the measures taken to cope with it roused much popular opposition. He writes to Elliot in May, 1898, of the troubles arising from the Resident and other British officers constantly coming in to inspect the arrangements. "These well-meant inspections," he says, "have a very tangible result on Native States." In fact, there were more strained relations with the Residency.

Other troubles arose in connection with the work of the Survey and Settlement Department, certain Rajputs of the *matadar* class in villages in Kadi banding together to resist Government survey measures. This culminated in an open defiance of the State at the village of Pilwai, necessitating the calling out of the troops, the storming of the village, and the punishment of the ringleaders by severe sentences of imprisonment. The Pilwai disturbances did not end till 1898.

In the following year a greater calamity befell Baroda. Hitherto, Eastern Baroda had been considered practically immune from famine, though the Western section of the State, like the rest of Kathiawar, had suffered severely in 1877-8. But now, in the monsoon of 1899, there was an almost complete failure of rain in Gujarat as well as Kathiawar, the grain-crops being ruined, prices rising over a hundred per cent., and the greatest distress occurring among the people. The unexpected visitation found few available means of combating it. Large purchases of rice, however, were effected from Rangoon, the Maharaja made a personal trip through the famine districts, and relief-works were started, which employed 55,000 labourers.

Some idea of the disastrous result of this famine, coming on the top of the plague epidemic of earlier years, may be gathered from the fact that the Census of Baroda in 1891 showed the population of the State at 2,415,396, its highest record; the Census of 1901 showed it at 1,952,692. Thanks to the lesson which has been learnt from the calamity of 1899, an efficient system has been built up of relief-work, which can be put in operation the moment it is required. Special care is taken that money shall not be spent on unremunerative work for the mere object of affording relief. Well-sinking, tank-making, drainage construction, and the building of new railway embankments and roads are the kind of work which is subsidised when famine threatens. In addition, loans on easy terms are advanced to the agriculturalists to enable them to sink private wells, buy seed, etc., and distress in all classes is alleviated by loans and, where necessary, by a State grant.

Only the beginning of this systematic method of famine-fighting was seen in 1899-1900; but it was then that the Maharaja determined on a consistent policy against one of the most serious enemies of his country's prosperity.

Through the troublesome period between his fifth and sixth visits to Europe His Highness was not distracted from his schemes of general improvement. We see him in his letters busy over questions of water-supply in the districts, drainage for Baroda City, a Contract Act for the State on the lines of the British Act, the assimilation of the State currency to the British—"a great boon to commerce at large"—and so on. In all such matters, particularly in those of the Contract Act and the currency, his personal labour was great.

At the same time he was keenly interested in his children's education. He had intended sending Prince Fatesingh to Eton or Harrow, but abandoned the idea in 1895, "as it would be necessary for him to work very hard to get entered, and I do not think it wise to subject him to a much greater strain than he is bearing at present" (letter to Dr. Nevins, September 24th). He resolved to have him prepared for Oxford in Baroda, entrusting him, with his half-brothers Jaisinh and Shivaji, to the charge of Mr. T. Harvey French. To Dr. Nevins he writes again in 1898 that the Prince has not done so well in the examination as he had been led to expect. "Rich children have their own dangers," he adds (letter of May 8th). In a letter to French, who accompanied the Prince on a trip to Japan after the examination, he rather amusingly expresses his desire that he shall not for the present learn dancing. "I do not wish Fatesingh to be initiated into the art of cutting capers yet. Good manners may be taught without bringing youngsters in too close contact with girls and young ladies" (letter of May 2nd, 1898).

Amid his multifarious concerns with public and private affairs, the Maharaja found time in the summer of 1899 to pay a visit to the new Viceroy,

Lord Curzon, at Simla. "He seemed," he wrote to a friend a few months later, "to be a very clever and businesslike man." Other aspects of Lord Curzon were to strike him later.

As there has been no convenient opportunity to mention the fact before, we may note here that Lord Curzon's predecessor, the Earl of Elgin, had, in November, 1896, been the second Viceroy to visit Baroda. Unfortunately, a serious accident among the crowd during the fête in the Public Park, resulting in a number of deaths, had marred the proceedings, and caused the cancellation of the remainder of the programme arranged in Lord Elgin's honour.

CHAPTER XII

THE CURZON CIRCULAR; AND THE 1903 DURBAR

In deciding to make another trip to Europe, Maharaja Sayajirao must have assured himself that he was leaving his State in safer keeping than, as turned out, he had left it in 1893. In his fragment of travel diary of 1900, he admits that he went "most reluctantly," with famine still prevailing in Baroda. But he had three strong motives for going: the desire to arrange for his children's education; the health of the Maharani, who required an operation that could not safely be performed in India; and his own health, which five years in India had not improved. Accordingly, in May, 1900, he left Bombay by the P. and O. s.s. *Caledonia,* accompanied by his wife and his five children.

Except for ten days in Paris, when he visited the Exhibition, His Highness spent most of the first three months of his trip in London. It is not surprising that he did not find the climate in August "either very bracing or very salubrious," though he had rented Bushey Hall as a residence. Nor was his mind at rest. Apart from his anxiety about the Maharani, who underwent an operation at the hands of Dr. Mary Scharlieb, known to their Highnesses through her medical work in India, he was seriously troubled by the issue of the

THE MAHARAJA.
From a picture by S. R. Samuel.

famous "Curzon Circular."* An allusion to both matters occurs in a letter which he wrote on August 8th to his Dewan Iyangar. "Allow me to remark," he says, "without wishing to injure the feelings of anybody, that our health and our interests are treated as nothing when a decision is being arrived at as to our trip to Europe. Had I the experience and assurance that we can always arrange our journey to Europe, and be also sure that during our absence the State affairs would be carried on smoothly, I should never have allowed Her Highness to suffer as much as she has done."

A week before this letter was written Lord

* This circular letter was not actually made public until late in August, 1900. Lovat Fraser, in his *India under Curzon and After*, says that it "obtained a publicity which, I believe, was never intended, and was the object of a good deal of criticism arising partly from lack of knowledge of the facts and partly from the indiscreetly literal manner in which the letter was interpreted by some Political Officers."

The Times of August 25th published, from its Simla correspondent, the gist of the circular, which was stated to have been issued to all local administrations, directing that all appeals for leave to visit Europe by native chiefs shall be submitted to the Government of India, who will exercise unfettered discretion whether to comply with or refuse them. The Government, it was pointed out, in return for its protection of the ruling families, was "entitled to claim that the ruler shall devote his best energies, not to the pursuit of pleasure nor to the cultivation of an absentee interest in amusements, but to the welfare of his own subjects and the administration."

The *Times* correspondent added that the letter should have a good effect on chiefs such as the Gaekwar of Baroda and the Maharaja of Kapurthala, who had acquired the habit of constantly visiting Europe and leaving their States in the charge of Dewans; and *The Times* itself, in an editorial on August 27th, endorsed this criticism.

Curzon had passed through Baroda, but had refused a State reception, asking to be received by His Highness in person in the following November. The Maharaja, as he now tells the Dewan, finds it almost impossible to return to India then, owing to Her Highness's and his own health. Nor did he then return; for, after a visit to Scotland, where he was the guest of Mr. and Mrs. Kent at Lochindorbe, a stay in Germany (in order that Her Highness might take the waters at Schalbad), and another visit to the Paris Exhibition, he went to Brighton in November, and was not back in Baroda until January, 1901.

His Highness's letters of this period are full of his views as to the attitude of the Government of India towards Indian Princes such as himself. Some of these letters are quoted, with others of different periods, in Appendix I. We need not, therefore, make extracts from them here; but two sentences from a letter to Mrs. Kent, after his visit to Lochindorbe, may be taken, to show how he felt over the Curzon Circular. " I do not think the Rajas are well treated in the Circular," he writes. " We are all supposed to be chiefs, but are treated worse than paid servants."

Nevertheless, this sixth trip to Europe had its pleasant memories for the Maharaja. Among those people with whom he renewed or made acquaintance were the Duke of Connaught, Lord Harris, Lord and Lady Reay, Lord Northbrook, Lady Tweeddale, Lord George Hamilton, Sir John Watson, Sir John Puleston, Sir Edward Lawson, Sir James Blyth; but he was specially gratified by an invitation from Queen Victoria to stay at

Windsor. The news of the Queen's death on January 22nd, just after his return to Baroda, came as a great shock to him. He had received many kindnesses at her hand, he wrote to the Acting Resident. He closed the public offices and schools as a token of sorrow, and contributed R. 100,000 to the Victoria Memorial Fund.

Outside England, what interested him most was the Paris Exhibition. Alluding to this two years later, in a speech made at the opening of the Industrial Exhibition at Ahmedabad, he told his audience how struck he had been by the thoroughness of the methods shown in Paris, especially in the German and American exhibits.*

One of the main incentives of His Highness's journey to England was, as has been said, to arrange for his children's education. He settled the three elder boys in Oxford under the care of T. H. French, Prince Fatesingh studying for the entrance examination at Balliol, while Princes Shivaji and Jaisinh attended the preparatory school kept by the late C. C. Lynam, known to his friends, through his enthusiasm for yachting, as "the Skipper."

"It is a very bold experiment on my part," wrote His Highness to Mr. French after his return to India, "to send Fatesinghrao to Europe for education. It will depend upon his wisdom to make a success of the experiment. Kindly impress

* In this same speech he tells how in London he had made enquiries with a view to finding "lucrative home industries for our women, and especially for widows," and was convinced that the education of women in decorative art would prove extremely profitable if the right steps were taken.

upon him the seriousness of the step" (letter of February 2nd, 1901). But at the time he had no doubt as to the rightness of his decision. In the already quoted article which he contributed to *The Nineteenth Century* for the same month he said, after reference to his own boyhood, "In regard to the training of my own sons in the transition period, I think it necessary to give them the best English education." As is shown in another article in *East and West*, January, 1902, the results of the education of Indian Princes in India appeared to him meagre, and not calculated to fit them to rule. Unhappily, what he failed to reckon with was the strength of the temptations which beset such Princes at an English University.

When he started back to India he took the other children with him, but left Fatesingh in Oxford in French's charge. The young Prince failed for the Balliol entrance examination in December, 1900, but passed successfully in the following July. In August, 1902, however, he returned to India, the College authorities having advised his withdrawal. He was set to work in Baroda to learn the duties of the military and other departments. In the meantime his half-brother, Jaisinh, whose not over-robust physique it was thought the English climate might benefit, was entered at Harrow, and Shivaji, who was of fine physical build, continued his education in India.

Another member of the family, His Highness's brother Sampatrao, remained in England, and intimated his wish to stay up at Oxford to qualify for his B.A. The Maharaja replied to the effect that "the Oxford B.A. degree is no unfailing measure of one's abilities." It is rare to find an Indian who does not set a very high, not to say excessive, value on degrees. But obviously His Highness implied no disrespect for University education apart from the mere letters after one's name. We have heard above of his own ungratified desire to spend at least a year at either Oxford or Cambridge.

The year 1902 was not to prove altogether peaceful for Maharaja Sayajirao. His health continued poor, and his doctors advised a sea-trip; but, as he wrote to F. A. H. Elliot in May, "the fear of the Government prevents us from thinking of this project." He contented himself with visiting Mysore, and during the rains was at Coonoor, whence he wrote ruefully to a friend on July 1st that his absence from Baroda would increase his reputation as a Maharaja who wished to be away from the scene of his work. From Coonoor he went to Ootacamund.

The arrangements for the Imperial Durbar of January 1st, 1903, to celebrate King Edward's Coronation were a source of heartburning to His Highness, as well as to other ruling Indian Princes. A letter from the Government of India had been conveyed to him by the Acting Resident at Baroda, Captain Carnegy, with a request for his observations. These he gave; but Captain Carnegy was not satisfied that they would be acceptable. His Highness, therefore, by the pen of his secretary, Manubhai Mehta, afterwards one of the best known of his Dewans, communicated his views to his own administration.

The main difficulty was over an elephant

procession in which the Government of India wished the Princes to take part at the Durbar. The Maharaja Gaekwar had demurred to this, but protested now against his unwillingness to join the procession being construed as a sign of disrespect to the King-Emperor. "His Highness," wrote his secretary, "is ready to withdraw his refusal, and would join the procession as if he were not asked about it at all; but it seems to him very hard that he should pretend to do willingly, spontaneously, as if it were of his own accord, what is only forced upon him under the threat of insult. . . . As regards the plea that His Highness is now in the good grace of the Government of India or of Anglo-Indian society, His Highness is aware that argument will always be brought forward when his hands are to be forced and he is to be coerced into a certain line of action."

He sent a second letter, signed by his own hand, to his Dewan, R. V. Damnaskar. "It is more than needless," he protested, "to bring in the person of H.M. the Emperor into this question, as it would be a folly, to say the least, to entertain the notion of any disrespect towards him. It is most inconvenient that such official matters should be so mixed up with questions of one's feelings towards high personages. . . . I may suggest that I am more in favour of the ceremonies observed when Lord Lytton arrived at Delhi at the time of the Imperial Durbar of 1877* than the present pro-

* It is a curious coincidence that Lord Curzon at Jaipur, during his Rajputana tour later in the year, said that he was "most anxious to provide that the Indian Princes should not be merely spectators at the (durbar) ceremony, as they were in 1877, but actors in it."

cedure, which, it seems to me, is lacking in respect towards the Native Princes" (letter of August 27th, 1902).

We have thought it right to devote some attention to this dispute, because it illustrates a marked characteristic of the Maharaja—his insistence on the rights and dignity of the Indian Princes, and his opposition to innovations calculated to lessen these. It is obvious that such an attitude is in no way inconsistent with complete loyalty to the Paramount Power. Unfortunately, however, under the Curzon régime there was a tendency to misinterpret the attitude; and a series of pinpricks, possibly not designed as such, were administered, which produced inevitably some reaction. One of these was a ruling forbidding the use of their regular scarlet livery by the Gaekwar's servants and followers at Delhi. A little tact would have, no doubt, avoided the creation of a feeling of resentment against an order to discard the State livery on this ceremonial occasion.

In spite of preliminary difficulties, Baroda was well represented at Delhi, where the Maharaja, with all his family (except Prince Jaisinhrao, still at Harrow), the Dewan, and a select number of his ministers and officers, arrived on December 31st.

On the following day he took his place among the Princes, and after the Royal Proclamation, the Viceroy's speech, and the reading of the King-Emperor's message, was the second of them to be presented to the Viceroy and then to the Duke of Connaught, who, with his wife, was at Delhi in honour of his brother's Coronation.

The other principal ceremony in which the Indian

Princes took part at Delhi was the investiture of the Orders of the Star of India and the Indian Empire on the evening of January 3rd. This was held in the public audience-hall of the old Moghal Emperors, and was a very gorgeous spectacle. It was noted that "the Gaekwar of Baroda wore his famous necklace, worth a quarter of a million sterling, with the historic Star of the South as a pendant" (*The Times*, January 5th, 1903).

The Coronation Durbar had passed off without a hitch. But His Highness was not inclined to drop the subject of the treatment by the Government of India of Princes like himself. His correspondence in 1903 is full of discussion upon it. He complains to his Dewan of the demand for a fixed programme in advance when a trip to Europe is contemplated. This would be intolerable in the case of a private person. For himself, the interference is worse when the Maharani and her ladies take part in the trip, for it is painful to Indian sentiment to answer enquiries where women are concerned.

Another grievance is the insistence on the inclusion in the suite of a Political Officer—not desired by the Prince, and a cause of unnecessary expense.

On the eve of a journey to Kashmir the Maharaja addressed a long letter to the Resident, Lieutenant-Colonel M. J. Meade, son of a former Resident at Baroda, in which he reiterated his complaints.* He spoke also of "ignorant and irresponsible persons and newspaper editors," who had attributed the basest motives to his frequent visits to Europe. He

* See Appendix I.

combated the idea of the extravagance of these visits, and asked pertinently whether the home-staying Princes (of whom he named some) had not acquired undesirable habits and run into extravagance. "The home-bred Indian idea of a Raja," he wrote, "is not that he should work hard and be a slave to duty, but that he should live at ease and enjoy himself, and anyone who did otherwise was popularly considered an idiot."

From Kashmir he wrote again to the Resident, authorising him, if he wished, to forward the above-quoted letter to Lord Curzon. Meade must have suggested, in reply, a meeting with the Viceroy, for in August His Highness said:

"I should certainly not mind a friendly talk with the Viceroy; but I have no confidence that they [the Government] will change their views on any important subject. The misfortune is that greatness, or apparent greatness, is severely dealt with in India. The wretched Princes have not even the right of a common Indian merchant."

One more controversy, if it may be so called, occurred between the Maharaja and Lord Curzon during the latter's Viceroyalty. In April, 1904, Lord Curzon wrote concerning the changes which he proposed in the Imperial Service system. The Maharaja replied on August 1st, enclosing a long and well-reasoned memorandum, in the drafting of which he no doubt sought expert advice, though the ideas are his own. Pointing out that the origin of Imperial Service in India was a spontaneous and individual offer by various Princes in 1889, as a result of the Russian scare four years earlier, he said that now it was asked that the Indian ruling chiefs should acknowledge the obligation to assist the British Government with money or troops in defending, not the Indian dominions of the Crown only, but all foreign interests of the Empire.

"The creation of the new obligation proposed," continues the memorandum, "would seem to demand the concession of a corresponding privilege, a recognised voice in the councils of the Empire. The privilege is the natural corollary of any general military federation, and would alone justify the creation of new burdens."

The suggestion of a Conference of Princes to consider the matter was welcomed, and of this idea, when it widened out into the scheme for the "Council of Princes," the Maharaja was a consistent supporter.

CHAPTER XIII

THE CALM BEFORE A STORM

THE attention given by the Maharaja of Baroda to external affairs at the period with which we have been dealing did not in any way diminish his zeal for internal reforms in his State. In 1902 he had put into operation the law permitting Hindu widows to remarry. The Infant Marriage Prevention Act followed two years later, as did definite legislation on Primary Education, the Penal Code, and Criminal Procedure. The Land and Revenue Questions were still exercising him greatly, and in August, 1904, he took the step of appointing as *Amatya*, or Revenue Minister, Romesh Chandra Dutt, a native of Bengal, for whose abilities he had much admiration. He had invited Dutt to enter his service as far back as 1895; but, being then Commissioner of Burdwan, Dutt had intimated that he would be unable to accept the offer until he should retire from his service with the Government of India. Now in 1904, at the age of fifty-six, he came to Baroda to reorganise and reform the Revenue Department, sure of a sympathetic reception of his financial theories. He was able to write to his brother on October 18th that His Highness had agreed to all his suggestions about Income Tax, Customs Duties, etc. "But the greater Land Question looms ahead," he added. "All Western India is watching my land measures in Baroda, to see if I have the courage to practise what I have preached to the British Government these years."*

To complete the story of R. C. Dutt's connection with Baroda, though this involves an anticipation of the order of events. In July, 1907, he ceased his work with the Revenue Department, having been nominated by the Government of India to serve on the Royal Commission on Decentralisation. He returned to Baroda in June, 1909, to take up the post of Dewan, which he agreed to hold for a year only. He overestimated his strength. The work was too severe for him. "Baroda," he had written to B. L. Gupta in 1906,† "is not like other Native States in India, where you can take things easy. It is hard grind here, and the hard-worked administrator is not his own master." He died in harness on November 30th, 1909, the immediate cause being heart failure. The story of his service in Baroda is one which does honour alike to him and to the ruler who brought him there; and his biography leaves the impression of a charming personality, which is not always the characteristic of an able statesman.

We must now revert to the year 1904, toward the end of which Maharaja Sayajirao accepted an invitation to preside at the Social Conference of

* Quoted from J. N. Gupta's *Life of Romesh Chandra Dutt*. The Maharaja says of this work that the author rather tends to exaggerate the achievement of his fellow-Bengali; but he himself on one occasion mentioned Dutt as an instance of India's ability to produce statesmen, though so often they are swallowed up by the machinery of the British Government and condemned only to rise to positions of minor eminence.

† *Life of Romesh Chandra Dutt*, p. 482.

the Indian National Congress at Bombay, and to deliver the inaugural address. In his speech he dealt mainly with the two great problems as he saw them of India: caste, and the status of women. Of the caste-barrier he said that to remove it was undoubtedly their ultimate object. If they could not do that at once, at least they would hold up boldly before all men the ideal at which they aimed; and in the meanwhile, since something was better than nothing, they would do well to clear away the externals, the useless minute forms which encumbered their daily life, and prevented the increase of fellow-feeling. They must not stop at externals, however, but must exorcise the spirit of caste.

With regard to women in India, he specified as their three handicaps: early marriages, too strict *purdah*, and the denial of education to them. In the two latter respects their ancestors of the Vedic period were better off than they were. "What is it that we seek?" he asked. "It is nothing new or revolutionary. Our real aims are the true and noble ideals of our forefathers, ideals eternally beautiful, eternally worthy of the search of men."

This speech of the Maharaja to the National Congress is an excellent exposition of his views as to what is required for the well-being of India today. But as these views are dealt with by us elsewhere, we need not quote from it more extensively.

The administrative year 1904-5 may be taken as the beginning of a new period in His Highness's reign, wherein his labours on the improvement of his State bore their due fruit. The year was marked by the coming into operation of three important Acts, concerning Co-operative Credit Societies, Religious Endowments, and the Customs. With these on the statute-book, the Maharaja in the spring of 1905 departed from Baroda on his seventh European trip, accompanied by his wife and younger children. On June 30th he was among the guests at Harrow School, when the King and Queen came for the opening of the new sports field. In London he had a busy programme, including such varied items as an address to the Society of Arts on the relations of Indian Princes and British Political Officers, and visits to the Horticultural College for Women at Swanley, to a working men's club in South Lambeth, and to the Leicester Galleries. At the end of July he crossed to Dublin, and made the acquaintance of Lord and Lady Aberdeen; and on August 12th he went to Paris.

The rest of the year was spent on the Continent, and in the spring of 1906 both Maharaja and Maharani visited first Territet and then Geneva. His Highness had now determined to fulfil his ambition of seeing a new part of the Western world, and from London on May 5th he started, with his wife and his brother Sampatrao, on a journey to America. All aspects of life in the United States interested him keenly, and he was constantly on the look-out for ideas which might be adapted to the requirements of Baroda. In particular he studied the system of education, and secured the services of an expert educationalist, Dr. Cuthbert Hall, to come to India to inspect the schools of Baroda and suggest improvements.

He enquired also into the questions of industrial development, agriculture, labour unions, child-rearing, and circulating libraries, on the last point with very fruitful results, as will be seen. He sent home from the United States various kinds of seeds to be experimented with in India, and, after a visit to Colorado Springs, conceived the idea of starting a paper-making industry in Baroda.

Altogether, his American trip was a very busy time, and suggested countless new schemes to the Maharaja. His admiration for the States was tempered with other feelings in two small matters. The rather naïve disappointment of the public at his not appearing before them as a bediamonded Raja, but in ordinary European dress, amused him; and the attentions of the reporters were little to his taste. When he was pressed by newspaper-men to give his opinion on the looks of American women, he was no more gratified than the Bishop of London in 1926 when asked for his views on shingling. In one instance a paper, which had failed to "draw" him as it had wished, published some statements that inclined him to bring an action for libel; but on legal advice he did nothing.

In August the Maharaja was back in England, where he took the opportunity of raising with Mr. John Morley, Secretary of State for India, the question of the desirability of greater autonomy for Indian States, so long as they satisfied the condition of providing decent government for the public. He sent a letter in this strain to Morley in September, enclosing some notes which he had drawn up on the subject,* and he took the opportunity at the same time of expressing approval of the idea of a Council of Princes, which was again under discussion at this period.

November 19th found the Maharaja once more in Baroda, after an absence of a year and seven months. The twenty-fifth anniversary of his assumption of the administration of his State was at hand. As, however, he had promised to deliver the inaugural address at the opening of the Industrial Exhibition at Calcutta in December,† it was decided to celebrate the Silver Jubilee on his next birthday, March 5th, 1907, and the five following days, which were to be public holidays.

The Silver Jubilee celebrations were on a grand scale in Baroda City, and were echoed throughout the State. As the general programme was much the same as on the occasion of the Golden Jubilee, described later, it is not necessary to give a full account here. At the Birthday Durbar, announcement was made of the concessions to be granted in honour of the event. Arrears of taxation were remitted to the extent of over R. 500,000. Vernacular education was made entirely free. Two new boarding-houses for the "Untouchables" were to be opened at Patan and Amreli. Five scholarships for students in Europe were founded. A new market was presented to the Baroda

* After his return to Baroda he sent his notes also to Lord Minto, with a covering letter similar in trend to that to Morley. He added: "It could not have been intended by the British Government to crush out all initiative and originality from these States and destroy their distinctive features altogether."

† See p. 91.

municipality, the Khanderao Market, a fine building not far from the gates of Laxmi Vilas Palace. Two charitable institutions for the poor were to be opened in the city, and four hospitals in the districts. A new open space, the Jubilee Gardens, was to be made in the crowded area north-east of the Sursagar Tank; and R. 550,000 were to be spent on providing public wells.

Two very important steps in the administration of the State were taken in this same year (1907), though not in connection with the Jubilee concessions. The work of the Settlement Department was submitted to a joint Commission appointed by Baroda and the Government of India; and sanction was given for the formation of a Legislative Council, which took definite form in the following year.

That the progress of Baroda did not escape notice in England is shown by the fact that in the House of Commons on March 31st, 1908, Mr. O'Grady asked the Secretary of State for India whether he was aware that the Maharaja of Baroda had separated the judicial from the executive functions, had restored local self-government, had instituted primary education throughout his State, and had further instituted popularly elected members in the Legislative Council; and, if so, would the Council of India consider the application of such reforms to other native States and to India as a whole. Mr. John Morley cautiously replied that the results of these measures in Baroda would be watched with interest; but he could not undertake forthwith to suggest the introduction of similar measures in the whole of British India, and certainly could not interfere with the discretion of the rulers of other States.

In 1908 another highly important scheme was carried out, when the Bank of Baroda, Ltd., was established under the management of Mr. C. E. Randle. It was not until two years later that His Highness transferred the State Treasury work to the Bank, agreeing that the State should maintain there a minimum balance of five and a half lakhs of rupees without interest; but from the very start the Bank was a remarkable success, and revolutionised the financial situation of Baroda.

A great domestic sorrow fell upon the Maharaja in September, 1908, when his eldest son and heir, Prince Fatesinghrao, died with unexpected suddenness. He left an infant son, Pratapsinghrao, who thus became heir to the throne of Baroda.

Owing partly, no doubt, to his domestic grief, there is a considerable gap in His Highness's correspondence at this period, which leaves us without the intimate insight into his thoughts possible at other periods.

In February, 1909, the time came for Lieutenant-Colonel M. J. Meade, who had been Resident at Baroda since 1901, and was the chief British representative at the Silver Jubilee celebrations, to retire from his post. The Maharaja gave a banquet in his honour, and made a very complimentary speech, in which he alluded to the fact that Lieutenant-Colonel Meade had among his predecessors at the Residency his grandfather, Major D. Malcolm, and his father, Sir Richard Meade.

The political sky in Baroda seemed absolutely unclouded, and there was no hint of any troubles

PRINCE PRATAPSINGHRAO.

to come, though the Maharaja, in common with other ruling Princes, was the recipient in August of a warning letter from the Viceroy on the danger of the sedition which was at the time rife in parts of British India taking a hold in the Indian States. It was, no doubt, on account of this letter that, in a speech made in Baroda in early September, Maharaja Sayajirao dealt with the view that education was partly responsible for the prevailing political unrest. Discontent, he maintained, was not necessarily an evil. The effect of education was to broaden men's minds and widen their aspirations. But the crimes in England had caused a thrill of indignation, and it was the Government's obvious duty to stamp out sedition. Fortunately, in Baroda there was no trouble, and he hoped that the good sense of the people would render repression unnecessary.

The crimes in England to which His Highness referred were the assassination at the Imperial Institute on the night of July 1st of Sir Curzon Wyllie, a noted friend of Indian students, and of Dr. C. Lalcaca, a Parsi physician who had bravely but vainly interposed himself between the assassin and his victim.

This horrible and senseless murder by M. L. Dhingra, a Punjabi student in London, for which he paid the due penalty of the law, was nearly outdone in India little over four months later. The Viceroy was on his autumn tour, in the course of which he had promised to visit Baroda. At Ahmedabad, as he was driving from the railway-station, a bomb was thrown at his carriage, which it fortunately missed.

On November 13th Lord Minto, with his wife and daughter, arrived in Baroda. The *Times* correspondent described his reception as a splendid success. He rode through the city escorted by Inniskilling Dragoons and Royal Horse Artillery, amid dense crowds, which gave him a cordial welcome. One of the principal events of the visit was a State banquet at Laxmi Vilas on November 15th. In proposing the toast of the Viceroy and Lady Minto, the Maharaja expressed the profound horror of India at the attempt on the representative of the King-Emperor, and emphasised the firm and unalterable loyalty of his House.

"Loyalty," he continued, "has always been considered in the East as one of the first virtues in a people; but loyalty, when merely sentimental, is of small value. It should be real, genuine, and active. To secure such loyalty, there should be a community of interests between the subjects and the ruling power. The former should have a proper share in the administration of the country, and should feel that the Government is their own. It is for this reason that I hail with pleasure those great measures of reform which Your Excellency initiated and His Majesty's Government have accepted. These reforms will open out to the people of India a larger field of activity, and inspire them with a greater sense of responsibility in the performance of their civic duties; and future generations will recognise in these statesmanlike measures a forward step in the progress of the country under the enlightened rule of Great Britain."

Lord Minto, in his reply, thanked his host

for the warmth of his reception in Baroda. With regard to the reforms in India, he said that there might be defects in their first working, but he was confident of their final result. He concluded with a tribute to the earnest desire which His Highness had shown for administrative efficiency in his own State. He particularly complimented him on his "bold attempt to separate the judicial and executive functions," which had "elicited the warm interest of the Government of India."

When the Viceroy left Baroda the next day, therefore, the omens seemed fair indeed for the continued peace of the country and its ruler. It is true that, on turning to the Maharaja's correspondence, we find him on November 19th, just after Lord Minto's visit, writing to him a letter in reply to a warning that seditious people were trying to establish their evil doctrines in Native States. His reply was that he did not know to what extent sedition had actually spread, but had had enquiries made and a note prepared by his ministers. This he enclosed, but the text is not included in the printed *Letters*.

Few people, assuredly, would be prepared, after reading the account of the Viceregal visit and the almost colourless terms of the Maharaja's letter of November 19th, to see him, little more than two months later, made the object of an attack which singled him out, alone among the Indian Princes, as lacking in loyal response to the requirements of the Government of India.

This matter, however, may be left to the next chapter, while we note that in the year 1909 Maharaja Sayajirao was very intent, and expended much personal labour, on the codification of rules of departmental work, especially that of the *Khangi*, or Household Department.

At the end of the year he had the gratification of learning that two of his children, Prince Shivaji and Princess Indira, had passed the examinations for which they had entered. He yielded to his son's wish that he might go to Oxford, while the Princess became a pupil at Baroda College.

CHAPTER XIV

THE STORM

THE Calcutta correspondent of *The Times*, in a message dated January 27th, 1910, stated that the publication by the Government of the opinions of the ruling chiefs on the measures required for suppressing sedition in India was having a good effect, and that the chiefs, *with one prominent exception*, had declared that they would gladly adopt any measure recommended. The exception, the message went on, was the Gaekwar of Baroda, who disclaimed knowledge of the extent to which sedition had spread in the Native States, and gave only a "qualified assurance" of his readiness to respond to any reasonable call for assistance against sedition. It was admitted, however, that the requests of the Baroda Residency for the surveillance of itinerant Indian preachers were complied with, and that offending newspaper editors were reprimanded.

In spite of this concluding admission, the message from Calcutta, with its hint of inspiration from high quarters, came as a violent shock to those who had the interests of Baroda at heart. What had happened to disturb the genial atmosphere prevailing at the time of Lord Minto's visit less than two months before? A slight clue to the solution of the mystery is given in the *Times* message, when it is remarked that the extremist Indian paper, the

Amrita Bazar Patrika, which, like others of its kind, was wont to play off one Native Prince against another, had eulogised the Maharaja of Baroda's reply to the Government.

This was undoubtedly true. The *Amrita Bazar Patrika* had taken the opportunity of bestowing praise upon Maharaja Sayajirao for what it assumed to be his attitude towards the Government's request. As we shall see, this was not the only instance of mischievous misinterpretation of his thoughts which was to injure the Maharaja. Discussing the matter many years after, in 1926, he protested, with patent sincerity, that he had never in his life made any attempt to influence the Press. He somewhat ruefully remarked that what he suffered from at the " sedition " period was an excessive popularity in India, due to his reforming zeal. The native papers, including those with whose opinions he was far from being in sympathy, extolled their view of his character. There may even have been talk—not, perhaps, in 1910, but at some time in the period now under notice—of the possibility, if ever India became a Republic, of his being the first President. Such talk he disregarded; but it may, in his opinion, have had some influence on Anglo-Indian officialdom at the time. A Native Prince must not become too popular, even when he does not court popularity.

The attack upon the Maharaja at the beginning of 1910 was but a faint premonition of what was to come later; and it was without misgiving that at the end of March he left Baroda on his eighth trip, this time taking in the Far East. He called at Hongkong and Shanghai, and spent the whole month of May in Japan, whence he sailed for San Francisco on June 1st. After seeing something of the United States again and of Canada, he arrived in London on July 19th, accompanied by his wife and daughter, and his son Jaisinhrao, who, after leaving Harrow, had proceeded to America to continue his education. The other sons, Shivajirao and the young Dhairyashilrao, were already in England, and rejoined their parents in London.

On July 21st the Maharaja called at the India Office, and had an interview of nearly an hour with Lord Morley. In early August he was in Oxford as a visitor to Dean Strong at Christ Church to discuss the question of Prince Shivaji's entrance there. On the 25th he went up to Scotland as Lord Middleton's guest at a shooting-party. The Maharani having returned from a cure on the Continent, the family were all together in October, and spent their time between a London hotel and Bushey Hall. On November 20th, just before starting on his homeward journey, the Maharaja, with Her Highness, was the guest at an "at home" of the Indian Union Society, where he had consented to deliver an address. Speaking of Indian progress, he gave his opinion that what was needed was a knowledge of science of different kinds, proper organisation, and tolerance of view on political matters.

The return to Baroda was made on December 16th, 1910. But little over four months later Maharaja and Maharani were on their way again to Europe. For Her Highness's indifferent health it was thought advisable that she should try another cure at Bad Nauheim; and also she wished to see the realisation of a literary project on which she had been engaged. The Maharaja's own motive for the trip was his desire to be present at the Coronation at Westminster.

On June 22nd, 1911, His Highness duly attended the ceremony in Westminster Abbey. A month later he was received by King George at Buckingham Palace, after which he left London for Inverness, while the Maharani went to Germany. In October, when they were once more reunited, the book which Her Highness had written, with the assistance of Mr. S. M. Mitra, *The Position of Women in Indian Life*, made its appearance and met with a favourable reception.* The objects of this short trip to Europe having been attained, husband and wife returned to Baroda, which was reached on November 10th, three weeks before the arrival of King George and Queen Mary in Bombay on their way to the Coronation Durbar at Delhi.

Their Majesties came to Delhi on December 5th, and after leaving the station, proceeded to the "Chiefs' Reception Pavilion," where there were presented to them in turn the Nizam of Hyderabad, the Gaekwar of Baroda, and the other ruling Princes in their due order of precedence. A week later the great Durbar was held in the same amphitheatre which had been the scene of those of 1877

* In her introduction to this book Her Highness sets out as the questions which her visits to the West had brought to her mind: "The co-operation which exists between Western men and women in public affairs is practically unknown in India. . . . What can be the reason for this great difference ? Should the Indian woman continue to be isolated from all public affairs ? What is the remedy, and how is it to be applied ?" The book endeavours to find the answer to these questions.

and 1902. Here, after the King-Emperor's speech had been read, the Viceroy, Lord Hardinge, approached the Throne, made his obeisance, and returned to his seat. The Commander-in-Chief and the members of the Governor-General's Executive Council followed him; and then came the representatives of Hyderabad ("distinguished, as usual," says *The Times of India*, "by the Spartan simplicity of his attire"), Baroda, Mysore, Kashmir, etc., right through the list of Princes, territorial chiefs, and others.

There is nothing in the first reports of the Durbar to indicate that aught had gone amiss at the ceremony; nor was Maharaja Sayajirao, on the actual day, aware that he was thought guilty of any offence. He had gone to the Durbar in a state of great mental disturbance, owing to the receipt that very morning of unpleasant news of an entirely private nature, and in his agitation, though he wore all his medals, he omitted to put on his sash of the Star of India. He wore a white costume, such as he is wont to appear in at all his own State durbars. This, it may be remarked, is scarcely of the "Spartan simplicity" attributed to the Nizam's attire!

When his turn came to approach the Throne, the Maharaja did so in an unenviable frame of mind. He had not been able to attend the rehearsal for the ceremony, but had sent one of his brothers to make notes for him. He did not observe what the Nizam of Hyderabad had done before him, and he was the second of the Princes to make their homage. He therefore advanced toward the throne and made one bow. As we shall see, he said that this was as he had been instructed to do by the Resident at Baroda, who also, he thought, might have drawn his attention to his omission of his sash, as he drove with him to the Durbar. Having bowed, he backed from the Throne. Not knowing where the exit was, he did not retire far enough before, looking for someone of whom to ask the way out, he appeared to wheel round and turn his back on the King and Queen. He then hurried from the presence.

He heard nothing of his mistake on December 12th. Calling at Government House after the ceremony, he was told that Lord Sydenham was not at home; but this did not enlighten him. The next day Mr. G. K. Gokhale came to him, whether at official instigation or not he did not know, and told him that there was a sensation over his behaviour at the Durbar, and that an apology was expected from him. Accordingly, he wrote a letter to the Viceroy in the following terms:

"Dear Lord Hardinge,

I hear the manner in which I paid homage to His Imperial Majesty the King-Emperor has been the subject of unfavourable comment. I take the earliest opportunity of writing to you to explain what actually occurred, and to assure you that the very last thing I intended, or could ever intend, was to do anything that could displease His Imperial Majesty, or lead him or anyone to doubt the reality of my loyalty and allegiance to his throne and person. To the British Government the Baroda State owes everything, and to that Government my State and I myself personally will always be truly grateful and loyal. When approaching and returning from the daïs at the

Durbar, I am said to have failed to observe that exact etiquette prescribed. If this was the case, it was due entirely to nervousness and confusion in the presence of their Majesties, and before that vast assembly. Only one chief, the Nizam, had made obeisance before me, and I had not had the opportunity of noticing others, and, in fact, in the confusion of the moment, I had hardly been able to note the details of what the Nizam did. After bowing, I receded a few steps and turned round to ask which way I was to go. I was under the impression that I actually descended by the proper passage, but I am told that I did not. Having turned to ask the way, I became confused, and continued to walk round. For this mistake I can only say how sincerely sorry I am. . . ."*

The Viceroy received this letter on December 14th, and on the 16th it was made public. The storm burst two days later in London, when *The Times*, in publishing Reuter's telegram dated from the Durbar Camp, Delhi, on December 16th (with a summary of the letter to Lord Hardinge), appended an article of nearly half a column severely reflecting on the Maharaja's conduct from 1905 onwards. It was alleged that many Indian extremists came from Baroda, or found employment in the State,

* The letter concludes with an expression of regret that some suggestions by the writer, in an earlier communication about the programme of the reception by the King-Emperor, had not been considered with favour. If Lord Hardinge wished, said the Maharaja, he would withdraw his earlier letter unconditionally. It may be judged by the reader of today, unaffected by the prejudice imported into the discussion of the affair in 1911–2, whether it was fair to describe this second letter, as a portion of the British Press described it, as "an abject apology."

and even in the Gaekwar's household; that the extremist Press studiously excepted him from their scurrilous attacks on loyal Indian Princes; and that neither His Highness nor the Maharani, " an accomplished but *exaltée* lady," when travelling in Europe in 1910, shrank from contact with such people as Krishnavarma and Madame Kama, open promoters in Paris of an assassination campaign in India. In recent months, it was added, there had been traced to a printing-press in Baroda, patronised by officials, an extensive circulation of seditious literature; and the assistance rendered by the State authorities to the British police enquiry had been " extremely lukewarm."

This article began by stating that it was no secret that " the behaviour of the Gaekwar at the King's Coronation at Westminster provoked a good deal of unfavourable comment amongst those present who were familiar with Indian customs and etiquette," and concluded with a hope that the humiliation which he had brought upon himself by his conduct at the Imperial Durbar would serve as an effective warning to him.

Further attacks, less temperately worded than the above article, appeared in the London Press; and even in Paris the *Temps* published a message from Delhi, alleging that the Gaekwar had never made a secret of his hatred of British rule !

The *Times* article of December 18th had been telegraphed to India and published in *The Pioneer*. On December 21st the Maharaja, through his secretary, telegraphed to *The Times* that the article contained statements, some greatly exaggerated and some absolutely false. " That His

Highness acted in any way contrary to Indian custom or etiquette at Westminster Abbey is untrue. There was no room for such behaviour, since he was present as a spectator only, nor have these allegations ever been heard before. His Highness did not meet Krishnavarma in 1910, and has not seen him for many years, and not since the latter left England. The press to which seditious literature has been traced was an entirely private concern, not connected in any way with the State. All possible assistance was promptly given to the British authorities by the Baroda Council in the investigations made. The case having broken down in court from lack of legal evidence, the Maharaja has already confiscated the press and banished the writer. The statements regarding the employment of extremists in the Baroda State and household, and regarding assistance given to anti-British campaigners, are unfair and misleading, and based upon gross perversion of facts."

There followed in *The Times* of December 27th a letter from S. Krishnavarma, editor of *The Indian Sociologist* in Paris. He pointed out that he had been introduced to the Maharaja by Lord Northbrook at the end of 1884, and had met him in India and elsewhere; but since his migration from England to Paris in 1907, he had neither met him nor corresponded with him. Moreover, in September, 1911, he had strongly denounced him in his paper for presiding at a luncheon in London in honour of the K.C.S.I. bestowed on Sir K. G. Gupta on the occasion of the Coronation.

On January 1st, 1912, fresh fuel was added to the flames by the publication in the London illustrated papers of excerpts from the film taken of the Delhi Durbar, showing the Maharaja rendering his homage; and a few days later part of a fatuous article contributed to *The Pioneer* by Mr. Keir Hardie, M.P., was telegraphed to England, which did His Highness very ill-service by contrasting his alleged conduct with that of some of his fellow-rulers, "taught to grovel low before the Throne, as becomes all who go near such a symbol of imbecility." Keir Hardie's praise was more unjust in its effects than all the attacks, of which the most scurrilous appeared in *The World* of January 9th. This touched the lowest depths of journalism.

After this the active newspaper controversy over the Durbar incident subsided for some time. On October 8th Viscount Hardinge, brother of the Viceroy, lecturing in London on the Durbar referred to the incident, which he declared much exaggerated. The Gaekwar, he added, had travelled more than any Maharaja in India, all over the world, and if he intended to be disloyal he was the boldest native he had ever seen, to be so in front of three thousand loyal Europeans and a hundred thousand loyal natives. His personal belief was that the affair was a matter of "nerves." Three weeks later *The Pall Mall Gazette* published an article by "One who Knows," alluding to Lord Hardinge's lecture, and warmly defending the Maharaja from the charge of disloyalty either at the Durbar or elsewhere. A reply by "One who Knows Better" appeared in *The Pall Mall Gazette*, though not until January 20th, 1913, in which the old accusations were reiterated with greater violence and more wealth of detail.

Here the campaign of abuse seems to have stopped, except that to the present day there are people who are ready in conversation, and even in the newspapers, to revive the charges in a form that has grown vaguer through the lapse of years. It is safe to wager that the majority of these people have made no attempt to investigate the justice of the charges which they repeat.

The immediate effect of the affair upon the Maharaja's mind can only be faintly gathered from the *Letters*, comparatively few of which refer to it. To the Resident he writes on January 3rd, 1912, that the attacks upon him in the English Press have surprised and pained him; to Lord Lamington, former Governor of Bombay, on January 5th, he protests that the statements about him are gross exaggerations and perversions. He goes on: "I deeply deplore the breach of etiquette for which I was responsible at Delhi. It was, however, quite unintentional, and due to unforeseen nervousness and confusion, which I do not think would have overtaken me if I had been in my usual health at the time. . . . I think that the very fact that I went, of my own accord, to London to attend the Coronation should give the lie to any charge of intentional disrespect on my part, either at Delhi or Westminster."

At the time of writing this he had not learnt that, in addition to the charge of turning his back, there was another of omitting to bow to the Queen. In a letter of June 26th, however, he says to Mr. M. H. Spielmann:

"I was told by the Resident to make one bow only, as the first few Princes were, I learn, asked to do. I am chivalrous enough to bow to a lady, and to make one bow only to the King did strike me; but one dare not ask questions on ceremonies in the framing of which we had no choice."

The accusation of countenancing sedition in Baroda clearly came to him as a very painful surprise. In the above-quoted letter to Lord Lamington he spoke of the injustice of the attack on him in *The Times*. Having been away from his State for so much of the past two years, he went on, he could scarcely be held responsible for happenings in his absence. Only one case had been brought to his notice, and he had banished the offender at the earliest opportunity. He did not point out to Lord Lamington, though he might have done so, that during 1910 and 1911 he had a British Dewan, Mr. C. N. Seddon, and a British head of police, Mr. Macrae, which should have been good evidence of his desire to rule his State in conformity with British ideas; or that during a Prince's absence the British Resident always has more power in a State than when the Prince is present.

Maharaja Sayajirao's policy at this difficult period of his reign is a curious example of his obstinate determination to be convinced of the rightness of any decision on his part before making it irrevocable. It also illustrates his view of his position in India as an ally of the British Government, but an ally to whom discretion as to his actions is not denied. Complaints came to him from the Government of India that a certain K. G. Deshpande, Subha of Amreli, was implicated in sedition, and his dismissal from Baroda service was demanded. The material proofs of the charge against Deshpande did not satisfy the Maharaja, nor could the State officials find anything to incriminate the man. When, therefore, obliged to dismiss him, His Highness felt impelled to award him R. 10,000 in compensation. Commenting on the case today, long after the event, he says that what he wanted was "evidence, not mere accusations." Without evidence, arbitrary punishment was not his idea of right conduct in a ruler.

At the same time he was prepared to take vigorous action with definite evidence before him; and, finding that there had been a recent growth in Baroda of disaffection with the Paramount Power, he issued a warning Huzur Order at the end of February, 1912. In this he stated that copies of a seditious book had been traced to a printing-press in Naosari, and that the author had been dealt with and the press confiscated. He expressed pained surprise to find that there were in Baroda certain sympathisers with the author; and a determination to punish sedition in any form within the limits of his State. His subjects must regard as an enemy to order and good government "every misguided person who attempted to excite ill-will, hatred, or contempt against the British Government."

In the course of the year, the Maharaja was called upon to consider a charge against another man in Baroda service, D. L. Purohit, Professor of Philosophy at the college. He had sent Purohit to England to study religious and social questions, the administration of charities, etc., and, on his return, commissioned him to travel about India with a view to comparing the ideas of the two countries on such subjects. In the course of his travels Purohit visited Pondicherry, and was induced by someone to call upon, and have a talk with, a man who was decidedly *persona non grata* with the Government of India. This was Arabindo Ghose, a native of Bengal, educated at St. Paul's School* and Cambridge, who had later developed anti-British views. For a time he was a professor at Baroda College, and also advised the Maharaja with regard to his English writings, speeches, etc. After leaving Baroda, however, Ghose had conducted the notorious newspaper *Bande Mataram*, and had finally retired to the French colony of Pondicherry.

Purohit's indiscretion in visiting one who was now looked on as a dangerous extremist did not escape notice, and the Government of India demanded his dismissal from Baroda service. The Maharaja, though he had at no time paid any attention to Ghose's political views, did not feel that he could resist the demand, and when Purohit, in November, 1912, offered his resignation, accepted it.

Incidents like the Deshpande and Purohit cases, and the recollection of Ghose's former connection with Baroda, were not allowed to escape censure. No doubt there were some who genuinely considered the Maharaja Gaekwar to have been hand in glove with sedition-mongers. There were certainly others who would have been glad to prove him so. In his bewilderment he wrote to

* The present writer was at school with him, and can bear witness to his brilliant attainments as a boy. It would have been difficult in those days to regard him as a firebrand !

an English friend: "I do not know whether the whole attempt was not to give the State a bad name. . . . 'Give a dog a bad name and hang it.' This proverb was well illustrated, in my opinion, in the instance of Baroda."

An impartial critic, while rejecting entirely the supposition that Maharaja Sayajirao had any sympathy with sedition, might, perhaps, hold that he failed to observe sufficient care lest it should make growth under the shelter of Baroda; and that his absence from his State could not serve as a complete excuse, since his choice of the officers whom he left in charge was unfettered. These officers could only act in accordance with his wishes, or they must lose their posts.

At the same time the Government of India, as has since been recognised, in those days badly lacked the power of discrimination between legitimate nationalist feeling and sedition. Was a Prince in the position of the Maharaja of Baroda entitled to attempt to discriminate? It was a dangerous course, and a leniency of view in doubtful cases was bound to bring trouble on the Prince's head.

There was no doubt that the Durbar affair and the subsequent charges made against his administration of Baroda had a lasting effect on the Maharaja's after-life; not, indeed, to lessen his loyalty to the Paramount Power, but to increase the self-repression already natural to him, and to render him less confident in his attitude in face of the Western world. He felt that he had been, not only misunderstood, but unjustly treated. Nor does this view appear unreasonable. An unintentional breach of etiquette (by no means unparalleled in the West, it may be said) had been made the excuse for a calumnious attack on his past character, which had not been called into question before. As for the political views of men whom he had employed in his State on work that was entirely unconnected with politics, was it fair to impute to him sympathy with those views when his own utterances and actions so clearly disproved the idea ?

It must be admitted that the crimes of the Indian extremists had inevitably disturbed the balance of minds which otherwise would have shrunk from unjust judgments. It was Maharaja Sayajirao's deep misfortune to lay himself open to accusations, however little grounded on fact, at such a time. The Government of India, wiser after the event, has since made amends to him for its share in the humiliation inflicted on him. The unofficial traducers of his character may have repented in private; but the probability is that they have not, or they would surely have tried to repair the wrong they committed.

CHAPTER XV

THE WAR YEARS

THE incidents, and the controversy arising out of them, which have been dealt with in the preceding chapter are, happily, but a short interruption in the history of a remarkably successful reign. Such troubles as hereafter vexed the peace of Maharaja Sayajirao's mind were not of magnitude sufficient to disturb seriously the well-being of Baroda.

Allusions to domestic affairs occur in a few of His Highness's letters in 1912. His daughter's refusal to marry the Maharaja Sindia of Gwalior thwarted his desire for tightening the bonds between two great Maratha States.* A worse blow was the departure from Oxford of his second surviving son, Shivajirao, in circumstances mentioned elsewhere. Further, his eldest son, Jaisinhrao, who since returning from America had been learning departmental work in Baroda, was thrown from his horse and had concussion of the brain. All these events occurred in the spring of 1912, and combined to accentuate the Maharaja's nervous unrest. He continued his labours on behalf of his State, notably carrying out an increase of the popular element in the Legislative Council. But in February, 1913, he was ill with gout and

* An attack was made upon him in an English newspaper for promoting this union, because Sindia was already married; but an orthodox Hindu is not limited to one wife.

fever, which only allowed him to be present at Prince Jaisinhrao's wedding in an invalid chair. It was decided that six months' absence from India and a course of waters at Evian-les-Bains would be advisable for his health. Accordingly, he left Baroda on May 3rd in the company of the Maharani and their daughter.

A few days before his departure he wrote to his Dewan, B. L. Gupta (who had succeeded C. N. Seddon at the beginning of the previous year), a letter in which he set out his views on the conduct of a Prince in his position. "My policy," he wrote, "has always been to be a friend to the British Government, to be a father to my people, and to safeguard the dignity, rights, and self-respect of the State and its ruler; always straightforward, honest, and sympathetic in dealing with subordinates and others, ever willing to do that which is right, exercising self-abnegation, probably to an extent which others can hardly realise, taking in the light of knowledge and truth from whatever quarter it may happen to come, high or low, with the sole desire to do justice to all interests concerned."

The tenth European trip was largely spent at St. Moritz and Evian-les-Bains. A visit was paid to London, but at the time of the marriage on August 25th of the Princess Indira her parents were in Switzerland. The Princess, who already, at the age of twenty-one, was a young lady of determined character, had decided before she left India to marry no one but Jitendra Narayan, Maharaj Kumar of Cooch-Behar. Her father had refused his consent, but now gave way to the ex-

H.H. THE MAHARANI OF COOCH BEHAR.

tent of allowing the wedding to take place, though only represented at it by his solicitor. The young Cooch-Behar Prince being a Brahmo Samajist, the religious ceremony at the Buckingham Palace Hotel was Brahmo. It may be noted how widely Maharaja Sayajirao's attitude over his daughter's choice of a husband differs from the ordinary picture of an autocratic Indian Prince.

When His Highness came to England in the autumn, he took the opportunity of discussing with Mr. M. H. Spielmann a scheme he had long cherished of forming a representative collection of European paintings for the Picture Gallery which he had had built in the Public Park in 1910. The result is the fine collection now housed in Baroda, side by side with a magnificent exhibition of Indian art, unrivalled anywhere in the world. Owing to the intervention of the War, it was not until April, 1921, that the Western collection could be opened to the public.

Early in November, 1913, the Maharaja was at home once more; but neither he nor the Maharani was in a satisfactory state of health, and in the following April they were on their way again to Europe, little dreaming what was to befall in a few months' time. Only two events of the winter-season in Baroda need be mentioned. In February Her Highness signalised her abandonment of *purdah* by sitting on the same sofa with the Maharaja at a prize distribution at the Nyaya Mandir; and on March 17th the Maharaja Holkar of Indore, on a visit to Baroda, unveiled the equestrian statue of his host, the work of the late Derwent Wood, and erected by public subscription in commemoration of His Highness's Silver Jubilee.

The eleventh European trip began with visits to the Riviera and North Italy. The Maharaja proceeded to cures first at Evian and then, after a short stay in London, at Vichy, while the Maharani went to Carlsbad. Thus they were separated when the War broke out. He was able to reach Paris, and ultimately London, without difficulty, but she was less lucky; for, though she was not molested by the Austrian authorities, it was only after a very long and tedious journey that she could get to Havre by September 3rd, on her way to London.

A reception by the King and Queen followed in the course of September—His Highness's first meeting with their Majesties since the unhappy accident at Delhi three years before. The times had indeed changed. There were no insinuations now in the Press of "the Gaekwar's disloyalty"; and, by a curious irony, the very journal whose attacks had hurt him most gave prominent notice to His Highness's offer to the Imperial Government of all his troops and the resources of his State. Back in Baroda on December 4th, the Maharaja continued to give remarkable proofs of the loyalty which should never have been doubted. His offer of troops could only be accepted to a limited extent, three European officers and 157 men from the State Army being allowed to join the British Army, while 200 *sowars* were sent to Muttra to help to train remounts. With non-combatants and labourers included, Baroda's contribution in men was about 1,500. The nature of the war precluded the use of more men than these. The inhabitants of Gujarat, it must be remembered, are not of a fighting stock.

The figures for money gifts are more imposing. His Highness himself gave R. 500,000 for aeroplanes; R. 500,000 to the War Gifts Fund; R. 1,500,000 for Ford vans; R. 210,000 to the Imperial Indian War Relief Fund; R. 30,000 to the Prince of Wales's Fund; R. 40,000 to the Red Cross; and, further, a general contribution to the cost of the war of R. 12,000 a month from January, 1916, to June, 1919, R. 504,000 in all. (This last gift was in lieu of offering to pay for raising, equipping, and maintaining one or more regiments for active service, an idea which he had entertained.) With other subscriptions, Baroda contributed altogether R. 3,396,000 to these various purposes; in addition to which, miscellaneous donations to institutions and relief funds in Europe and India totalled nearly R. 76,000.

There were also material gifts by His Highness, such as horses from the State cavalry and tents for hospital use in France; and his Bombay residence, the Jaya Mahal Palace, was lent as a hospital for officers.

Finally, the purchases of War Loan Bonds by His Highness alone amounted to R. 10,000,000. The total of Baroda purchases of bonds was R. 11,224,000.* It cannot be said that Baroda failed in its response to the call of the War.

* * * * *

The influence of the world upheaval on the Maharaja's manner of life was naturally profound.

* The above figures are extracted from the *Gazetteer*, i., 621-2, where further details may be found.

There could be no more visits to Europe in search of health or ideas until the issue of the struggle was clearly decided. The twelfth trip, in fact, did not take place until near the end of 1919. In the hot seasons His Highness had to be content with the climate of the hills to build up his strength. His longest journey was in June and July, 1915, when in the Maharani's company he travelled, mainly by motor-car, through Southern India to Cape Comorin, paying on the way State visits to the Raja of Kollengode and the Maharaja of Travancore. On the return journey he saw for the first time the ruins of the great Hindu city of Vijayanagar, destroyed by the Mohammedans in the sixteenth century.

In the following year he spent the months from May to October in Kashmir. The old Maharaja, Sir Pratapsingh, had paid a brief visit to Baroda in March, and was most anxious to make a return for the welcome he had received. The heat of the Kashmir capital, Shrinagar, proved very trying, and at the end of June a move was made to Gulmarg, a beautiful spot 8,500 feet up, which reminded His Highness of St. Moritz, with its flowers and pines and snow-topped mountains.* Here he spent a pleasant time, rejoicing in a nearer approach to family life than was ever possible in Baroda—and particularly in the company of a little grandson. The presence of his son, Shivajirao, was evidently less welcome; for, though he had consented to it, he had told him that "the idea of

* Letter to Sir John Watson, July 9th, 1916. In another letter His Highness reminds the Raja of Kollengode that "the Persian poet calls this place a Paradise."

change to a cold place for young men is being carried too far in our family," and the young Prince's reckless ways were a sore trial.

The Maharaja, when he came to Kashmir, had no intention of taking a complete holiday. His letters to his new Dewan, Mr. (afterwards Sir) Manubhai Mehta, show him determined to keep his fingers on all the strings in Baroda. In a long communication sent from Shrinagar he urged the necessity of pushing on a new railway-line in Kadi; the importance of better inspection by Subhas and Naib Subhas of the work of their subordinates; the need of more reports to himself from his officers when appointed to new posts; the duty of the Accounts Department to check the carelessness of other departments, etc. A little later, at Gulmarg, the duties of the Police and *Abkari* (Preventive) Departments are his chief concern.

In August, however, the necessity came of a complete rest from work, in spite of which, at the end of the month, the Maharaja was writing to his Dewan about the policy of the Education Department as regards the translation of useful foreign books into the vernacular. "I should like to see every year at least ten to fifteen books translated into easy, simple Gujarati," he says. It may be noted that this provision of translations for the Gujarati-speaking population of Baroda has been consistently carried on, and that, through the Maharaja's interest in it, a great deal of Western knowledge has been made available for the linguistically less accomplished of his subjects.

Early in October the visit to Kashmir came to

an end. The Maharaja proceeded first to Simla, where he stayed for a few days with the new Viceroy, Lord Chelmsford, an old friend, to whom he had written in July warmly congratulating him on his appointment. From Simla he went to Kapurthala, on the invitation of its ruler, another friend of long standing; and so to Baroda. But he had only been home about a week when he set off again to Delhi to attend the Conference of Princes. As we have heard, he had from the beginning been favourable to the idea of the Indian Princes taking a part in the Council of Empire. It is characteristic, however, that he now went to Delhi with reluctance, trying to excuse himself from attending. He did not consider the agenda of the conference of any importance, and for mere ceremony he had no liking. In the following year, when Mr. E. S. Montagu paid his visit to India, Maharaja Sayajirao had worked out a scheme for useful co-operation by the Princes in the Government of India. This is explained in a letter to the Maharaja of Nabha:

"I think that the formation of a separate Council of the representatives of Princes, something after the model of the German Bundesrath, might meet the case. . . . I had suggested a somewhat similar idea to the Viceroy some years ago. I offer these suggestions with considerable hesitation, as I feel that this is a matter which lies more in the province of the scientific constitution-framer. . . .

"I have no doubt that if any matters which concern the Princes of India come into discussion the Government of India will consult the Princes before coming to any conclusion. There are, however, many questions of policy which it is essential for the Princes to open up on their own initiative. . . . It would be better for the Princes to restrict their attention to the following universally important matters:

"(1) The formation of a Council of States;

"(2) The formation of a properly representative Court of Appeal in matters of dispute between the Government of India and Indian Princes. . . .

"The Princes should not lose sight of the fact that these reforms are only the means to an end. The end is the reduction, or even cessation, of interference in purely internal matters and the right to be consulted in matters which affect both the Native States and British India equally."

This letter (dated November 7th, 1917) is of considerable importance as showing Maharaja Sayajirao's views as to the rightful position of the "Native" States within the Empire—views by no means in agreement with those of Indian Nationalists, and still less in agreement with old-fashioned Anglo-Indian ideas.*

The projected Conference of Princes at Delhi in November, 1917, did not come off, being post-

* In a letter written the following year (November 10th) to the Maharaja of Kolhapur, His Highness elaborated his views, proposing among other things that there should be in India Provincial and State autonomy, all questions relating to internal interest to be dealt with by the Provincial Governments and the States respectively, and that for the discussion of Imperial matters and internal affairs affecting British India and the States jointly there should be established a House of Princes' Representatives, to meet simultaneously with the Imperial Legislative Assembly.

poned, on account of the disastrous influenza epidemic, until the following January. The Maharaja did not attend it, having gone on a tour in the districts which were suffering from the effects of the failure of the monsoon in 1917 and the consequent rise in food prices. Nor, again, did the agenda of the conference seem to him of sufficient importance.

It must not be thought, however, that His Highness, because the Conference of Princes was not given such scope as he considered it should have, was unwilling to recognise that it performed some useful functions. Two of his letters to Lord Chelmsford, in January and in October, 1918, show that this was not the case. In the first he expressed his satisfaction that in a Resolution on Minority Administration in Native States the Government of India had been guided mainly by the advice of the Princes at the 1916 conference. Similarly, in the second letter he noted with pleasure that a memorandum on the rights of succession, etc., in Indian States had accorded due consideration to the views of the Princes at that conference.

We have been anticipating the order of events, and must return to record a few happenings in 1917. At the beginning of the year a note came from the Resident that the honour of the G.C.I.E. had been bestowed upon the ruler of Baroda. In February Lord Willingdon paid a two days' visit. In May the Maharaja, who was suffering from severe gout, retired for the hot weather to Ootacamund. Here the news reached him of the grave illness of his elder brother, Anandrao, and he started back for Baroda; but at Bangalore he learnt that it was too late, for pneumonia had proved fatal on June 21st, and he returned to Ootacamund, being himself too ill to attend the funeral. He felt the loss severely. "He was a good brother," he wrote, "and a wise, sensible man, of good common sense. He would have been fit for any big office, had he educated himself" (letter to Shrimant Sampatrao).

In October His Highness was sufficiently recovered to go to Simla, spending four days of his visit as guest at Viceregal Lodge. Plague was rife this winter in Baroda, in consequence of which the cold-weather months were spent in Mysore and Bombay,* and finally at Devlali, near Nasik, which the doctors recommended. Only in April was a visit paid to Baroda for the wedding of His Highness's grand-daughter, Princess Indumati, to the elder son of the Maharaja of Kolhapur. Most of the rest of 1918 was spent at Ootacamund, Gulmarg, and Dehra-Dun. Influenza was bad, with a high mortality rate, in Baroda; and at Dehra-Dun both Maharaja and Maharani were able to try electrical treatment for their complaints.

However, in November a return was made to Baroda, and here the tidings came of the end of the War. Writing to Lord Reay on December 8th, His Highness described India as "devoutly thankful." "All the country has celebrated the triumph," he added, "and in Baroda we have

* His Highness met Mr. Montagu in Mysore and again in Bombay, where he received a visit from him while confined to his hotel with a cold. In a letter to the Yuvaraja of Mysore he described Mr. Montagu as "a very nice man."

spent three days in festivities and feeding the poor."*

The Maharaja had been very anxious to secure a visit by Lord Chelmsford to Baroda during the Viceregal winter tour of 1918-9; and on March 24th he had the gratification of receiving His Excellency in his capital. The culmination of a two days' programme was a State banquet, at which Lord Chelmsford paid a well-deserved tribute to "the ruler who has for forty-three years devoted so much care and thought to the promotion of his people's welfare," "the wise promoter of a system of political and social order aiming at the combination of all that is best in Eastern and in Western civilisation."

By a curious coincidence, just as after the brilliant Viceregal visit to Baroda in November, 1909, we found Maharaja Sayajirao replying to a warning from Lord Minto on the prevalence of sedition, so now, after Lord Chelmsford's visit, we see His Highness on April 28th, 1919, acknowledging the receipt of a letter with a copy of a resolution regarding the violent agitation against the passing of the Anarchical and Revolutionary Crimes Act. "I am glad to inform Your Ex-

* He wrote in the same strain to General Birdwood ten days later. In both letters he alluded to the sufferings of India through high prices, profiteering, and shortage, aggravated by the failure of the rains and by epidemics.

Speaking of the War many years after, His Highness scouted the idea that India had ever wished for a British defeat. He admitted that some were not unwilling to see early disasters as a corrective of the excessive pride with which they were unhappily familiar in some Britons in India, but loyal support was given to the Government nevertheless.

Photograph by Vernon & Co., Bombay.

THE MAHARAJA AND HIS FAMILY.

cellency," he writes, "that, so far as I am aware, the contagion has not spread to my territories. Your Excellency may certainly count upon my full support and co-operation in the suppression of outbursts of lawlessness."

Happily the coincidence did not extend any further. Though there were grave disturbances in British districts of Gujarat adjoining Baroda State, there appears to have been no attempt to implicate the hand of Baroda in them. On this occasion history did not repeat itself.

CHAPTER XVI

TRAVEL AGAIN; AND TWO BEREAVEMENTS

As was only to be expected of so passionate a lover of travel, Maharaja Sayajirao, now that the termination of the War once more made it possible for him to leave India, began to think of another visit to Europe. There was, however, a special reason for his twelfth European trip. His eldest son, Prince Jaisinhrao, was seriously ill, and the doctors advised that the only chance of an improvement in his condition lay in a change from the climate of India.

The Maharaja had gone to Kashmir at the beginning of June, 1919, accompanied by the Maharani, Prince Shivajirao, and his family. Shrinagar proving too hot, they went to Gulmarg; but even there, in July, the heat became excessive, and His Highness was confined to bed by a severe attack of gout. It was decided to return to Baroda, where the bad report on Prince Jaisinhrao precipitated another move. The Prince was sent on ahead to Europe, and on September 22nd his parents followed him, to see that the best should be done for him. For the Maharaja himself a rest-cure had been recommended, and he was just preparing to go to a nursing-home in London when the stunning news arrived of Prince Shivajirao's death on November 24th. He was only twenty-nine; but his originally fine physique had been undermined by his manner of life, and influenza found him an easy victim. Thus, of four sons, only two now were left, the elder of whom was in a nursing-home, without prospect of any speedy betterment in his condition.

The Maharaja's own movements are recorded in a letter written by him to Lord Chelmsford in April, 1920. A rest cure of nine weeks in London had been followed by stays first at St. Moritz and then at Montreux—" like going from winter into spring," he writes. " This has been my first experience of nursing-homes and nursing, and although the cure was rather exacting I am hoping for results which will make it quite worth the trouble and loss of time. I am still taking the after-cure, and have not yet regained my normal strength; but I think that Eastbourne will set me up."

He stayed in Eastbourne until July. In August he was in Scotland, after which he spent most of the rest of 1920 at Hartsbourne Manor, Bushey Heath. In another letter to Lord Chelmsford he mentions the reception of the Maharani and himself by the King and Queen on November 29th, and his own reception by the Prince of Wales on the following day. To the Prince he expressed the hope that during his projected Indian trip he would honour Baroda with a visit, a matter on which he had already written to the Secretary of State for India.

Before the end of the year Prince Jaisinhrao had been moved from London to Berlin, where he seemed to make better progress; and his parents followed him to the Continent, Her Highness going to see him in Berlin previous to their return to Baroda, which was reached on February 5th.

This trip had unexpectedly extended to over a year and four months. But the Maharaja's ill-health, aggravated by the shock of Shivajirao's death and by the anxiety about Jaisinhrao, had reduced him to a state of inactivity indeed unusual in him. Not only physical, but also mental rest had been compulsory; and there is singularly little in his letters of the period about the affairs of Baroda.

An interesting and gratifying event had happened to Baroda during his absence, in the restoration to the Maharaja Gaekwar's administrative control of the westernmost part of his hereditary dominions. The Okhamandal *taluka* of Amreli, as it was then counted, today separately administered,* had had a curious history. At the beginning of the nineteenth century it was independent of the Gaekwar's authority. Its most notable inhabitants were a fierce and restless tribe, the Vaghers, said to be named after the tiger. Fishermen by original occupation, they had taken to piracy and general robbery under arms. In 1804 certain of the pirates among them seized a Bombay vessel off their coast and threw all on board into the sea. The Bombay Government was not strong enough to inflict immediate punishment, but in 1807 Colonel A. Walker, who as Major Walker had five years earlier been the first Resident appointed to the Court of Baroda, and who had wielded great influence there, was ordered to put matters right.

* See Chapter XXII. for some details about Okahamandal.

Accompanied by a Baroda force, he marched on Dwarka, occupied it, and imposed a fine of R. 110,000.

The Vagher chiefs reluctantly agreed to the fine and promised to be of good behaviour in future. Their depredations recommenced, however. Another expedition was necessary; but it was not until 1814 that one-third of the fine was extracted from them. Still they and allied chieftains continued troublesome, and at last Bombay decided to reduce them to subjection, which was done in 1816. In view of the fact that Okhamandal contained shrines so important to the Hindus as those at Dwarka and Beyt, a free gift was made of the *taluka* to the Gaekwar of Baroda, who conceded certain privileges to the Honourable East India Company in return.

Okhamandal was then incorporated in the possessions of the Gaekwar in Kathiawar, which went under the name of the Amreli *prant*. The administration of the place, however, proved very difficult. Risings occurred in 1818 and 1819, and only with British aid in 1820 was order restored.

A period of comparative peace followed; but by 1857 the weakness of Baroda control over Okhamandal was such that the Vaghers and other tribes were constantly raiding Kathiawar. Insurrections broke out in each of the next two years, which necessitated British intervention. In disgust Maharaja Khanderao expressed to the Resident at Baroda his desire to transfer the conduct of affairs in the *taluka* to the British. The insurgents, believing in the stories of the collapse of British rule in India, put up a strong resistance to an expeditionary force from Bombay, but, after Dwarka had been stormed and the tribesmen driven into the jungle, peace was reached by the end of 1859.

By the new arrangement the Gaekwar of Baroda still retained his sovereignty over Okhamandal. But a British Political Officer, appointed by Bombay and acting under the immediate orders of the Resident at Baroda, was stationed at Dwarka in charge of affairs, and having exclusive administrative control over the Vaghers and allied tribes. So matters continued for sixty years, though in 1909 the Government of India agreed that Baroda magistrates should have second-class powers over the Vaghers, reserving higher powers to the Assistant-Resident in Dwarka.

In 1919 it was suggested the resumption of complete control of Okhamandal might now be entrusted to the Baroda administration, and the Government of India agreed. At the beginning of May, 1920, the Resident, Lieutenant-Colonel C. J. Windham, went to Dwarka, and in the presence of the Dewan, representing the Maharaja, informed the Vagher chiefs of the transfer. "In view of the altered habits of the Vaghers," he told them, "and of the efficiency of the Baroda administration, in which the Government have every trust, the Government of India now wish to relax the stringent control which has been exercised by the Resident, and to make over the charge of the Vaghers to the Government of Baroda, whose subjects they are and have always been."

With the control of the Vaghers there was handed over to Baroda the Okha Battalion, originally recruited from the Vaghers alone, but in 1865 thrown open to other Indian races. This battalion still remains part of the Baroda army, its strength being about 400.

Since their return to control by Baroda the improvement in the habits of the Vaghers, which began during British control, has continued, and in 1924 the system of issuing passes to any of them wishing to go out of Okhamandal was abolished, except in the case of men of bad character. Education is making some small headway among them; and, as mentioned elsewhere, they have an excellent Boy Scouts company.

When Baroda regained full administrative powers over Okhamandal, it was decided that its former status as a *taluka* of Amreli should be changed. It was separated from Amreli *prant.* It has not yet, however, a *Subha,* but is under a Commissioner, who exercises the powers of *Subha* and District Judge.

* * * * *

The Maharaja's return to Baroda in February, 1921, was only in the nature of a flying visit; for in seven weeks' time he and the Maharani were again on their way to Europe. The last of his collected *Letters,* addressed to the Maharaja of Mysore in December, 1920, serves as a kind of apology in anticipation to those who might censure his long absences from his State. "You must not think," he wrote, "that I have given up my interest in India and am going to settle down in Europe. . . . The importance of health is not wisely and fully recognised by our people, and for temporary convenience they often incur permanent loss in the way of ill-health. I am trying to avoid this as much as I can."

The thirteenth European trip, however, was only for seven months and a half, being cut short by the Maharaja's determination to receive the Prince of Wales in person, now that he had accepted the invitation to include Baroda in his Indian tour. The Maharaja was back in Baroda on November 11th, 1921, and only twelve days later the Prince of Wales arrived.

Owing to the crowded programme of his tour, the Prince's stay in Baroda was very brief. He had to be at Udaipur on November 25th. He was, however, enthusiastically greeted. The *Times* correspondent telegraphed that apparently the whole population was in the streets to greet him, and that the arrangements for his entertainment were admirable. Naturally, like every distinguished visitor to Baroda, His Royal Highness was taken to see the Crown jewels at the Nazar Bag Palace, which, by the way, were valued by experts about this time at over three crores of rupees (R. 30,000,000), the chief diamond necklace for wear on State occasions being alone priced at forty lakhs (R. 4,000,000) and the largest diamond, the "Star of the South," at nine lakhs. The collection of emeralds is also magnificent, and a belt, or stomacher, of graduated pearls is unmatched in the world.

At the concluding State banquet at Laxmi Vilas the Prince expressed his gratification with his reception. "I shall," he said, "retain the most pleasant impressions of Baroda—the first Indian State which I have visited in the course of my tour—and of the wonderful sights which I have seen here. I have but one regret, that my stay with Your Highness must necessarily be so short. But, short as it is, it has enabled me to strengthen and revive the ties which bind your House and mine; and the most pleasant of my Baroda memories will be the pleasure which I have experienced in making the closer acquaintance of Your Highness."

After the departure of the Prince of Wales Maharaja Sayajirao spent four months of the Indian winter and spring at home. At the beginning of April, 1922, he started again with the Maharani for Europe. The fourteenth trip was destined to be a long one; in fact, His Highness's longest absence from Baroda during the whole of his reign. It was, however, far from being a visit of pleasure and sight-seeing. Apart from the affliction caused by constant ill-health to both Maharaja and Maharani, another great sorrow befell them in the death of their eldest son. After many years of illness this unfortunate young man passed away on August 27th, 1923. His Highness had now lost three sons, Her Highness two; and only one remained to them. What made the shock worse was that all had reached manhood successfully, though Prince Jaisinhrao had always been less robust than his brothers. Their decline had come later, when they were masters of their own fate.

Speaking once at Grant Medical College, Bombay —it was on the occasion of the prize-giving in

March, 1901—Maharaja Sayajirao said: " It would be a mistake to think that Indians have less wish to live than Europeans. I believe they are as much in love with life, and if they do not take as much care to preserve it, it is partly owing to poverty, but *still more to their ignorance of the laws of health.*"

It might be thought that a tincture of Western training would bring with it an appreciation of those laws of health. Unhappily, for Princes especially, there is also an insidious element in the teaching of the West which it requires an exceptionally strong character to resist.

CHAPTER XVII

THE FIFTEENTH EUROPEAN TRIP

It is not surprising, with the sad associations of his last visit to Europe, that Maharaja Sayajirao found his bodily condition unsatisfactory; and the return to India made it worse, the chief trouble being his old enemy, gout. In the course of five months from his landing in Bombay in November, 1923, he was hardly well for three weeks at a time. About the middle of January his ill-health took an acute turn. As Chancellor of the Hindu University, Benares, he had promised to read a paper at the annual convocation. On the journey from Baroda he was seriously indisposed, in consequence of which he had to ask his Dewan to read the paper for him. He spent five weeks at Benares and two at Delhi before being able to return to Baroda, where he had a month in bed with influenza complications. The doctors recommended a visit to Matheran, followed by a trip to Europe.

His Highness was carried on a stretcher from Laxmi Vilas to Baroda Station to meet the train to Bombay, *en route* to Matheran, and, though his condition improved after a fortnight, he had to proceed straight to Bombay by special train and to be carried on board the s.s. *Macedonia* in an invalid chair.

The large party from Baroda which came to see

him off on April 26th were seriously alarmed at their Maharaja's state, and had fears of not having him with them again; while the Maharani accompanied him to Europe. A nurse also travelled with the party, which, however, was small, as usual, the total staff only comprising two A.D.C.'s, a secretary and assistant-secretary, and His Highness's physician, Dr. V. Y. Modak.

The necessity of such a trip to Europe was completely vindicated. The Maharaja began to recover speedily on board, and as early as Aden he was able to give some attention to State affairs again. He landed at Marseilles, and, after eleven days in Paris, crossed to England, going into residence at his new house, "Russells," Watford, on June 3rd. While there he paid half a dozen visits to the Wembley Exhibition. Then another access of gout forced him to miss not only Henley and Ascot, but also the Royal Garden Party at Buckingham Palace. A cure at Evian was decided upon, and the last three weeks in July were spent here. Visits to Chamonix, Aix-les-Bains, and, finally, Bagnoles de l'Orne followed, the Maharani being already at the last-named place for a cure.

It had been intended that their Highnesses should both return to India in early November, but circumstances caused a complete alteration of plans. News of Prince Dhairyashil's illness made the Maharani, who had hoped to see Norway and Sweden, take the first available ship for Bombay, leaving Genoa on September 13th. It was not thought that his son's condition was so grave as to necessitate the Maharaja's immediate return. Moreover, his own health was far from satisfying the doctors whom he had consulted both in England and in France, and they advised that a winter in Europe and a complete rest from work would be desirable. Accordingly, his passage to India was cancelled, and after a little sight-seeing in France* he left for Switzerland in the middle of December, to take his share in winter sports. Like many Indians who have had experience of both climates, he proved himself more tolerant of European cold than of Indian heat, and was able, with a brief interval, to stay at Gastaad until the beginning of February, 1925, when he went to Nice for two months. At both places he took regular physical exercise, and at the end of this period his health was reported excellent.

During the winter His Highness had completed negotiations for the purchase of a house in Paris—6, Avenue Van Dyck, close to the Parc Monceau—and here he took up residence on April 8th. The return of his secretary from India next day enabled him to resume the work from which he had been compelled to abstain almost completely during the winter. In three or four days, it is recorded, he had disposed of the arrears of as many months.

Among the arrivals in Paris this spring was the Maharaja Sindia of Gwalior, so many years His Highness's friend. He had left India in serious ill-health, had been obliged to have an operation

* One of the sights which interested him most was the colony for railway servants, established at Tergnier by the Compagnie du Nord, which he visited on October 5th. In Baroda now there is the large railway quarter at Goya Gate (referred to in Chapter XXII.), one of the institutions on which His Highness prides himself, with good reason.

on the voyage, and now was in a most critical condition. Maharaja Sayajirao, who had intended to go to England, postponed his departure so as to be able to afford the comfort of his companionship to his fellow Maratha Prince, visiting him often twice a day. But the efforts of the doctors were in vain, and on June 5th the Maharaja Sindia was dead. After attending at his cremation next day His Highness left for England.

Though he spent only thirteen days in London and at "Russells," His Highness had a busy time for the last seven days. On June 19th he paid a call on Lord Reading, then on leave, at Lowndes Square. Next day he entertained the Mayor of Watford and about two hundred local residents at a garden-party at "Russells," and in the course of the afternoon received Lord Birkenhead and his elder daughter. As the Secretary of State for India was going that same evening to an open-air meeting of representatives of Conservative clubs in the Watford division, he asked to be allowed to accompany him, and was prevailed upon to address the audience, alluding to himself in his speech as "a colleague of the Empire," and insisting on the community of ultimate aim between England and India. On June 24th His Highness entertained Lord Birkenhead to dinner at the Carlton. On the 25th he attended the luncheon given to Lord Reading by the British Indian Union and proposed the health of their guest. Lastly, on the 26th, he was present at the reception by His Majesty the King at Buckingham Palace, being received in private audience beforehand.

Leaving for Paris next day, he had intended to

travel by air, but was dissuaded. Ten days in Paris were followed by a fortnight at Evian and a visit to Lausanne, unfortunately spoilt by a recurrence of gout, which necessitated a return to Paris and the use of an invalid chair. On his recovery, the last days of August were spent at Biarritz, with visits to San Sebastian and the Pyrenees region. A night and a day were spent at Lourdes, where the annual festival was in progress, and the sight of the pilgrims stirred up recollections of similar scenes at famous Indian shrines.

The fifteenth trip was now approaching its end. On September 1st His Highness returned to England and spent a month, mostly at "Russells," while many business affairs (including the sale of that house) were carried out. The chief social event was a luncheon-party at the Carlton to the members of the India Council. October was spent in Paris, where also business affairs demanded attention, and at last, on November 7th, His Highness left Marseilles in the P. and O. s.s. *Ranpura*.

We have dealt with this trip in greater detail* than any of its predecessors, because it is specially instructive as showing how the Maharaja spends his time in Europe, now that the passage of years no longer allows him to immerse himself in State

* This has been rendered possible with the assistance of the report on the trip of Mr. B. V. Desai, who was, first, assistant, and then sole, secretary to His Highness in Europe. Official accounts are prepared of every trip, but are privately printed, and contain much information not intended for general publication.

work to the same extent as formerly, but compels him to put the recovery of health to the fore. He had urgent reasons for wishing to be back in Baroda in 1925, seeing that May 27th of that year was the fiftieth anniversary of his accession to the throne; but he could not disregard the advice given to him, that in the interests of his health, perhaps even of his life, he should not return to India until the cold season had set in.

CHAPTER XVIII

THE GOLDEN JUBILEE

MAHARAJA SAYAJIRAO landed at Ballard Pier on the morning of November 20th, 1925, after having been greeted by a salute of twenty-one guns and conducted from the *Ranpura* by the representatives of Sir Leslie Wilson, Governor of Bombay, who was himself absent at the time. He proceeded to the Jaya Mahal Palace, and the same night left Grant Road Station in his newly-built saloon car, reaching Baroda at 9 a.m. next day.

At Baroda Station he was welcomed by the Assistant-Resident and by his own ministers, while a British guard of honour was drawn up on the arrival platform. Outside the station was another guard of honour from the State Army. After inspecting both guards His Highness drove straight to Laxmi Vilas, escorted by cavalry, elephants, etc., along gaily decked and crowded streets. At 5 p.m. a durbar took place at the Palace, at which about a thousand people were present, half military and half civilian, the uniforms of the former helping to make the scene a very brilliant one. The durbar, through the presentation of so many people, lasted an hour and a half. It is typical of the Maharaja's energy that within a short time of its termination he took a drive from the Palace and paid an unexpected and informal visit to the Guest-House, to see whether the new quarters, which had just been completed for the reception of State guests, were comfortable. One guest must confess to having been discovered without coat or waistcoat when His Highness walked into his room !

The day after the Maharaja's return was observed as a public holiday, and on the following day also all offices and shops closed, owing to the receipt of news of Queen Alexandra's death. The date of the Jubilee celebrations was still some time ahead, as they were now fixed to take place in January. His Highness was thereiore able to devote himself with few interruptions to the task of going through with his ministers all the questions which had arisen during his long absence from Baroda and of planning for the future. His first public appearance of note was on December 11th, when he went to the Kareli Bag to open the *Arya Kumar Ashrama.* Some account of this ceremony is given in Chapter XXI.

The next distraction from routine work was on December 13th, when a visit was paid to the historic town of Dabhoi, about twenty miles from Baroda City. His Highness likes to keep in touch with all the country districts, but he had not been to Dabhoi for several years. On the present occasion he took with him his grandson and heir-apparent, Prince Pratapsingh, a small suite, and a couple of guests. The trip only occupied two days, and the procedure was much the same as usual on *swari,** so that no special description is required. The neighbouring country as far as the frontier to south and east

* See Chapter VIII.

was visited, and the irrigation problem was discussed. An interesting feature of the second day was a ride round the town on elephants, accompanied by a cavalry escort, amid enthusiastically loyal crowds lining every street. The opportunity was taken to inspect the celebrated temple of Kalika Mata and the fine gateways, not entirely destroyed by the Mohammedan raiders at the end of the thirteenth century. Before leaving Dabhoi His Highness formally opened a new boarding-house for boys at the local High School, built by public subscription, and was the guest at a garden-party of the club recently founded in the town.

From December 23rd to 26th the seventh annual Hind Vijaya Gymkhana was held on the Gymkhana Ground, opposite the gates of the Laxmi Vilas Palace, their Highnesses and all the family being present at the prize-giving at the last day.* On the 30th, for the popular benefit, there was an exhibition in the arena, outside the Pani Gate of Baroda, of wrestling, elephant fighting (which now can only be seen in Baroda and is freed, as far as possible, from any risk of serious injury), and other contests and games. The Maharaja's party, with guests and suite, filled the Grand Stand, and every part of the seating accommodation was packed to overflowing.

On the New Year's Eve a State banquet was given in the Durbar Hall of Laxmi Vilas, at which the guests, Indian and European, numbered over eighty, and would have been considerably more numerous but for the prevalence of a certain amount of illness in Baroda at the time and the

* See p. 64.

absence of most of the British officers from the Camp for army manœuvres.

The Jubilee celebrations were not due until January 11th to 13th, and His Highness decided to spend part of the time before them in a tour of Kadi *prant*. He started from Baroda City on January 2nd, and changed at Ahmedabad Station from broad to metre gauge railway, the latter being the gauge all over Kadi. He paid a short visit to Kalol, proceeding to Kadi town, the former district capital, on the afternoon of the 3rd. Here he was lodged in the excellent little rest-house which he had caused to be built outside the town, while his suite and guests had tents close at hand. On the following morning a durbar was held, with the usual ceremonies, and in the evening a drive was taken through the town and a reception attended within the old fort. The townspeople, who had not seen His Highness for four years, were very enthusiastic in their demonstrations, and the dust for which Kadi is famous rose in clouds as the children pursued the procession through its streets. After dinner there was a firework display, of which a good view could be had from the camp. Fireworks, by the way, are a minor industry of Baroda, and they are of admirable quality.

During the stay at Kadi His Highness devoted attention to the questions of water-supply (which is acute) and the cotton-ginning industry, for the development of which there are great hopes, provided that water can be procured.*

On January 5th the journey was continued to

* See Chapter XXII.

Bechraji, across an intervening strip of British territory. The village appears in the *Gazetteer* under the name of Bechar, Bechraji being the name of the goddess whose temples give the locality its importance.* At one season of the year about 100,000 pilgrims visit the holy spot, and the rest-houses built by and for the pious are very numerous. The tank near the principal temple has a great reputation, and the pilgrims make a point of washing in it. It cannot, however, be said that its waters look inviting, whatever their virtue.

The object of His Highness's visit to Bechraji was connected with water, but not the water of the temple tank. There is another tank, of large size, which could supply the country round, but in January, 1926, was used for growing wheat and onions principally. An artesian well was being sunk near-by, and the discovery of sweet water in sufficient quantity would solve a very pressing problem.

From Bechraji His Highness visited the surrounding country, which is an agricultural centre of great promise if its water-supply can be made independent of the vagaries of the monsoon. On the morning of January 7th he was back in Baroda.

At last the opening day of the Jubilee celebrations arrived, and at 9.30 a.m. on January 11th the public durbar was held in a great marquee on the Warashia parade ground, north of Baroda City. Maharaja Sayajirao rode to this from Laxmi Vilas in a golden *ambari* on his own special elephant,

* Bechraji has also a well-known temple in the suburbs of Baroda City, which was a special place of devotion for Maharaja Sayajirao II.

which wore its massive gold anklets and was decorated with gorgeous fantasy. He was escorted by cavalry and followed by infantry and the gold and silver guns drawn by white oxen. In the marquee he took his place on the *gadi*, on a raised daïs, with the Maharani at his side, while gold and silver chairs were on either side for the various members of the Gaekwar family, including the widowed Maharani of Cooch-Behar, who was on a visit to Baroda for the Jubilee.

The presentation of congratulatory addresses made this durbar a long ceremony. These were read on behalf of His Highness's subjects in general; the Millowners' Association; the Mohammedan community; the Parsis; the Roman Catholics; the Shikshana Prasaraka Mandali of Poona; the All-India Hindu Maha Sabha; the Surat municipality; the Maratha Samaj; Naosari District; the Sunni Anjuman of Baroda; and the Antyajas. The languages employed were Marathi, Gujarati, Hindustani, English, Persian, and Arabic.

When the addresses had come to an end, His Highness replied in English without notes. Beginning with the lesson drawn from the words they had just heard from members of various races and religions, he emphasised the point that they were all animated by one object, to live in harmony with one another. Their differences, therefore, could be obliterated by the ideal of common nationality. With regard to his own work for the State, he claimed that it was actuated by no whim, but was part of a fixed, deliberate policy which he thought it his duty to pursue. When they had privileges and rights given to them,

THE GOLDEN JUBILEE PROCESSION: THE START FROM LAXMI VILAS PALACE.

however, they must have the moral strength to use them with wisdom and courage. They must seek after the attainment of nationhood, and banish sectarian ideals. As for the past, they must not brood over it, but must adopt from it what was best and press its lessons into the service of the present. Then if they went forward with courage and determination, he felt sure that the future would repeat the success of that past civilisation for which India was noted.

Outside the marquee the selected troops of the State Army were drawn up, and at the appointed time the artillery fired the salute and the bands played the Baroda national anthem.

A second durbar was held at Laxmi Vilas in the afternoon, after which their Highnesses drove to the Nyaya Mandir, in the hall of which was held the Children's Gathering, a ceremony which is a charming feature of public celebrations in Baroda. In the evening the whole city was illuminated, and a firework display was given at the edge of the Sursagar Tank.

The only public event on January 12th was a People's Fair, which was held in the Public Park at 6 p.m., their Highnesses paying a visit to it and spending some time in the various tents, where singers, dancers, acrobats, etc., gave their performances.

January 13th began with a grand review of the State Army on the parade ground near Makarpura Palace at 8.30 a.m., the brilliant uniforms of the troops making a very picturesque spectacle. A distribution of food and of clothes to some thousands of the poor took place in the afternoon.

In the evening the Maharaja was "at home" at the Palace to all the leading people of Baroda and the European community, and in the illuminated grounds many tents of entertainers of all kinds played their parts throughout the evening. A notable performance was an open dance by a troupe of Bhils, men and women, who afforded an astonishing contrast to the more usual forms of Indian dancing. The guests, about five hundred in number, had not all taken their leave until nearly twelve o'clock.

On the morning of January 14th a *Gazette Extraordinary* was published, announcing the concessions made by His Highness to his people on the occasion of his Golden Jubilee. These included a remission of arrears of Land Revenue, amounting to about three-quarters of the sum due at the beginning of 1926, or R. 300,000 in all; a suspension of the collection of cotton excise duty; a promise of the installation of telephonic communications between all the large towns of Baroda; and the release of a number of convicts under sentence at the Central Gaol and of the boys at the Reformatory.

The Jubilee celebrations had come to an end. There was, however, a function in the same week which was closely connected with them, since it marked the fulfilment of a desire of His Highness to leave to his subjects a memorial of the past history of Baroda, with which might be associated once a year a day of remembrance. On the morning of January 15th he proceeded to an open space near the Royal Cemetery on the bank of the Vishvamitri and adjacent to the large temple known as Kadareshwar, and there laid the foundation-stone of a Kirti Mandir (Temple of Fame, or Hall of Remembrance). In his address to those assembled to witness the ceremony he told them how it had long been his ambition to found in Baroda an equivalent of the Pantheon or of Westminster Abbey, in which could be honoured the memory of distinguished persons and benefactors of the State, and, first of all, the past rulers and devoted members of their families. He recalled how in his early days, in the old Moti Bag Palace, he had been impressed by the Indian paintings of the former Gaekwars, and how later he had had the paintings photographed and bronze busts and studies in relief made from them. Now he proposed to honour them further in this Kirti Mandir, and in the annual commemoration he was considering the idea of including a Golden Jubilee memorial lecture upon some great personality.

His Highness then laid the foundation-stone and performed the Hindu ceremonies proper to the raising of a *Chatri* in honour of his predecessors on the throne, at which *sraddhas* (offerings) might be made at the due time. *Sraddha*, he had emphasised in his speech, was not meant to be a mere empty form, but to express some of the noblest feelings of mankind, to "enshrine the best of filial virtue, of reverence for virtue, and to be an inspiration to faithfulness to one's kith and kin."

On the evening of this day Maharaja Sayajirao was the guest of the club which had been founded by his officers, and had been named after him

Sayaji Vihar.* With him came H.H. the Maharani and the members of the Gaekwar family, and an Indian banquet followed, at which the attendance of club members was very large. After the speeches there was an open-air entertainment by singers and dancers.

On January 21st another short round of festivities began, His Excellency the Viceroy paying his promised visit to Baroda, accompanied by the Countess of Reading, a suite of about 80, and an escort of 260 of the Welch Fusiliers. He was received at Baroda Station and conducted to Makarpura Palace, in which, and in tents in its grounds, the whole party was lodged. On the following morning, after a drive to see the State jewels and other treasures at the Nazar Bag, His Excellency had a visit from Maharaja Sayajirao, his son and grandson, the Dewan, and other high officials of Baroda. This visit was returned at mid-day, when Lord Reading drove to Laxmi Vilas and was received in the Durbar Hall. Her Highness the Maharani and Lady Reading also exchanged visits.

Later in the day came arena sports and a

* Originally instituted as a club for heads of departments only, in 1909, with His Highness's cordial approval, the Sayaji Vihar was thrown open to junior officials also. Later non-officials were admitted, and still more recently Europeans. Lastly, on February 11th, 1926, it was resolved to permit ladies, hitherto only allowed to come as guests on exceptional occasions, to join as members. This is indeed a revolution in Indian club life!

The Sayaji Vihar has three good hard courts for lawn tennis, two billiard tables, and facilities for badminton, table tennis, and cards. An enlargement of the premises is contemplated.

garden-party at Laxmi Vilas, at both of which Lord and Lady Reading were present; and in the evening a State Banquet in the Durbar Hall, when the guests numbered 150. At the banquet His Highness proposed first the health of the King-Emperor, and then that of the guests of the evening, Lord and Lady Reading. In his second toast, after a tribute to His Excellency's work in India, which had laid her under a debt of gratitude, he alluded to Baroda's unswerving loyalty to its obligations during nearly a century and a quarter of the British connection, to his own efforts for fifty years to follow out his ideal of a modern State, and to his hope that, though much remained to be done, he could claim for Baroda an honoured place in the Indian Empire. He spoke of the deep interest with which they of the Indian States had watched the progress of British India from stage to stage of self-rule, and of his own earnest wish that the claims of the Indian States should not be forgotten.

"In the new era," he continued, "the Indian States now claim a place in the sun, and, believing in the justice of the British people, they hope that their ancient rights and dignities will be fully revived. For my own State it is only natural in me to hope that its original sovereignty will be restored. Over a hundred years ago the British Government elected to mediate between my House and its tributaries . . . to collect the tribute on our behalf free of charge. It was a sacred trust then undertaken. A hundred years of British peace, progress, and order have now ensued. In the interests of efficient government, and, with the utmost solicitude for the good of the Empire, I suggest to the British Government that the ancient privileges be now fully restored to their friends and allies of old."*

In conclusion, His Highness expressed the pleasure which was felt that Lady Reading (who had been seriously ill and was at first not expected to be in a fit state to accompany the Viceroy from Delhi to Baroda) had been able to visit them, and assured her of an abiding place in the affections of the Indian people, due to the splendid manner in which she had fulfilled the exalted functions of her post.

The Viceroy's reply gave high praise to Baroda's "long and glorious record of loyalty" and to its people's progress, social and economic, under His Highness's beneficent rule. With regard to the future position of Indian States there need be no apprehension, he said, lest in any enquiry concerning constitutional advance in British India this position and the privileges of the Princes should run any risk of being ignored. He could not discuss special representations made regarding Baroda, for they were still under examination; but His Highness might rest assured that they would receive the most careful and impartial consideration.

On the following afternoon, previous to the departure of the Viceregal party for Delhi, Lord Reading laid the foundation-stone of a new Science Institute in the grounds of Baroda College. To found such an institute had for many years been one of Maharaja Sayajirao's cherished hopes;

* See p. 235.

and he had made up his mind, during the Golden Jubilee celebrations, to realise it rather than an alternative scheme to erect a modern building for the better housing of the Public Library. There was a large gathering of Baroda notabilities and British guests to witness the ceremony. The Dewan, Sir Manubhai Mehta, opened the proceedings with a speech in which he spoke of the scope of the institute to be, the proposal to add a Faculty of Law to the College curriculum, and the dream of providing ultimately an University for Baroda, or perhaps for the whole of Gujarat. Then, in response to the Maharaja's invitation, Lord Reading, with a graceful tribute to the many-sided intellectual activities of Baroda, laid the stone.

The Viceroy's visit ended the same evening; but on his arrival at Delhi he sent a telegram of warm appreciation of his reception and of what he had seen in Baroda. His Highness replied with a telegram of thanks.

In contrast to the preceding months, February was mainly spent by Maharaja Sayajirao in travel, though not to any great distance from his capital. Beginning with a trip eastward, in the course of which he visited the famous Ajanta Caves and paid a State call at the Court of Gwalior, he returned to Baroda on February 10th, only to set out next day for Kathiawar. His main object was the formal opening of the pier which he had caused to be constructed by the firm of Meik and Buchanan at Adatara, in the westernmost portion of his territories, Okhamandal, lying on the Arabian Sea and the Gulf of

Kutch.* He also desired to take part in certain religious ceremonies, including the opening of the *Sharda Math* at Dwarka, in Hindu eyes the holiest spot in all Baroda, which he had not visited for five years.

Accompanied by a large party, including his brother and son, the Assistant-Resident, and other guests, His Highness travelled by train through Ahmedabad, Viramgam, and Jamnagar (where the journey was broken to lunch with the Jam Saheb's brothers, the Jam himself being away at the time), and arrived at Dwarka on the evening of February 12th, twenty-six hours after leaving Baroda City. For the next three days he stayed at the small house formerly occupied by the Assistant-Resident during the British administration of Okhamandal, while the rest of the party were accommodated in other buildings or in tents on the picturesque rocky cliff overlooking the Arabian Sea and within a short distance of the vast temple, or rather temples, of Dwarkadish.

On the 14th the train was taken to Adatara, where in the afternoon the ceremony of opening the pier took place. At the preliminary durbar His Highness, replying to an address of welcome, expressed his satisfaction with the completion, which they saw that day, of the great and costly harbour works, and his hopes that his people would avail themselves fully of the facilities afforded by the scheme he had so many years had in view. The Dewan followed with a brief speech, announcing the Maharaja's intention of presenting with

* See Chapter XXII. for some account of Okhamandal, its railway, and its harbour (now called Port Okha).

THE PIER AT ADATARA (PORT OKHA).

poshaks (robes of honour) those chiefly responsible for the work on the harbour. It is characteristic of Baroda that these were a Briton, Mr. Berry, ex-resident engineer; a Chinese contractor; and an Indian naval engineer. After the durbar His Highness cut the cord at the entrance to the pier, and the whole party proceeded to inspect it and to see over two ships which had come to moor alongside in honour of the occasion. One of these, running from Bombay to Karachi, was over 6,000 tons, and therefore a good test of the capacity of the harbour.

The Maharaja had already paid a visit to Dwarkadish and called upon the much revered Shankaracharya;* but an unfortunate indisposition prevented him from opening the *Sharda Math*, which he had to depute to Prince Dhairyashil. He left Dwarka on February 15th, and after stopping at Jamnagar to dine with the Jam Saheb, now back in his capital, proceeded to Amreli, where a durbar was held and the leading men of the *prant* were presented to him. Thus he completed his district tours for the winter of 1925-6, having visited in turn Baroda, Kadi, Okhamandal, and Amreli *prants*. Through lack of time he had to content himself with such glimpses of Naosari as he got when passing through the *prant* by rail.

His Highness was only back in Baroda a few days when he started out again on a journey which he had planned for many years, but had hitherto been unable to make. This was to revisit, for the first time since he had left it in 1875, the home of his family and his own birthplace, Kavlana. He

* See p. 230

was accompanied by his son, his brother, and other immediate kinsmen. Some of his impressions of this visit have been recorded in Chapter I.

At the beginning of March it was necessary for the Maharaja to be in Baroda again for the last ceremonies before his departure for Europe. His passage had been booked by the P. and O. s.s. *Rawalpindi*, leaving Bombay on March 13th. Almost to that day he was harassed by the idea that he ought to cancel his passage and stay in Baroda. The strain of official work, however, in which he had been unremittingly engaged since he landed in India the previous November, whether in his capital or on *swari*, had told on his health. At Dwarka he had been far from well, and now his nerves were in an irritable state. Moreover, in India it was impossible for him to observe the same strict rule of diet to which he was accustomed in Europe, and there was the fear of another access of gout hanging over him. With reluctance, therefore, he took the decision which he knew to be unwelcome to his people,* and arranged to make his sixteenth foreign trip.

* This is no mere polite formula. The Maharaja's presence makes all the difference to the social life and gaiety of Baroda, which, without him, to say the least, languish. Students of English history will remember the effect produced by Queen Victoria's retirement from the public view after the Prince Consort's death, and from that form some idea of what happens to Baroda with its Prince away.

He is well aware of this; but, as he says, the question is whether he serves Baroda best by husbanding his energies until he can safely hand over his power to his successor, or by wearing himself out in a possibly brief space of time. The memory of his prostration in April, 1924, abides in his memory.

A few public appearances marked the remaining days in Baroda. On March 4th there were military sports on the Warashia *maidan*, at which His Highness presented the prizes; and on the evening of the same day was a performance in Marathi of *Twelfth Night*—curiously and ingeniously converted into a sort of musical comedy—at the Maharaja Theatre. On the 5th were held at Laxmi Vilas a farewell durbar in the morning and a grand garden-party at night. On the 10th His Highness formally opened the Baroda Poor House, the first institution of its kind in the State, near the Kareli Bag. In his speech he contrasted the old reputation of Baroda, the *Dharma Raj*, for indiscriminate charity with his present intention to provide for extreme cases of destitution among the aged, unable to earn their own living and with no one to care for them, and foreshadowed the future establishment of a similar institution in each *prant* of Baroda.

The objects which had necessitated his stay in India until the growing heat of the sun had begun to be enervating in the plains of Baroda had now been attained; and on March 12th Maharaja Sayajirao left his State in the capable hands of Sir Manubhai Mehta, embarking the following morning on the s.s. *Rawalpindi*, and reaching Marseilles on the 26th.

PART II

CHAPTER XIX

THE REFORMER

SPEAKING of his aspiration towards reform, Maharaja Sayajirao maintains that it was innate in him rather than implanted by his teachers. This does not mean that he failed to appreciate the labours of those who guided him during his minority. In particular, it must not be thought that he undervalued the example set in the management of the State by Sir T. Madhavrao. It is obvious that he saw the excellence of the example, and that he continued, after his assumption of full powers, along the wise lines of government initiated by his old Dewan. But he insisted on thinking out matters for himself, and personally working over the details of every scheme which suggested itself to his mind as desirable for Baroda. No reformer can be entirely uninfluenced by the teachings of others. The Gaekwar, however, can justly claim that he did not want an outside stimulus to urge him in the direction of reform.

He was, for all the " dullness " and the " slowness at acquiring information " which might be attributed to him in early Baroda days, intensely observant from his youth upwards. This quality has remained his throughout life. There is nothing which escapes his eye, hardly anything which may not prompt him to enquire about it. This is not mere curiosity, but a right inquisitiveness, stirred, in his travels in the West, by the desire to discover whether what he sees working efficiently there cannot be adapted to India. Wherever he has gone, he has tried to glean new ideas to that end. To new ideas he must have been born open; and even when he does not at once welcome one, at least he never says, "No, this cannot be done in Baroda."

Seldom has his inquisitive tendency been more displayed than on the occasion of his visit to Europe in 1923, when he was already sixty years of age. In that summer he spent a month in Berlin, a full programme having been mapped out in advance, which involved work from 9.30 a.m. to 6 p.m. daily. He inspected research and educational institutions, dyeworks, wireless-set factories, etc., and had interviews with countless people. In the same year he manifested a great interest in the subject of agricultural banks, cabling to his ministers in Baroda to ask whether a Land Mortgage Bank could not be established there on the lines of the Crédit Foncier and the Egyptian Agricultural Bank. While in Rome he collected all available documents concerning the International Institute of Agriculture.

On his American visit of 1905, too, he was exceptionally busy and interested. American ideas of education were his chief study, and he secured the services of an expert educationalist, Dr. Cuthbert Hall, to inspect the Baroda schools and suggest reforms. Circulating libraries attracted much attention from him, with a result which was notable later. Other subjects which occupied his mind were industrial development, agriculture, and labour unionism in the United States.

It may be said that nothing is too trivial for him which may serve a useful end. For instance, hearing once in England that someone whom he knew was going to a poultry show, the Maharaja insisted on accompanying him, in order that he might consider the possibility of improving the egg-laying qualities of Indian fowls. Travelling from Europe by the s.s. *Ranpura* in November, 1925, he was struck by the system of ventilating the cabins and saloon by " punkah louvres," and ordered enquiries as to whether they could be introduced into Baroda buildings. Again, being told of a patent night-lamp in the American Mission in Baroda, which kills mosquitoes and other insects coming in contact with it, he suggested its adoption in the Laxmi Vilas Palace.

To his gift of keen observation is allied a power of mastering detail, a very necessary asset for a reformer in India, where grasp of detail is decidedly not a common trait. A genius for hard work has been his throughout his reign. No single officer of his has so much knowledge of the State as he has, because he has always insisted on doing his own work. He has a mind, too, as one who is very well acquainted with him has observed, which can go from one end of a subject to the other and back, like a pendulum. There is a disadvantage in this, now that he is older, since it is apt to tire him out and to bring on his peculiar form of gout.

In his youth he suffered much from insomnia, and would lie in bed for hours without sleeping, unable to shake off the ideas which came into his mind.* Even then the effect upon his health was prejudicial. "Thinking is my disease," he says himself; and he fully realises the inconvenience, striving to concentrate upon the broader issues and free himself from excessive attention to detail.

To help him in his hard work, however, he has a great possession—namely, that he is a thorough optimist, to whom nothing is impossible. Opposition only makes him stiffen, and then, as the close acquaintance quoted above expresses it, he "hammers." His own way of putting it is that, from the first days of his actual rule in Baroda, he had a "strength" which carried him through when there was a tendency to resist his views. He could stand up to his early ministers, and, when they thought to guide an inexperienced youth as they wished, could insist on having the full powers of his predecessors. He would make no compromise or concession to gain an end which seemed to him right.

At the same time, when he has met with very determined opposition, he has shown an ability to keep quiet for years, waiting to find the right man to carry out the object which he has kept in view. The man being found, the reform is put through.

A shrewd observer sees in His Highness not one, but two personalities: the Idealist, out-and-out, and the Realist, the man-of-the-world. This causes a conflict, sometimes one and sometimes the other personality prevailing. On the whole, however, the Idealist has remained on the top.

* "When Maharaja sleeps well, his officers are happy!" is a saying not unknown in Baroda.

Perhaps it is the realisation of this conflict which has caused him to be very cautious in the introduction of many of his reforms. It is not that he doubts the correctness of his theory, but that the man-of-the-world in him has misgivings about the application of the theory. Therefore he will not force the pace. Quite early in life he made up his mind as to this. In a letter to his Khangi Karbhari in April, 1888, when he was only twenty-six, he writes of the impossibility of reforms being carried through in a hurry, and adds: "Never be afraid of being late in an undertaking, so long as you have it in view." This attitude of mind comes out well in the history of such reforms as the setting up of a system of compulsory education and the extension to his people of a share in the government of the State.

He is nowadays more than ever convinced of not merely the wisdom, but the absolute necessity, of slowness in many progressive measures, even when he has them very much at heart. Particularly is this the case where the religious susceptibilities of his subjects are involved. He marked, after his wont with books as he reads them, a passage in Stanley Rice's *The Challenge of Asia* about the choice with which, in India, the Government is often faced, of either not doing what is felt to be right or else offending long-cherished susceptibilities; and in conversation upon the subject soon afterwards he insisted that no religious reforms, such as caste-intermarriage, the remarriage of widows, or the cessation of child-marriages, can be carried out in India by compulsion. If made compulsory, the reforms would not last. Persuasion, not force, is the better way. Therefore, he said, he would never compel, even if he had the power to do so, which, of course, he has not, from the very status of Baroda in the Indian Empire. The Maharaja's inclination in the matter of child marriages, for instance, would be to make the punishment imprisonment, not merely a light fine. But the British attitude is " Don't stir up a revolution "; so that he dare not go so far as he thinks right.

Although well aware, as he remarked on another occasion, that " in India one must always be pushing people from behind," he has declined to exercise violent pressure. Even if he has the ambition, as has sometimes been said of him, to carry out what the Government of India has thought impossible to achieve in the way of reforms, he has not let that ambition vary his policy of *festina lente*.

As might be expected, there are in India today critics who consider that the pace chosen by the Maharaja of Baroda is too slow, and that with increasing years he has lost his enthusiasm for progress, letting Baroda fall behind certain other Indian States. Particularly do they complain that he has not introduced in its fulness that " popular government " which is to make everyone so happy. At the beginning of 1926 an article appeared in *The Servant of India*, which, discussing the celebrations for His Highness's Jubilee, said that, " with all his desire to model his State on Western lines," he had never been known to favour popular government.

" Though perhaps Baroda [the article continued]

was among the first to admit its people into consultation on legislative and administrative bodies, these are still in the same rudimentary condition in which they were at the start, while some other States, coming into the race at a later period, have long overtaken it. Mysore and Travancore are, in respect of popular government, a generation in advance of Baroda. It was hoped that His Highness would be pleased to announce a substantial instalment of constitutional reforms on the occasion of the Jubilee celebrations, but these hopes have been sadly disappointed."

In the previous October, before Maharaja Sayajirao's return from Europe, there had been a debate in the Baroda State Assembly, when some members pressed for an enlargement of the Assembly, for two-thirds of its members to be elected, for it to become a responsible instead of an advisory body, and so on. The Dewan made a conciliatory reply, in which he assured the members of the Assembly that the Government in no way thought them unfit for power.

It was left for His Highness to answer more definitely the suggestions for increasing the pace of constitutional progress. This he did at the State Durbar in the Laxmi Vilas Palace on November 21st, the day on which he reached Baroda after his fifteenth trip to Europe. There were many addresses of welcome, in some of which the desire was expressed for further progress in constitutionalism and in local responsibility. At the end of a brief speech in reply His Highness remarked gravely that in the past he had, of his own accord and unasked by his people, introduced constitutional reforms and bestowed privileges. He would continue to do so in future, at the proper time; and he advised them, when differences of opinion arose, to accept his opinion ungrudgingly.

These words were uttered in the usual level tones in which the Maharaja is wont to make his durbar speeches, and without any appearance of severity. Nevertheless they were clearly a warning, to those who wish to speed up the progress of Baroda towards democracy, that he who so long has guided the State does not mean to cease that guidance yet. It is he still who must decide when the time is ripe for the introduction of further reforms.

His view appears to be—and here the best opinion in his State is with him—that today his work has to be consolidated, and the machinery of government made efficient, rather than new measures introduced. "If my people are really progressive," he said on one occasion, in private conversation, "they have now in Baroda all the facilities necessary for progress. But they must themselves prove that they are progressive." In the past he gave them everything which has made Baroda what it is, gave all free of charge, except the land tax, and, for such as it affected, the income tax, introduced between 1897 and 1905. It is time that they should show that they have deserved this treatment, and show also some willingness to contribute towards the cost of the benefits which they enjoy.

Such an attitude of mind is eminently reasonable. But the reasonable is apt to be slighted alike by the ardent "progressive" and by the taxpayer asked to pay more, which accounts for the ebullitions of discontent, not very grave, which at its close disturbed the harmony of His Highness's sojourn in Baroda for his Golden Jubilee. He was not unduly troubled thereby. He has always maintained that his people are "a very good people," and, where they have sufficient work to occupy their minds, very loyal. To the truth of the latter statement anyone who has accompanied him on a country tour can testify. It is only in the big towns that there is a hint of disaffection.

Complete sympathy with his ideas the Maharaja has not expected to find. He feels himself, in many ways, more Western than Oriental; and it is hard to make his officers and his subjects, who have not had the education that he has had, comprehend what is in his mind. He stands, in his own words, "in a gap between two civilisations, Western progress and Indian tradition." He wants to keep what is good in the traditional life of India, and at the same time, where the methods of the West are better, to adapt them to the East. His problem has been to get men educated on quite different lines from his to see eye to eye with him. Where the government of the State is concerned, an appeal to reason is not enough to secure support, not because Indians have inferior reasoning powers to Europeans (for this he will not allow), but because their education is inferior. Therefore, for the good of Baroda, he fears to leave the helm yet.

CHAPTER XX

THE EDUCATIONALIST

To the direct question, put to him during his voyage to India in November, 1925, which did he consider was the greatest success among the reforms introduced by him into Baroda, Maharaja Sayajirao replied without hesitation, "Free and compulsory education."

Certainly, if we judge merely by statistics of what has been accomplished, we can hardly doubt that the readiness of his answer was justified. At the end of his predecessor's reign Baroda spent on such education as was imparted by State agency little over R. 32,000. In 1876-7, when Sir T. Madhavrao was treating the question of schools with that "wise liberality" which P. S. Melville commended, the amount had risen to nearly R. 111,000. In 1881, when His Highness's personal administration began, it was nearly R. 156,500. The latest available figure, that of 1925, is R. 3,056,866. The number of children receiving education of any kind in Malharrao's reign was under 9,000,* including very few girls. In 1876-7 Sir T. Madhavrao puts the total school-going population of Baroda between 22,000 and

* Precise figures cannot be given. In 1871, 822 children attended Government schools, while the number attending private elementary schools was estimated about the same time at 8,000.

23,000. In 1881, though we have no complete figures, there were over 17,000 pupils in the vernacular primary schools alone, and there were then eight girls' schools, with some 600 pupils. In 1925 the total school-going population was 217,000, including 67,000 girls.

Under Malharrao no Education Department existed. Some progress, indeed, was made in his reign, the High School and four Government primary schools, two Marathi and two Gujarati, being founded in Baroda City, and an Anglo-vernacular school at Petlad. The headmaster of the High School had the general superintendence of all these schools; but otherwise education in Baroda was in private hands and was of a most elementary kind. The old Indian system of popular instruction, with which Maharaja Sayajirao likes to compare the system which he has established, had lost its effectiveness owing to the decay of the village communities on which it was based.

In 1875 a Vernacular Education Department was set up in Baroda, to which was entrusted the control of fifty-five primary schools. The number of these schools steadily increased until, in 1881, it reached 180, all but eighteen of them Government schools. In 1885 sanction was given for the expenditure of from R. 50,000 to R. 60,000 annually on the building of new schools. By the tenth year of Maharaja Sayajirao's personal rule 558 primary schools were under the Department.

In this year, 1891, His Highness took the first practical step towards the foundation of a system of State-aided popular education in the country districts. He ordered that, in every village where there should be found sixteen children ready for elementary instruction, a school should be opened; and the village schoolmasters in general were, for the future, to be reckoned among the servants of the village, with a monthly salary paid by the Revenue Department, and, in addition, such fees as the pupils' parents were prepared to pay. The cost of upkeep of these schools was eased by a grant-in-aid from the Education Department. In two years' time 632 new primary schools were thus opened and maintained.

So far there was no compulsion to attend school. This idea, however, had for some time been in His Highness's mind, and a commission had been appointed to consider the position. In a letter to the Dewan, Manibhai Jasbai, dated March 16th, 1893, he writes that he has on the previous day obtained the necessary information and is proceeding to give the order for the introduction of compulsory education in his State. Such defects as there might be in the scheme must be rectified later.

"We do not wish," he says, "to be mere enthusiasts, doctrinaires, or hobbyists, but rather the reverse. We are most willing to set our mistakes right. I must say that it will be a serious question whether the State will be able to afford much money. We are already spending almost as much as our income, and this is not satisfactory."

Characteristically, His Highness decided to make a partial experiment with the new scheme. It was to be introduced at first only in the town of Amreli and the villages of the *taluka* of which it was the headquarters. The estimated cost of this was over R. 31,000; for the whole of Baroda the estimate was between twelve and fifteen lakhs. "I cannot determine a policy," he writes, "till I can definitely find out by experience whether the State can bear the burden of such an expensive plan of education. Nothing would be worse than to pledge what you cannot carry out."

He adds, nevertheless: "Education is absolutely necessary for the realisation of my ambition and wishes, and for the success of my policy. The one important point that we must bear in mind is that educated people require a stronger and firmer government,* a want which I hope our successors will try to meet."

Although a beginning was thus to be made of compulsory education, there was to be, at first, no punishment for failure to attend school, His Highness believing that the majority, if not all, of the parents would send their children voluntarily. Moreover, religious and social prejudices were to be considered. All castes and communities were to be provided with the means of education. In particular, the objection of the upholders of the *purdah* system must be respected. "It is not necessary that they should send their girls to Government schools. All that they will be expected to do is to educate their girls and boys to the standard fixed by the Government from time to time."

No better instance than this could be found of Maharaja Sayajirao's cautious policy of reform. He does not sympathise—this is an understatement,

* The truth of his warning has been realised in his lifetime, the spread of education having made the government of Baroda a far more responsible task than it was when he wrote this letter to Manibhai Jasbai.

as is shown in Chapters XIX. and XXI.—with such things as caste prejudice. But as long as thirty-three years ago he recognised that they could not be overcome by legislative violence. They must be slowly conquered.

In 1896 the post of Director of Vernacular Education was remodelled, the holder being henceforward styled *Vidyadhikari* and Commissioner of Education. Nine years later some diminution was made of this officer's powers, the control of the village schools being handed over to the *panchayats* (councils of elders, local boards) which in 1902 had been provided for every village of a thousand or more inhabitants. It was found, however, that the *panchayats* exercised this control badly, and on the recommendation of an Education Commission in 1910 it was handed back to the Department of Education.

In the meanwhile the extension of compulsory education was proceeding. By 1904 the number of schools under the experiment in Amreli *taluka* had risen to fifty-two, with an attendance of 5,201 pupils in the compulsory standards and 939 in higher standards. The number of girls alone was over 2,200. The experiment was felt to be justified, and by an Act of 1906 primary education was made compulsory and free throughout Baroda. Originally it was contemplated that only 40 per cent. of the pupils should be admitted free. It was felt, however, that the element of compulsion made a charge illogical, or at least open to objection. The infliction of fines for non-attendance, except where exemption had been granted, was at first in the hands of the Revenue Department, but in

1914 was transferred to the local boards, the bulk of the money recovered going to the erection of school buildings and the giving of assistance to necessitous children.

The school age was at first fixed at seven to twelve for boys and seven to ten for girls. In 1913 the last year was raised to fourteen for boys and twelve for girls. If even now the maximum age seems low to Western ideas, the physical differences of India and the West must be borne in mind. Indian boys and girls are far maturer for their age, and in agricultural districts—a term which applies to most of Baroda—there is both a call for their labour and a chance of earning wages when they are still quite young.

In particular was opposition offered by the agriculturalists to the education of their daughters. Female education, in any case, was a strange notion to them. Compared with working in the fields, working in school seemed to them waste of time for girls. This prejudice against girls' schools, though it did not manifest itself in open revolt, had to be fought steadily; and the fines inflicted for non-attendance were too small to have much effect. It was found advisable to relax the rules somewhat for the benefit of the agriculturalists, and to trust to the gradual spread of enlightenment. Nowadays, Maharaja Sayajirao thinks, if a plebiscite were to be taken in his State it would probably be in favour of a continuance of female education.

Generally speaking, as has been said above, he looks on free and compulsory education as his most successful reform. As regards the male sex, he points out that learning is an historic

BARODA COLLEGE.

tradition in India, and that under British rule it has been an easy task to get a "literary caste." He has seen, however, the evil as well as the good side of this, which has caused him more and more to aim at imparting a practical character to the education of his subjects. The aim of compulsory education was to place "the three R's" within the reach of every child in Baroda. Some would keep education for the few, he says, to help in the preservation of the caste system. His idea, on the other hand, is to educate *upwards*. "Give the mass of the people elementary education, and the demand for more follows." When this demand has been created, it must be directed in the right way.*

What this right way is, in his opinion, is shown in an extract from Huzur Orders:

"Education should no doubt be given in all subjects, but . . . technical subjects like agriculture, commerce, and industry should follow next after primary education. Such technical instruction should preferably be in the vernacular, as otherwise it would not permeate, and take root in, the State. The public are prone generally to move in the trodden paths of education, and we see the students flocking to the hackneyed Arts course in colleges and showing reluctance for scientific subjects."

Again, also in Huzur Orders:

"Education abroad is an important item. . . . Students should be sent to foreign countries to learn technical subjects, as such an education will

* For some criticisms of the shortcomings of popular education in Baroda, see Chapter XXIII., p. 249.

pave the way for the opening up of new industries in this country."

The ultimate goal of education being, as His Highness remarks in yet another order, to make good citizens, his view is that those who avail themselves of free primary education in Baroda should go on to work for the good of the State by devoting themselves to pursuits such as will promote its development and progress, rather than to those leading to posts in offices. It is not that he despises mental culture or even clerical efficiency; but the need of the moment in Baroda is technical ability.

In the cause of technical education Baroda was in 1925 spending over R. 130,000 a year. As early as 1886 His Highness had the idea of founding a school of technical instruction. Two years later he set up a committee to consider ways and means. In August, 1890, the Kalabhavan (" Home of Art ") was opened, which combined scientific, industrial, artistic, and literary activities. The literary side was closed in 1876; the artistic is languishing, though an attempt is being made to reinvigorate it; but the practical side, if we may so call it, has made great advances. After a critical report by Professor Alfred Hay, an expert from the Indian Science Institute of Bangalore, in 1921, the Maharaja was inclined to close the Kalabhavan altogether, as incapable of fulfilling the functions for which it was intended.* In the end, however, he wisely decided to reorganise rather than to shut down. A thorough reorganisation consequently

* An observer, albeit a great admirer of the Maharaja, has remarked that he is rather apt to pull up the seeds of his reforms to see how they are growing.

took place in 1924, involving revision of the existing training courses, the introduction of new ones, increase of staff, and purchase of fresh machinery, etc.

The expense has been heavy and is not yet done with; for the very necessary reconstruction of the workshops is now in progress. But the money will not have been spent in vain if the improvement in efficiency since reorganisation can be maintained and increased. The civil engineering, electrical engineering, dyeing, bleaching and calico-printing, weaving, and soap-making courses are producing good results; and a small school of commerce is doing useful training work in typewriting, book-keeping, etc., in the early hours of the day.

The Kalabhavan's activities are supplemented by four industrial schools—at Amreli, Naosari, Petlad and Patan respectively—and two more are contemplated. An earlier attempt at decentralising had proved less successful. Speaking at the opening of the Industrial Exhibition at Ahmedabad in December, 1902, His Highness told how he had had branches of the Kalabhavan set up in various parts of his kingdom; "but the response among the people was so faint that after a time the institution had to be contracted within narrower limits." Now again expansion is the order of the day, with better results. In these district schools the instruction is given in Gujarati, whereas at the Kalabhavan half of the higher training is imparted in the English language.

It has been thought best to relegate certain observations on education in Baroda to an appendix. The scope of the present chapter is only the Maharaja's principal aims in educating his people. Roughly, he has put the rudiments within reach of all, and while he has afforded ample facilities for higher learning—a point which has not been dwelt on in this chapter—he had endeavoured to guide the products of the primary schools into the most useful channels of work in the interests of the State. Complete success is a matter of time and money; and, as he says, "the State cannot afford too much money." The Budget of 1923-4 showed that education was absorbing nearly one-sixth of the total State disbursements—R. 2,899,235 out of R. 18,894,454. This, too, was after a series of retrenchments in educational expenditure. In 1925 that expenditure went up again to over R. 3,000,000, a figure which it had reached before retrenchment.

Part of the success of free and compulsory education is due to the fact that it is free. Of this His Highness is well aware, and he feels that the limit has been reached to which the Government should go in paying for popular education. If the children get the elements taught to them without any cost to their parents, it is right to expect the parents, or at least those parents who are not indigent, to give money towards higher education.

"No doubt," runs one of the Maharaja's comments in Huzur Orders, "any Government can secure popularity easily by such measures as the opening of new (high) schools and the preparation of new textbooks. But as the Government has many other functions, equally or even more useful, the public should be given an opportunity to show its philanthropy and evince its keenness for its own welfare by contributing liberally to the maintenance of educational institutions."

It is in the matter of primary education that Baroda can claim to be the pioneer State of India.* The State has also a leading place where female education is concerned. In 1885 the Maharaja announced his resolve to give special attention to this. Before he assumed full powers there were in Baroda only eight girls' schools, with 600 pupils. As the result of his zeal, by 1901 the number of schools had risen to ninety-six, with 8,380 pupils. Another 3,662 girls were then attending mixed Government schools, and in all 13,381 girls were receiving education in Baroda. In ten years the schools numbered 351, with some 28,000 pupils, while the total of girls receiving education was over 60,000. Progress then became slower, for in another decade the figures were 372, 30,000, and nearly 62,000 respectively. Since then there has been further progress; † but the chief difficulty, apart from the necessity of overcoming popular prejudice against female education, is, as it has all along been, the scarcity of women teachers. The excellent Women's Training College in Baroda City, which

* "Long before the rest of India," say the compilers of the *Gazetteer of Baroda* with pardonable pride, "had done more than think of the free and compulsory education of the people as something desirable, but hardly attainable, His Highness . . . had introduced it into his dominions, and he has since witnessed its successful development in the face of extraordinary difficulties."

† The report, *Education in Baroda in* 1875–1925, gives the number of girls' schools as 385, and the total of girls receiving primary instruction as over 67,000.

sprang in 1893 out of a previously existing training class, has less than seventy members. Many of these are young widows, to whom there are few other callings open. There is also a training class for women teachers at Mehsana. The Government is spending over R. 21,000 on these two institutions, including scholarships to all the members of the Women's Training College; but the supply of teachers falls far short of the demand, and it is difficult to see how the situation can be remedied for many years to come.

"Women regulate the social life of a people, and men and women rise or fall together," said Maharaja Sayajirao in a memorandum of 1885, announcing his resolve to give special attention to female education. He has certainly striven hard to extend to his female subjects the same educational advantages as his male subjects possess. But that there is a long way to go before his desire can be gratified is shown by the statistics of literacy in the last Census of Baroda. Literacy being interpreted as the ability both to read and to write, it appears that 240 per 1,000 males and 47 per 1,000 females over five years of age are literate. Among literates thirty years of age and over, only 9 per cent. are women, which (as Mr. S. V. Mukerjea, the compiler of the Census, says) points to the comparative recency of educational advance among women.

Some of the Hindu castes, notably the Prabhus, and the Nagar and Deshastha Brahmans, show a fair approach to female equality with males in the matter of literacy. Among the Mohammedans, on the other hand, female illiteracy is very marked. The dearth of women teachers is extreme, and only the devoted efforts of Mrs. Tyabji and a few helpers enable Baroda City to show so good a figure as 154 literates per 1,000 Mohammedan females; for the State generally the ratio is only 48 per 1,000.

There are some complaints among the Mohammedans that they do not receive equal educational opportunities with the Hindus in Baroda. But the Government schools are open to them, as to all; and His Highness no doubt feels that he has no call to foster Moslem exclusiveness with regard to their women when his policy has so long been the emancipation, through education, of his female subjects in general.

It would not be just to overlook here the share which Her Highness the Maharani has taken in raising the status of women in Baroda. Writing in *The Nineteenth Century* in 1901, her husband bears witness to her conviction that the seclusion of women, as practised in India, was bad, though she realised that at present no one could lift the veil. Subsequently, in 1911, Her Highness published, in collaboration with the late S. M. Mitra, a book entitled *The Position of Women in Indian Life*, in which she suggested that the failure of many progressive schemes in India might be due to the lack of systematic female co-operation. There is no doubt that she is right, and her endeavours to remedy the situation in Baroda deserve all praise.

CHAPTER XXI

RELIGIOUS VIEWS

It is a very complex State, in its religious aspect, over which the Maharaja Gaekwar rules. In a population of over 2,000,000 there are, in round figures, 1,742,000 Hindus; 163,000 Animists, the unconverted aborigines, chiefly of the Naosari *prant*; 162,000 Mohammedans; 43,000 Jains; 7,500 Parsis; 7,400 Christians; a few Sikhs, and still fewer Jews. The subdivisions of the main religions are many. The Hindu castes and sub-castes are over three hundred in number. There are Hinduised Animists and Animistic Hindus. Among the Mohammedans the majority are Sunnis, but a little under 10 per cent. are Shiahs. The so-called "*Pirana* sectaries" are a blend between Hinduism and Islam, of whom 8,000 returned themselves in the last Census* as Hindus, 2,000 as Mohammedans. The Jains fall into three sects, though the *Svetambaras* vastly predominate. The Parsis are not without a few schismatics, and Christianity shows seven sects among its Indian converts in Baroda.

An Indian Prince called to rule over so diversely religious a State has no light task. Baroda is more than four-fifths Hindu, and the Maharaja is, in theory, a Hindu, of the warrior caste, brought up

* The chapter on religion in Mr. Mukerjea's *Census Report of* 1921 is the most interesting and instructive in the whole book.

in boyhood strictly in the Hindu faith.* But the non-Hindu minority is no inarticulate mass, content to give precedence to the religion of the majority over its own various creeds. It has been suggested recently that the reason for the general absence of religious-racial outbreaks in the "Native" States, as compared with parts of British India, is that in the former minorities dare not express themselves. It is certainly not the case in Baroda that the ruler exhibits religious partiality. It is true that he observes the Hindu festivals and performs the rites which his Hindu subjects expect him to perform. But he also patronises the Moharram and other festivals of the Mohammedans, and when the Jumma Masjid, the great mosque of his capital, was renovated, he contributed R. 55,000 between the years 1908 and 1914.

In Huzur Orders may be found many instances of His Highness's religious impartiality. In 1883 he expressly laid down that no action by people of one religion must be allowed to annoy or interfere with the freedom of people of other religions. In 1885 he ordered the translation of the historical books of the Jains. In 1904 he sanctioned a grant of R. 500 for a book on comparative religious history. In 1908 he asked for the preparation of a volume each year on Buddhism. In 1911 he proposed the opening of a class for the study, historical and comparative, of Christianity, Jainism, Zoroastrianism, Islam, Buddhism, and Hinduism. In 1918 he pointed out the desirability of encouraging Arabic and Persian, as well as Hindu,

* "My tutors and guardians wisely, as I think," he writes in his *Nineteenth Century* article, "left me a Hindu."

scholars in Baroda; and in 1921-3 he insisted on the need of attracting the Parsis into the service of Baroda.

In such orders, as in his delight in calm discussion with friends of all faiths and in the study of the most varied religious literature, he has shown a toleration based on the belief in the common principles underlying the different creeds. "Serve humanity" is his religious ideal, which has produced an aloofness from any one form of religion. He claims that it was his ideal, perhaps not so conscious as it has since become, from the early days of his reign. People thought he might change as he grew older; but he has not. To the strictly orthodox Hindu he appears a *nastik*, or atheist. The application of such a term to him is as futile as it is to so many unprejudiced and broad-minded thinkers. He has, indeed, displayed a very real concern in the welfare of the Hindu religion and a keen desire to remedy its distortions.

In his early days in Baroda he was called upon to take part in the elaborate rites which marked the daily life of the Palace under the past Gaekwars, and to witness the superstitious ceremonies on which the Brahman priests insisted, to their own no small profit, since the performance brought them food and rich gifts. While he submitted to the demands made of him he formed his opinions, and at last determined to effect a change. A letter which reveals his ideas is one addressed to F. A. H. Elliot in October, 1896. He finds, he writes, that the religious ceremonies in the Palace savour more of the corruption of priestly times than of the Vedas.

"Personally, of course," he tells his old tutor, "I have very few religious preferences, and really could not say whether I think the Vedas more authoritative, or the Bible, or the Koran, or the Avestha. But socially the people attach a high importance to these ceremonies. It is a pity that they are so sunk in ritual as never to understand the principles of their religion. In their apathy they fall in blindly with the interested inventions of the priests. It is with this view I want to make the change. I think it better, since importance is attached to forms, to have the right one, which clearly conforms with religious principles, than acquiesce in an importance which only feeds self-interest and fattens priestcraft."

There was a struggle. The established priests clung to their theory that the Vedic *mantras* were only to be recited at a Brahman's house, the Puranic *mantras* sufficing for a non-Brahman's. But the Maharaja won; the old staff of priests were turned away, and a new staff installed, who would comply with their Prince's wishes.

Other Brahman pretensions, such as that to daily *Gopradan*, the gift of a cow or its value in cash, were curtailed, and the examinations in Sanskrit learning held in the month of *Shravan*, formerly open to them only, and the source of valuable prizes to those who were successful, were thrown open to all Hindus regardless of caste.*

* The measure dealing with the qualification of *purohits* finally became law in December, 1915. This both required any *purohit* officiating at a religious ceremony to obtain Government authorisation and allowed any Hindu to qualify as a *purohit*.

An investigation was further made into the condition of the large number of Hindu temples in Baroda City and State which were in receipt of Government subsidies. As a result, now only those temples which are considered deserving get fixed annual sums for fixed services, the temple managers are under obligation to keep accounts, subject to inspection by the officials of a department separately set up, and the priests have to pass examinations before being appointed to temples. The principle has been established in Baroda that Brahmans and priests must work for their living like other men.

An instructive passage on the religious idler occurs in a speech made by the Maharaja in December, 1904, his inaugural address at the eighteenth session of the Indian National Social Congress. "We have already," he said, "a large body of men who might be doing some of this (social reform) work for the country, such as the great religious orders of the Middle Ages did so much for Europe. I refer to the countless body of *Sadhus* who are roaming over the country. But they must be trained, and they must have something useful to say. For asceticism is evil unless it be a humane asceticism, one not divorced from philanthropy. He who surrenders life to help his fellows is a saint, but not he who becomes a beggar to avoid labour or responsibility, or retires to a jungle to save what Kingsley would have called 'his own dirty soul.'"

A feature of Hinduism which has always pained His Highness is the caste system. In India, he says, there is great social tyranny, though not so strong among the Marathas as in some other races. To end this caste must go, for it is a most inhuman thing. Real contact with the West would kill it, but the vast majority of Indians only know the West in theory. If, however, they cannot all get into practical contact with the West, they can get into contact with one another. That they should be induced to do so has been his constant aim in Baroda. He found his State, like the rest of India, a place where the very presence of one man might pollute his fellow-men, where the idea of drinking the same water, dining or even sitting in the same room, was unthinkable. His fight has been uphill; but now, although it must be admitted that very much more remains to be accomplished, a very remarkable picture has already been seen in Baroda, unparalleled elsewhere in India. At a great banquet in the Laxmi Vilas Palace in November, 1925, all the leading men of the State sat down to eat together in the same room, presided over by the Maharaja and his brother. That is even more astonishing than the fact that the members of the Legislative Council have among them one of the "Untouchables."

This question of the "Untouchables" is one which has greatly exercised His Highness for very many years. He can justly claim to be the pioneer of the humane treatment of these unfortunate people.* In the Appendix to this book dealing

* This is not ignoring the work done by "Mahatma" Gandhi; for, though both have devoted much labour to the campaign against the cruel oppression of the *Antyajas*, the Maharaja Gaekwar has been able to carry his idea into practice, which Gandhi has not. "We Hindus," wrote the latter in

with education in Baroda some attention has been given to his efforts to raise the *Antyajas* out of the ignorance to which they were formerly condemned. The great difficulty at the beginning was that he could get no teachers except Mohammedans (to whom the idea of caste is strange) and a few enlightened Hindus. He showed his appreciation of the superiority of example over precept by personally visiting the *Antyajas* in their homes and in their schools. Many centuries in a servile position made them shy, and he tells how pupils at the schools were at one time afraid even to take prizes from his hands. But he was determined to conquer the prejudice which separated a large section of his Hindu subjects—their number by the last Census was nearly 177,000—from the mass of their co-religionists. He has instituted a system of schools and hostels for them, with a well-equipped teaching and superintending staff. The second hostel in the Baroda City area was opened on December 11th, 1925, when His Highness delivered a notable speech defining his views.

This opening of the *Arya Kumar Ashrama*, as it is called,* was made the occasion for a great demon-

---

1925, after referring to the treatment of Indians in South Africa, " refuse to see the incongruity of treating a fifth of our own co-religionists as worse than dogs." Gandhi is a Kathiawari, and at Wadhwan, in Kathiawar, the municipality in 1925 prohibited the *Antyajas* from using the pools in the river-sands. Gandhi, of course, could not prevent that. Princes have an advantage over preachers. The combination of Prince and preacher is a fine one.

* *Arya Kumar* is a new and more honourable synonym for *Antyaja*.

stration by the Aryasamajists, not only the small body in Baroda itself, but also many visitors from other parts of India. His Highness expressed the keen sympathy which he had always felt for the *Aryasamaj* movement where its activities were directed to the removal of the disabilities of the depressed classes. "For India to be a nation," he said, "and for the progressive development of society and of the country, it is necessary that a social and national consciousness shall be created among the people. Therefore, friendly and sympathetic relations must be created between the various castes and communities. Those that are backward must be brought on the same level as the more advanced, and the responsibility for doing this rests on the latter."

With regard to the caste system, he continued, it is not ancient; nor can it be tolerated in the future. "Nowadays, any organisation which prevents an individual or a race from sharing in the general advancement of the world cannot be accepted without questioning. An organisation responsible for keeping various sections in watertight compartments and denying certain communities the common privileges and advantages of civilisation does not secure the best interests of society. It is necessary that we learn to forget caste consciousness. If not, we cannot hold our own, either as men or as a nation,* against the rapidly advancing civilisation of the whole human race."

* "India is not a nation," said His Highness on another occasion, "and cannot be made into a nation while split up into religions and castes as it still is."

In conversation a few weeks previous to this speech the Maharaja explained to the present writer his resolve to give the "Untouchables" their full and proper share in the life of the State. He had found them, at the beginning of his reign, inarticulate, and unable to overcome the disabilities imposed on them. By education and by combating the feeling against them among the conservative Hindus he was giving them the opportunity to create a balance in the State to which their numbers entitled them.

It may be added that His Highness is loyally supported by his ministers in his efforts on behalf of the depressed classes. In laying the foundation-stone of the *Antyaja Mandir*, or Untouchables' Temple, at Amreli in November, 1925, the Dewan, Sir Manubhai Mehta, spoke strongly against the idea of "untouchability," which was to him the darkest spot in Hinduism, and made him a little nervous about the preservation of the religion in its integrity. The idea of one Hindu being polluted by the touch of another was illogical. They must see that in purifying the "impure" they would purify themselves.

Beneath the surface of officialdom, no doubt, the old prejudice remains. It was not long ago that an *Antyaja* officer and his wife, being sent to reside in quarters with Hindus, found themselves socially ostracised, with the result that the unfortunate officer resigned his post.

Apart from the question of the ban against the *Antyajas*, Maharaja Sayajirao found many serious evils existing among his Hindu subjects, owing to the prevalence of caste-consciousness in the higher castes. He has made war on these evils, particularly where they concern marriage. By strict caste rules marriage must be performed, not merely within the caste, but within the sub-caste, the penalty being excommunication. The remarriage of widows, however young, is forbidden among the Brahmans and Vanias (traders), the penalty again being excommunication. Early marriages are, or were, usual, though not compulsory.

On these three points His Highness has not feared to run contrary to strict Hindu ideas. Caste-intermarriage in Baroda is easier than in British India, there being no necessity for a declaration by people marrying outside their castes that they belong to no particular religious body. A Brahman, therefore, may by law marry a lower-caste woman—an idea horrible to the old-time Indian. His Highness suggests that the Government of India feared a revolution if they went so far as he has done. That is the advantage of being, to some extent, an autocrat! But, as he says, he had to carry the reform through quietly. He could make caste-intermarriage legal and could encourage it. He could not declare the caste rules illegal.

Similarly, with regard to the remarriage of Hindu widows, what he has done is to encourage the practice, and as far as possible, to prevent the victimisation of those entering into such unions. He has had to educate both men and women up to the idea, in order to remedy what he rightly calls "a cruel state of affairs."

In the matter of child-marriages he has found

a great difficulty. These marriages were not expressly ordered by religion, but they were, as has been said, usual. He could no doubt have declared them illegal. But he does not believe in reform by compulsion against the weight of popular susceptibilities.* By the Infant Marriage Prevention Act of July, 1904, he fixed the permissible age of marriage at sixteen for boys and twelve for girls. The penalty for infringement of the law was a small fine, and exemptions were granted in the case of girls between nine and twelve in special circumstances. A further concession was made later to the peculiar sect, the Kadwa Kanbis, whose ancient custom was to have periodical marriages.†

"In the first seven years of its existence," says the Census Report of 1921, "the law had to encounter the sullen opposition of the people. It was at first applied with little strictness, and the proportion of rejections of applications for permission to marry infants was only about 5 per cent. There were 23,388 convictions under the Act in the first seven years of its operations, or 3,341 per year. . . . There was a total of 40,510 convictions in the last decade, or 4,051 annually."

In 1922-3 and 1923-4 the numbers of cases brought for offences against the Act were 15,801 and 9,103 respectively, with percentages of con-

* See Chapter XIX., p. 193.

† "Once in every nine, ten, or eleven years priests and astrologers connected with the temple of *Umia Mata* fix a day on which marriages take place in the whole caste. Tiny children, and even unborn children, are then married" (*Gazetteer*, i., 198).

The Kadwa Kanbis number nearly 189,000 in Baroda State.

THE MAHARAJA IN 1925.

victions of 86 and 81·8. The Administration Report for the latter period remarks that " infant marriages have been prevailing more among the lower classes; the higher classes, on account of spread of education, have been perceiving the advantage of marriages at a comparatively advanced age."

It might appear, from the slow progress made, that the Maharaja was not very determined in his campaign against infant-marriage; but to think so is to underrate what he appreciates at its true value, the strength of custom sanctioned by religion. In a speech on social reform made during a visit to the Chief of Bhor not long after the passing of the Act, he put forward his views very plainly. " I think it a great mistake," he said, " to get the girls married at their eighth or ninth year, without duly thinking over what is really meant by the old *Shastras*. . . . You should think over your own *Shastras*, and discuss what changes should be made to suit the present times. Early marriages will never make you rise. They have a bad effect upon our worldly career. If you wish for heavenly happiness, and if you think that early marriages tend to produce bad effects, put a stop to them !"

CHAPTER XXII

THE RAILWAY BUILDER

ONE of the greatest successes of his administration of Baroda, in Maharaja Sayajirao's own opinion, with which no visitor to the State would be inclined to disagree, has been the provision of a railway system connecting all the towns and the principal villages.

The first beginning of railway enterprise in Baroda territory dates back as far as 1856, when Maharaja Ganpatrao, shortly before his death, ceded a strip of land for the construction of the Bombay, Baroda, and Central India Railway, on condition that he should be compensated for any loss of transit-dues. This, however, was a British enterprise, and the British had full sovereignty, including civil and criminal jurisdiction, over the ceded strip. The first train left Baroda Station in 1860.

Ganpatrao's brother, Khanderao, must have the credit for starting the first line of any kind for Baroda itself, when, toward the end of his reign, he resolved to build a light railway from Karjan, on the B.B. and C.I. Railway,* to the important trading centre Dabhoi, twenty miles to the east. The original idea was to employ bullock-traction, but the Maharaja was finally persuaded to import

* The station is known by the name of Miyagam, which is a village less than three miles away from Karjan.

three light engines from England, and to have carriages and trucks built in India. Old rails were used, and in 1869 a narrow-gauge line (2 feet 6 inches) was opened at the cost of R. 50,000.

The experiment was not a financial success. Before he died, Khanderao consented to a thorough overhaul of the line, the working of which was for the future to be entrusted to the B.B. and C.I.R. It was reopened for regular traffic on April 8th, 1873, in the reign of Malharrao, being the first native-owned railway to be seen in any Indian State. Thus, at the beginning of his minority, Maharaja Sayajirao found his territory provided with twenty miles of light railway, in addition to the British-owned mainline running across the State from south to north.

We have heard how Sir T. Madhavrao, though enthusiastic about the provision of good roads for India, was driven by the prohibitive cost of them in Baroda to consider the question of cheap light railways instead. The fact that the Karjan (Miyagam) to Dabhoi line was even now paying less than 4 per cent. was not very encouraging; but in the *Administration Report* for 1876-7 the Dewan urged the need of more railways. Proposals were in the field to connect Dabhoi north-westward with Baroda City, eastward with Bahadapur, and southward with Chandod. The last two sections of line were opened in 1879, and the first named in 1880, while in January, 1881, a two-mile extension in the immediate neighbourhood of Baroda (Goya Gate to Visvamitri) was added. When His Highness took over the administration, there were fifty-nine miles of State-owned light railway in working order.

So far State enterprise had only concerned itself with Baroda *prant*. But already, in 1880, the suggestion had been put forward by the Bombay Government that it would be desirable to construct in Kadi *prant* also feeder-lines for the B.B. and C.I.R. and for the branch from Ahmedabad, the Rajputana - Malwa Railway. The Baroda Government consented, and asked that Mehsana should be made the central station from which the feeder-lines should run, its situation in the middle of Kadi making it an obvious choice. In deference to the wishes of the British engineers, Baroda agreed that the Kadi railways should be metre-gauge, like the Rajputana-Malwa line.

The first section of the new railways, from Mehsana north-eastward to Vadnagar, was opened in March, 1887, and an extension to Kheralu at the end of 1888. In 1891 Mehsana was joined up south-westward with Viramgam, in British territory, and north-westward with Patan, so that by the tenth year of Maharaja Sayajirao's personal administration Kadi was provided with over ninety miles of branch railways.*

* * * * *

His Highness's study of the question of communications in his State soon made him an ardent advocate of railways, and his work in this direction may be judged by the fact that Baroda now has 642 miles of line—roughly twenty-one miles of

* Including the section of the Viramgam line outside Baroda territory.

broad-gauge (Anand - Petlad - Tarapur), 304 of metre-gauge (in Kadi, Amreli, and Okhamandal) and 316 of narrow-gauge (in Baroda *prant* and Naosari). The broad- and metre-gauges are worked by the B.B. and C.I.R., who charge Baroda State the working expenses at which they have arrived on their own system. Up to 1921 the narrow-gauge, too, was managed by the B.B. and C.I.R.; but the working expenses mounted after the War, until in 1920 they came to 104 per cent. The Baroda Government decided to assume the management, taking over a loss of R. 4,802.

The genuine personal interest which His Highness takes in railway enterprise is shown by his frequent suggestions in Huzur Orders for new lines. In one order he emphasises the point that a railway, though it may not be directly remunerative, always tends to develop backward country and facilitates the transport of produce. The actual development of many country districts in recent years is an eloquent testimony to the soundness of his views.

Moreover, the people have come to "love the railway," as he said once in conversation. Not only do they look on it as a great convenience, but also they are relieved by it of such perils of the road as dacoity. Certainly they show their appreciation by the extent to which they use the trains. During the last four years for which figures are available the numbers of passengers carried appear as 2,574,630 in 1922, 3,271,432 in 1923, 4,000,572 in 1924, and 4,736,723 in 1925. And these are the figures for the Gaekwar's Baroda State Railways only, 339 miles of line.*

Particularly admirable are the networks of railway in Baroda and Kadi *prants*. That in Kadi, of metre-gauge throughout, connects practically every *taluka* (subdivision of the *prant*) with the others, and radiates from Mehsana.

Mehsana, as a town, has been made by the railway. Previously it had but 6,000 inhabitants. By the Census of 1921 it had 11,888. It has fine Public Offices, originally built for a Palace by Stevens in 1904 at a cost of R. 443,532, and intended as a residence for Prince Fatesinghrao. On his death in 1908 the building was made over to the municipal authorities, except one portion, which is reserved for the Maharaja when he visits Mehsana. There are also large and excellently planned Police Barracks, completed in 1922, at a cost of over half a million rupees, with lines for three hundred police; a Jail outside the town, which can hold sixty prisoners, and a police-station, with a temporary lock-up, in the town; a well-equipped Hospital, with one medical officer, three assistant surgeons, and a nurse-midwife; a Veterinary Hospital, where in 1925 667 animals, chiefly cattle, were treated, and eighty-nine operations were performed; a High School, built in 1908 at a cost of R. 38,000, wherein nineteen teachers give instruction to nearly three hundred pupils between the ages of ten and nineteen; a Hostel for twenty of the High School boys; a Public Library

* Including the twenty miles from Bodeli to Chota Udaipur, worked by Baroda and financed by a loan made by Baroda to the State of Chota Udaipur.

with 5,000 books; a branch of the Bank of Baroda; a large Rest-House and commodious bungalows for the Subha of the district and other officials; and an Officers' Club.

Mehsana is in the centre of a good cotton and oilseed district, but there is a great scarcity of water, the curse of all Baroda, except Naosari. The great Tank, when the present writer visited Mehsana in January, 1926, was practically dry, a playground for children, and a short cut to outlying villages. There is a fair supply of brackish water, especially near the railway-station; but recently, by boring to the depth of 300 feet, sweet water also has been found, and an overhead storage-tank has been erected to hold 42,000 gallons. This will make a tremendous difference to Mehsana, which may be expected to grow bigger and bigger, and to boast of far more than the three cotton-ginning factories that were in existence in 1926.

The railway, as has been said, made Mehsana; for roads are impossible save for primitive methods of progress. No road-metal is available near at hand, and the cost of transport is prohibitive. There are, indeed, two fine roads laid out by His Highness, one leading from the railway-station to the Tank, and the other at right-angles to it, leading to the Public Offices. Elsewhere, however, motor-traffic would be out of the question, if there were any motors in the place. Even horse-traffic has little scope. The ground is more suitable for camels.

It can be seen, therefore, that the Maharaja has had great difficulties to overcome in establishing

Mehsana as a district capital. It has become so, however—the smallest capital of the largest district of Baroda—and has taken the place formerly occupied by the town of Kadi, which in consequence has fallen into decay. Historically Kadi was of some importance, and it has the remains of a large fort, various other ruins dating from the Mohammedan times and those of the early Gaekwars, many picturesque but dilapidated houses showing fine wood-carving, and some considerable temples. But its population by 1921 had fallen to under 12,000. (One is tempted to believe that there are quite as many dogs as human beings; for the pariah flourishes, or rather languishes, here, as all over Kadi *prant*, owing to the religious prejudice against its destruction.) The town is very full of dust, even for Western India, and the water question is acute. There is a big tank, but since the bottom was cleaned some time ago it will not hold water. Artesian well-boring has been tried to remedy the deficiency; but the drills struck rock, and much money was spent to no purpose.

Only a Naib Subha now resides at Kadi, which has fallen from its high estate. The railway makes some towns but injures others, which cannot be helped, as His Highness says. Mehsana's situation pointed it out as the town to be encouraged. Kadi was out of the way, and only sentiment could urge its retention as district headquarters.

The case of Mehsana has been taken at some length as an example of what the Maharaja's railway policy is doing. Needless to say, in the central *prant* of Baroda his activities have been marked; and the capital is now linked up with every outlying place of importance.

In Naosari and Amreli not so much progress has been made. But in Okhamandal we get another example of Maharaja Sayajirao's long vision, which, in this instance, events have yet to justify. This distant portion of Baroda territory, still over a day's journey from the capital, was originally accessible only by a most tedious march across Kathiawar, or else by sea. It is not an important district agriculturally, being rightly described in the *Gazetteer of Baroda* as " a dull and generally undiversified verdureless plain," though inland there is some fairly fertile soil. Its average rainfall is 15 inches a year, the lowest in all Baroda, and sweet water is extremely scarce. Dwarka, the only town of the district, has to procure its water from a distance of four miles.

With an area of only 275 square miles and a population at the last Census of 21,507, Okhamandal might be thought negligible by the railway builder. It has some small interest for the sportsman, though game is not preserved as in the neighbouring Jamnagar. There are pearl fisheries off the coast, but the pearls are of no size. The district derives importance, however, from containing Dwarka and Beyt, two holy places of pilgrimage, the former being the spot where Shri Krishna died, and having, among many other temples, the vast one of Dwarkadhish, which can be seen twenty miles out at sea, and the latter, an island, being the site of numerous temples of Krishna, his consorts, Hanuman, etc. Dwarka is also a seat of Hindu learning from of old, which, after a sad decline, was revived under the pious Shrimant Shantyanand, whose death, "with his life's desire gratified,"* took place on February 16th, 1926, a day after the last visit paid to him by the Maharaja Gaekwar.

For the convenience of the many thousands of pilgrims visiting Dwarka and Beyt at festival seasons it is clear that a railway across Kathiawar could do much. There were other objects in such a railway, as we shall see.

The difficulty for Baroda of a trans-Kathiawar line lay in the fact that it must run almost entirely through foreign territory—British and Indian ("Native") States, the latter, though tributary to Baroda, being outside her political control. So, although a line in Okhamandal was Baroda's concern only, to link it up with the general railway system of Baroda was quite another matter. The State principally affected was Jamnagar, the territory of the Jam Saheb, famous on the cricket-field as Kumar Shri Ranjitsinhji. Any line extending eastward from Okhamandal must run through Jamnagar. When, therefore, in 1904, the Baroda Government decided to approach the Railway Board about the cost of surveying a line in Okhamandal, it also requested the Resident to enquire whether the Jam Saheb would co-operate in connecting the line with his capital, and offered to make a loan to finance him.

* His own words not many hours before his death. Presumably the *Shankaracharya* referred to his ambition to interest some of the ruling Princes in his work of restoring Dwarka's good name and reviving orthodox Hinduism. He had shortly before received the Maharaja of Mysore.

The Jam Saheb, however, was at first unwilling to accept a loan, except on conditions which imposed delay. Finally, in 1908, he consented; and, Baroda's engineer-in-chief having recommended the route which seemed to him best for the line and the adoption of the metre-gauge (uniform with that of the existing Kathiawar railways), the preliminary negotiations were settled at Baroda in 1910. Next year the construction of earthworks was sanctioned by the Government of India, and operations began. They were twice suspended by Baroda, owing to the lack of a definite decision about the section between Jamnagar City and the Okhamandal frontier. At last, in 1920, the Jam Saheb's Government, with a loan from Baroda and the help of the late Sir Vithaldas Thakersey and other private persons, felt itself in a position to proceed. The construction of the line in Okhamandal, running from Kuranga in the south, through Dwarka, to Adatara on the north-east coast, was resumed, and in November, 1922, it was open to traffic. After the link between Kuranga and Jamnagar City was completed, Okhamandal and the rest of Baroda were at last in railway communication.

But this was not the end of Maharaja Sayajirao's ambition for Dwarka. Apart from the attraction which the neighbourhood has for pilgrims, its climate is better than that of Baroda in general. Lying as it does in the angle between the Arabian Sea and the Gulf of Kutch, and visited by breezes in both winter and summer, Okhamandal is comparatively cool. It has, therefore, possibilities as a health-resort. Again, its soil yields plenty of stone, which would be very valuable in the other *prants*, and gives Dwarka itself the opportunity of erecting good houses. Above all, between Adatara and the island of Beyt is an excellent natural harbour, calm even in monsoon time, and sheltered from the waves of the Arabian Sea.

As long ago as 1882 the Maharaja conceived the idea of utilising this harbour, improving it, and equipping it with a pier. He saw a future port of call for vessels bringing goods from abroad for Northern India, cheapening and shortening their transit, and yielding at the same time a good revenue to Baroda in port dues and freight charges. Might not Adatara, indeed, become in time a rival to Bombay and Karachi ?

True to his principle of "Never be afraid of being late in an undertaking, so long as you have it in view," His Highness did not until forty-four years after the conception of his idea see its realisation ! The harbour improvements were completed in November, 1925, but the ceremony of opening the pier at Adatara by the Maharaja only took place on February 14th, 1926. The main reason for the delay was the cost. The pier has taken twenty-four lakhs of rupees—which is very dear—and the total expenditure in connection with the harbour is about R. 2,800,000.

Adatara Harbour is eleven miles distant by rail from Dwarka. Whereas at the latter place, on an open rocky coast, ships cannot come in close, and passengers can only land by being transferred in turn to smaller boats and man-borne chairs, at Adatara there are three channels of entry, two of them good, and disembarkation can now be made by gangway straight on to the pier, alongside which ships of up to 7,000 tons can moor. As a port of call between Bombay and Karachi, therefore, Adatara has great advantages. What remains to be seen is how the passage of goods can be facilitated. Apart from the necessity of getting steamers to call,* a doubling of the railway track and the provision of sufficient trucks are essential. Even then the question of transit costs is formidable. Between Adatara and either Mehsana or Ahmedabad trucks must pass through Baroda, Jamnagar, Rajkot, Morvi, and British territory.

An example of the inconvenience at present suffered is that while in parts of Okhamandal salt-pans yield a good supply, British interests prevent the salt being sent to Baroda. For the benefit of the Salt Revenue it was agreed, during Sir T. Madhavrao's administration, that no manufacture of salt or collection of earth-salt should be carried on in the *prants* of Baroda, Kadi, and Naosari. Kathiawar is outside the "salt-line," and the manufacture of salt from sea-water or brine is permitted in Okhamandal; but its importation into British India or any Indian State, even to any

* In the course of his sixteenth European trip His Highness had the satisfaction of arranging for the institution of a regular service of steamers to Adatara, or Port Okha, as it is now to be called. In August, 1926, and subsequently, conferences were held in London with Sir John Ellerman, as a result of which the Ellerman Company agreed to run a monthly service to Port Okha, without guarantee or subsidy, but with the condition that if there is no cargo for the outward voyage the company may cancel the sailing. Further, an associated American line has agreed to run steamers from America to Port Okha.

part of Baroda outside Kathiawar, is forbidden. In consequence, while Okhamandal merchants may export their salt as far as Zanzibar, the people of Eastern Baroda have to pay nearly three times as much for salt as those of Western Baroda.

Another example is that of cement. His Highness in December, 1921, opened in Dwarka a cement factory, the largest in Western India, and put it under American management. The cement was of good quality; but it was found that, after the transit dues for crossing Kathiawar had been paid, it could not compete in price with cement exported to Bombay from Europe. In consequence, the factory is now closed down.

Such obstacles to development, coupled with the scarcity of sweet water in the Dwarka neighbourhood, which deep boring has so far failed to remedy, make the pessimists despair of any considerable success for trans-Kathiawar railways. Not so His Highness, however, who, while fully aware of the obstacles, still hopes in time to overcome them. Moreover, he and his advisers have given some attention to an even more ambitious scheme of penetrating Kathiawar by an extension of the short line now running from Anand, on the B.B. and C.I.R., to Tarapur. This extension would cross the Sabarmati River, and run south-westward to Dhola, a station on the Bhavnagar Railway, whence a connection would be established with the Gondal-Porbandar Railway, and ultimately, by a suggested line through Western Jamnagar, with Okhamandal.

This proposition, with its obvious advantages to Baroda, including the bringing nearer to the capital of scattered portions of Amreli *prant*, would also make a great advance in the communications of Central India with Kathiawar and the Arabian Sea. Against it are the complications entailed by a railway running through several States; and, of course, the expense.

For the political complications one remedy would naturally suggest itself to a ruler of Baroda familiar with the past history of his State. In Chapter XVIII. some passages have been quoted from Maharaja Sayajirao's speech and Lord Reading's reply at the banquet in the Laxmi Vilas Palace on January 22nd, 1926, referring to the possibility of the restoration of Baroda's original sovereignty. The allusion by His Highness on such an occasion to his ambition that his House should be once more not only fiscal, but also political, overlords of Kathiawar—for that was the real meaning of his words—was perhaps unexpected by the Viceroy, who could only assure him that any representations which he had made in the past would receive careful and impartial consideration.

It is no place here to enter into the vexed question of the future position of the Indian States under the régime apparently contemplated for India in general. We have only to bring out the high aspirations for the development of Baroda cherished by the Maharaja. What chance have his schemes of success? "It is not failure which is a disgrace, but a low aim," is an expression of his. Certainly in his railway policy, and all that is bound up with it, he has had no low aim.

* * * * *

Baroda was the first Indian State to build railways on an extended scale; she has kept to the front, and clearly means to stay there in the future. The mere question of return on capital has not been allowed to obscure other considerations.* With the development of the districts and the encouragement of the taste for travel, the comfort of passengers has been studied. The permanent way is being constantly improved, the engines and rolling-stock compare favourably with those of other Indian railways, and now the carriages are being fitted with electric light and other conveniences.

Mention must not be omitted of the workshops at Goya Gate, two miles to the south of Baroda old city, where European visitors may well be surprised at the up-to-date character of the concern. Here everything connected with railways is turned out, except wheels, axles and springs; and repairs, particularly of boilers, are a speciality. Here there is a power station manned entirely by Indians, with the exception of the engineer-in-chief, which has two electrical engines, with floor-

* The question as to whether the railways "pay" could only be answered by elaborate statistics, for which there is no space here. But from the Railway Department's Report down to the end of 1925 (to which I am much indebted in this chapter) it appears that on all the State railways to that period the capital invested had been R. 42,024,889, and that the net earnings in 1925 were R. 1,836,144. In the last year the Anand-Petlad line was paying over 16 per cent. on capital, the Mehsana railways over 8 per cent., the Gaekwar's Baroda State Railways (in Baroda *prant*) nearly 3 per cent., the small Kijadia-Dari line in Amreli over 1 per cent., and the Okhamandal line (in its third year) 0·65 per cent.

space for more units, and supplies the needs not only of the railways,* but also of all private consumers in Baroda City. The Electrical Department, once a separate concern and housed in the grounds of Laxmi Vilas, is now amalgamated with the Railway Administration under one control, all at Goya Gate, which it has long been the Maharaja's intention to make the industrial quarter of Baroda.

Figures in themselves may convey little, but it is worth while to note that, while the total capital sunk in the Goya Gate enterprise is over R. 3,000,000, the annual receipts from the sale of electric energy are now R. 300,000.

The story of the Maharaja as a railway builder is one of the most instructive chapters in the annals of his administration, illustrating at once his quickness to see what will be for the good of his State and his patience, yet persistence, in carrying out his ideas.

* The electrification of the suburban lines has been under consideration, but, pending their further development, is not thought to be justified.

CHAPTER XXIII

DEVELOPMENT: AGRICULTURAL AND INDUSTRIAL

EVERY chapter in the history of Maharaja Sayajirao is a record of the economic development of his State. But, while no attempt will be made in this book to compete with the accounts given in the *Gazetteer of Baroda* and other works* of what he has accomplished, his biography would be very incomplete without at least a short section on the subject.

Agriculture has been, and still is, the main occupation of the inhabitants of Baroda. The Census of 1921 showed 640 out of every 1,000 persons in the State to be supported by it; and out of a total area of over 4,960,000 acres of land in Baroda, nearly 4,100,000 acres are arable, over 3,338,000 of these being occupied and under cultivation. The principal crops are cotton, tobacco, oilseeds, and food crops (*juwar*, *bajri*, rice, and pulse). It is, therefore, of immense importance to the people that agriculture shall be enabled to flourish to the fullest extent possible. The effect of bad years is eloquently told by the figures after the great famine of 1899-1900, the Census of 1901 showing not only a fall in the total population of over 19 per cent., but a reduction of the

* Particularly the *Report on Agricultural Indebtedness in Baroda State*, by M. B. Nanavati (1913), and the *Report of the Baroda Economic Development Committee*, 1918–9.

number of people maintained by agriculture to 519 per mille.

Mr. Nanavati well calls this famine a landmark in the history of the economic conditions of Baroda. Gujarat had hitherto, since as long ago as 1813, come to be regarded as a land of plenty, afflicted at times, it is true, by scarcity, due usually to failure of rain, but never by famine. Kathiawar had not been so lucky; but the deficiencies of one section of Baroda could to some extent be met by the other. In 1899, however, the general failure of water and loss of crops, followed by countless deaths of men and cattle, and the frantic selling of property at nominal rates to avert ruin, disorganised the whole State. Not only was it necessary to institute a campaign of relief work (to which allusion has been made elsewhere), but also attention was focussed on the position of the agricultural classes, which had become more than precarious. The ryots, to keep themselves alive, had got heavily into debt, the only alternative being to abandon agriculture for some other means of livelihood.

The Maharaja, after his efforts to relieve immediate distress, turned his mind to this question of indebtedness, and early in 1901 ordered a census to be taken of the ryots' liabilities. Later in the same year he set up committees in each *taluka* of the State to report on not only agricultural indebtedness and the measures necessary to reduce it, but also the right steps to enable the people to resist famine, the best organisation for agricultural banks, the possibility of grain storage, the reduction of the social expenses of the people—this was a matter which had long exercised His Highness—and their physical improvement.

Thus the Committee's terms of reference were wide, and it is not surprising to hear that the progress of their work was slow. They evolved a scheme for the compulsory conciliation of the ryots' debts, which, when embodied in a draft measure in the Legislative Council, was strongly opposed by the high officials as well as by the money-lending classes. The measure was rejected by the Council in 1907 as too drastic.

The Committee continued its work; but it was not until Mr. Nanavati, who returned from a course of study in the United States in 1911, was charged with the duty of making a final report that definite, practical proposals were put forward. Considerations of space forbid that the report shall be dealt with at any length here. Briefly, it found a reduction of the population through famine and plague; a displacement of the best-class agriculturalists by inferior exploitation of the land as an investment; a physical deterioration through insufficient nourishment; a lessened fertility of the soil through lack of cattle, implements, manure, etc.; a rise in prices, including the cost of labour; excessive rate of interest charged by the money-lenders;* an increase in drinking; a lack of education among the older population. An improvement of the Agricultural Department was urged, and the

* It was estimated that about 60 per cent. of the *khatedars* (registered landholders) were in debt in 1901, to the extent of R. 460 per head, and that of the remaining 40 per cent. nearly half were money-lenders of various classes, who had come into possession of the soil in liquidation of old debts.

institution of a Board of Economic Development. Also the restriction of the subdivision and alienation of land was strongly recommended.

Up to 1909 agriculture in Baroda had been under the supervision of a branch of the Revenue Department. In that year an independent Department of Agriculture was set up, and in 1912 V. M. Samarth, who had rejoined the Baroda service as *Amatya*, took charge of it and endeavoured to give expression to the agricultural policy contemplated by the Maharaja. This included the rescue of the farmers from the grasp of the money-lenders by the grant of State loans at a low rate of interest, and still more by the establishment of Agricultural Banks; the fullest possible co-operation between the Department of Agriculture and the cultivators by means of demonstrations, lectures, and shows; experimental work, the benefits of which were communicated to the farmers; the sale to them of improved implements at less than cost price; and a serious attempt to deal with the evils of subdivision and alienation of land.

The subject of Agricultural Banks was one which keenly interested His Highness even before 1899. In that and the two following years he directed the opening of three of them, two in Naosari and one in Kadi, with liberal help from the State. Subsequently, another was opened in Kadi, one at Amreli, and one at Bhadran, Baroda *prant*. With the exception of the Kadi banks, success attended the ventures; but in 1913 it was decided that the Co-operative Credit Society system offered better prospects, and no more banks have been opened. Of the Co-operative Credit Societies, legalised in Baroda by an Act of 1905—only one year later than the Act, on which it was modelled, in British India—there were in 1921 over 500, 461 of them being agricultural.

The weakness of the Co-operative Credit Society system is that it only enables small short-time loans to be made; and now a proposal is under consideration to establish a Land Mortgage Bank,* to make loans for a longer period, and so keep the cultivators from seeking extra aid from the money-lenders. This proposal contemplates a financing by the State at first, the State capital to be gradually replaced by the borrowers themselves on co-operative principles.

The education of the agriculturalists by demonstrations and general propaganda work has made great strides, though the class which has to be dealt with in Baroda is not easily taught modern methods. His Highness has been under no illusion in the matter. "The great obstacle in effecting improvements," he notes in a Huzur Order, "is the natural disinclination for agriculture among men of education, owing to the physical labour required, and owing to the small profits compared with those from other professions. Students in agricultural schools and colleges are actuated by the desire rather of securing some post than of following the profession, and do not all of them possess hereditary instincts for agriculture."

* A scheme for such was prepared as early as 1916 by the Department of Commerce and Industry, but it was considered too ambitious until more experience had been gained of the question of debt-redemption.

Nevertheless, progress has been made. The work of the Model Farm of eighty-four acres, situated about a mile from Baroda Station, and at present under the direction of Mr. C. V. Sane, who studied agriculture first at Poona and later at Wisconsin and Kansas, is most instructive. Started as a practical training-ground for students in 1892, when Mr. (now Sir) Thomas Middleton was Professor of Agriculture at Baroda College, the Farm subsequently languished until a succession of expert Directors of Agriculture, two of them Cirencester-trained, raised the level of its utilities. It is today largely used for experimental purposes, fruit crops, oilseed plants, cotton, and tobacco having special attention. The rotation of crops is another branch of research. But no more important work is done than in connection with tractors, with a view not only to testing comparatively their suitability to the soil of Baroda, but also to the encouragement of their use among the cultivators. A tractor instruction class is held at the Farm for about ten weeks annually between July and September. This was attended in 1925 by nearly forty students. In addition, the Agricultural Department lends the services of a tractor operator and an engineer, at a nominal charge, to cultivators in the State.

A publicity branch issues quarterly, in Gujarati, a magazine describing the experiments made at the Farm and their results, an annual agricultural calendar, and various pamphlets for free distribution.

The labour on the Model Farm is supplied by good-conduct men from the jail, who live on the

Farm on parole, and have the opportunity of earning a fair sum of money by the end of their sentences. This is an example of His Highness's general reformatory policy with regard to prisoners.

Before the establishment of the Farm a special Agricultural Vernacular School had been opened in Baroda City. The class at Baroda College was started in 1900, followed by an agricultural class at the Kalabhavan and another at the Men's Training College. Mention is made elsewhere of the instruction in agriculture of the *Kaliparaj* boys at Songadh and Vyara. A small farm on the lines of the Model Farm has long been in existence at Jagudan, near Mehsana, and orders have been given for the starting of another in Amreli district. There are demonstration-plots in various places—*e.g.*, one about three miles from Dabhoi, where cotton and rice crops are being grown, and, if more water can be secured, sugar-cane and fruit will be tried.

In each district there is an Agricultural Inspector, who is in charge of propaganda and conducts tests on the farms for the farmers to follow, such as of tobacco at Petlad, wheat in Kadi, etc. The need of intensive cultivation is everywhere sedulously preached. But it is recognised that the question of water-supply is the most vital of all. The many years of scanty rainfall which succeeded the great famine have encouraged the suspicion that the climate of Gujarat has changed, and the possibilities of well-boring have had the anxious attention of the Maharaja and his advisers. His Highness, since first in 1883 he spoke publicly of his desire to see irrigation works opened all over Baroda, constantly reverted to the subject. He is still as keen, but the failure of water from overhead has driven him to seek it under ground.

Agricultural well-boring is under the charge of the Agricultural Engineering Department, not, like the general water-supply question, under the Public Works Department. The work is that of the development of already existing wells rather than the boring of new wells. It was started in 1911 with the help of a demonstration at the Model Farm by the Superintendent from Nadiad, in British territory, near the Petlad *taluka* of Baroda. The purchase of a boring machine was sanctioned, and a student was sent to Nadiad to be trained. Since then the advance has been steady, twenty machines being now in the possession of the Agricultural Department, 971 successful boring operations out of 1,247 attempts having been made in the fourteen years down to the date of the last report (1925), and the increase in the quantity of water made available thereby being about 437,500 gallons an hour. The State does the work for the cultivator who applies, charging him for the cost of bringing the machine to his well, labour, repairs to machine, etc.; but if the operation is unsuccessful, the State writes off the labour-charges.

It will have been seen from the above that very serious efforts have been made since the disaster which befell Baroda at the end of the last century to lift agriculturalists from the plight which overtook them, and to equip them with better means of making their living in the future. The vagaries of

Nature, such as produced the famine, cannot be prevented; but the organisation in advance of measures to fight them and the introduction into the raising of food-supplies of better brains and better methods are the scientific remedy. The main obstacle is in the character of the people on the land, sapped by so many centuries of under-education and the sun of Western India. "The strength of accumulated inertia," said His Highness once in a different connection,* "must in the end baffle the most actively benevolent Government."

Nevertheless, it is no unpleasant picture that the visitor gets who travels through the villages and fields of Baroda State, especially in the early hours before the sun has begun to assume his full powers. Rather there is a primitive, idyllic charm about it, touched to quaintness by the proximity of railways and telegraph poles, and occasional advertisements of English goods. In a time of peace, such as the winter of 1925-6, happiness did not seem far—were there only more water and less dust!

* * * * *

The Report on Agricultural Indebtedness had recommended the institution of a Board of Economic Development for Baroda. The Maharaja did not immediately accept the recommendation; but in January, 1918, he appointed an Economic Development Committee, to whom Government officials were ordered to submit suggestions as to methods of increasing soil productivity, improving cattle-breeding, and developing the arts, commerce, and industry. Again

* Speech at Grant Medical College, Bombay, March 29th, 1901.

His Highness had given his committee a very wide field to cover.

This was not, of course, the first beginning of the Maharaja's interest in the economic development of his State. In the early years of his reign, however, he had not found much time to devote to the building up of new industries. In the second period, which may be said to have begun with the foundation of the Kalabhavan in 1890, he endeavoured to stimulate progress in many ways;* but at the end of twelve years he had to confess himself dissatisfied. "I have tried various measures in my own State," he told his audience at the opening of the Ahmedabad Industrial Exhibition in December, 1902, "but I am sorry to say that the results are disappointing. A sugar-mill, a cotton-mill, and an ice-factory were tried, but were not a success. A State fund for the advance of capital and other assistance to manufacturers also failed. I found that the managers were not sufficiently interested in the scheme, and not impartial in the working of it. I am convinced, however, that the fault lay not

* "A number of students were sent to Europe to acquire first-hand knowledge of industries, railways were built all over the State, loans were given to new industries at a low rate of interest, and custom duties were revised. The result of these various activities was the rise of a number of small industries. . . . As was to be expected, those met with varying fortunes" (*Gazetteer*, i., 406).

In Huzur Orders His Highness was constantly making suggestions for the starting of fresh enterprises—*e.g.*, a glass factory, a leather factory, a stone quarry, sericulture, pearl fishing, wax production, a castor-oil factory, flour mills, a paper mill, etc. These suggestions come within the period of 1891-1906.

with the industries themselves, but in the fact that they were State enterprises."

Undeterred by the non-fulfilment of his hopes, the Maharaja in 1905 began a new campaign. So far the supervision of industrial development had been merely one of the duties of the Revenue Department. Now a special branch of the department was set up to look after commerce, industry, agriculture, the customs, etc. The work proved too heavy. Soon it was found necessary to appoint a Director of Commerce and Industry, and in 1909 the Department of Commerce and Industry was separated from the Revenue Department.

Meanwhile, in 1908 the Bank of Baroda had been founded, one of the most important duties of which has from the start been to finance industries.

Towards the end of 1909 export, import, and octroi duties were abolished throughout the State. Certain inland customs in Kodinar (Amreli) and Okhamandal were revived in 1912, but in 1922 they were also abolished.

These three steps cleared the way for a real advance in the direction of industrial progress in Baroda.* But the report of the Economic Development Committee after its enquiries in 1918-9 had many disquieting features. As we have heard, the Committee's terms of reference included the study of the agricultural position, to

* Mention must not be omitted of His Highness's appointment in 1914 of an Industrial Advisory Committee, with a proportion of non-official members, to study local needs and advise the Department of Commerce and Industry.

which, indeed, it devoted much of its attention. It found three prominent facts in the lives of the population of Baroda: (1) Low income—about R. 45 per head per annum; (2) low vitality, the expectation of life being, as in India generally, only twenty-six years; and (3) illiteracy, especially among the women.

The report did not hesitate to speak of "the pernicious results of the present education," including the migration of the rural population into the towns, the purposeless activities of the people, and the aversion from manual labour. At the same time it quoted figures showing that in 1881 nearly 18 per cent. of the population were supported by industries (other than agricultural), and in 1911 little over 12 per cent. Popular education, therefore, had tended to neither agricultural nor industrial efficiency. Educated boys were unwilling to follow their fathers' trades, but looked for State or similar service. The great need was for vocational training, which must be attended to in the upper primary schools, and still more so in the secondary schools. The whole educational system should be divided into urban and rural, with appropriate studies and specially trained teachers.

The recommendations of the Committee on the matter of education fell in with His Highness's own views,* and due weight has been given to them since. In the matter of the encouragement of commerce and industries, except by preliminary training, the report was not very suggestive. But the policy of the Government was decided by

* See Chapter XX.

the time that the report was published. It was indicated in a notification of March 23rd, 1920, laying down on what conditions a person or company desirous of starting a new industry in Baroda might receive State aid.

Briefly, if the Director of Commerce and Industry should consider the application *bona fide*, and an enquiry into the prospects of the venture worth while, he would estimate the cost of the enquiry, of which the Government would bear a portion, usually a half, the applicant depositing his share. If the enquiry should show that the industry could be organised profitably, the applicant must bear the whole cost. Otherwise the Government would refund the applicant's deposit.

The system of "co-operative investigation of industries" was reinforced by financial assistance from the State in the shape of debentures, a generous sum being laid aside for the purpose. The old policy of State enterprise was thus abandoned in favour of State-aided enterprise. The new policy is sketched in one of those comments in Huzur Orders which we have so often quoted:

"Private enterprise is preferable to State investment, as Government interference can thereby be obviated; but the Government must take the lead, and must also offer substantial assistance, owing to the present apathy of the public. Further, it is advisable to invest a portion of the State's money within the limits of the State itself. . . . Due precautions must be taken against a large increase of expenditure or assistance to private firms. . . . No concession or help should be promised to industries unless the Government is assured of their profitable working."

It is too early yet to estimate the likely effect of the new industrial policy of His Highness's Government, the general trade depression and financial stringency affecting Baroda like other States. In the *Administration Report* for 1923-4 no application under the Co-operative Investigation of Industries scheme is recorded.* On the other hand, the Director of Commerce and Industries had no less than three hundred interviews during the year with persons engaged in, or desirous of starting, new industries; and two loans, amounting to R. 27,500, were sanctioned by the Government in aid of industrial ventures.

Industrial development in Baroda is still in the making, agriculture being, as was said at the beginning of this chapter, the population's main occupation. No one is more alive than the Maharaja to the dangers of a desertion of the land for the city, in the hope of better wages. The only wise course is that which he has adopted, to encourage sound industrial enterprise, but to endeavour at the same time to induce the cultivators of the soil to use their brains to the best advantage for the improvement of their own profession.

* In the following year there was one by the Alembic Company, Ltd., of Baroda, which contributed R. 1,500 to the cost of investigation.

CHAPTER XXIV

CONSTITUTIONALISM AND ITS PRICE

"I LOOK upon the introduction of the elective principle as a grave change in the policy followed up to this time by the Government of India. It is clear that the principle, being so great, should be but cautiously introduced. I am in favour of granting a limited number of elected members. A combination of elected and nominated members, in proportion, ought to meet all requirements for the present. I should have a certain number of persons as permanent members, to represent the significant and widespread interests of India, like agriculture, commerce, etc., and add special members whenever a special question is raised. An attempt should be made always to secure members of the class actually following the profession, instead of the people who don't follow the interests of the avocation they are expected to represent."

So wrote Maharaja Sayajirao in April, 1890, to Colonel E. R. Bradford, whose acquaintance he had made when that officer was in attendance on Prince Albert Victor of Wales (soon to be Duke of Clarence) during his Indian tour.

At the time when His Highness wrote, Baroda had still eighteen years to wait before possessing a regular Legislative Council. A State Executive Council,* presided over by the Dewan, had been

* Of the division of the work of administration it is observed in Huzur Orders:

THE MAHARAJA AND HIS DEWANS, 1875–1925.

in existence since 1887. But it was not until 1904 that the Maharaja ordered a scheme to be prepared for an additional council, with one elected member for each of the districts of Baroda, on the lines of the Legislative Councils of Bombay and Bengal, but with modifications to suit local circumstances. In 1907 the formation of the *Dhara Sabha*, or Legislative Council, was sanctioned and its constitution was framed. On His Highness's suggestion, the questions to be discussed by it were to be such as the various departments of State could not deal with, and the language to be employed by it was to be Gujarati.

At first the number of members of this council was fixed at seventeen. In 1912 the elected members were increased, and two nominated members, representing the *Sardar* and merchant classes, were added; while in 1913 a member was nominated to represent the depressed classes. At the present day, the Legislative Council has a membership of twenty-six: the Dewan and five other *ex-officio* members; ten nominated members, six official and four unofficial (the latter representing the Gaekwar family, the *Sardars*, the merchants, and the depressed classes); and ten elected members, three each from Baroda and

---

"Under the existing arrangements, certain matters are reserved for His Highness's orders, due provision being made for urgent cases. All other items exceeding the powers of the Minister are allowed to be disposed of by the Executive Council, and all reserved matters are submitted to His Highness with the Council's opinions."

Orders passed by the Executive Council, it may be added, are liable to be modified by the Maharaja.

Kadi districts, and two each from Naosari and Amreli.

In 1917 His Highness dropped a hint that the right of interpellation, which had been given to the *Dhara Sabha*, should not be abused, and that members putting questions should refrain from vague assertions and produce evidence for their statements.

The position of the *Dhara Sabha* is that it may interpellate and may divide on resolutions, but its resolutions are not binding on the Government. Legislation may be referred to it for opinion, but again its votes are not binding; nor are all new laws referred to it, some of the most important having been passed without its cognisance. In 1924 it was accorded the right of discussing the annual Budget; but it may not vote upon the subject, nor are its criticisms necessarily regarded.

As might be imagined, a Legislative Council of this kind does not satisfy the ardent advocates of democracy in Baroda or in India generally. His Highness has considered the idea of a more fully developed assembly, and in a confidential letter of October, 1922, desired the preparation of a draft constitution for his State, embracing the creation of Upper and Lower Houses of Legislature. The late Dewan, Sir Manubhai Mehta, in the following year produced a carefully thought out sketch of the outlines of such a constitution on the foundation (as he insisted was necessary) of " the inherent and unalterable sovereignty of His Highness the Maharaja Gaekwar, who is, and will always be, the head of the State of Baroda, the supreme executive head, as well as the 'source and sanction of law,'" although "under the ægis of the Sovereign all men are born and continue equal in respect of their rights."

Both the Dewan and Mr. S. V. Mukerjea, whose suggestions for constitutional reform in Baroda were published by order of the Government in 1924, endeavoured to meet His Highness's desires as to the creation of two Houses of Legislature. The former would have a directly elected* Representative Assembly to initiate all legislation, with a partly nominated, partly elected Legislative Council, whose assent would be required before any measure could become law. The latter proposes a Legislative Assembly, largely directly elected, but with the retention, at first at least, of some nominated members. All ordinary legislation, not involving alteration of organic laws, will be the work of this assembly; but for the purposes of extraordinary legislation there will be a second body, something like Japan's "Elder Statesmen," to whom also the Dewan may refer laws passed by the Assembly.

No further progress has been made in the direction of constitution-building. In Chapter XIX. we refer to the complaints which Maharaja Sayajirao has had to endure for not going ahead as fast as his critics would wish. Increasing years, some of them try to make out, have caused him to abandon his former liberal ideas. His Highness's reply on one occasion, as recorded in Chapter XIX., was sufficiently dignified; and no one who is not

* The elections for the existing Legislative Council were by the *Mahal* (*Taluka*) *Panchayats*, but His Highness had expressed a wish to consider the question of direct election.

infatuated with the idea of the supreme virtues of Democracy can quarrel with it.

In conversation some time later the Maharaja amplified his views. The day has not yet come, he said, for a further extension of democratic principles to Baroda. The people are not, in the mass, educated up to such a point. Those who talk so much about the necessity of popular government are not "the people," but a small class of literates. The masses take no interest in the matter, and, as far as direct suffrage is concerned, would not trouble to vote unless they were compelled to do so. He was ahead of British India in conferring some measure of representation on the people; but he refuses to go so far, in a small State like Baroda, as the Government of India has gone today.* For small Indian States princely rule (given a conscientious Prince) is the best. Even for India as a whole the ideal would be a strong ruler, though with large concessions to the right of popular initiative. There must be force in the background, however, for by the show of it "the man with the *lathi*" must at the last moment be compelled to run away.

Pure Democracy—we are not now using His Highness's words, but attempting to interpret his

* He points out that in British India the Government has succeeded in interesting certain classes in politics, such as the Brahmans and some of the *Bunnias*; but it has left almost untouched great sections, like the *Sardars* (demoralised since their old military occupation has gone) and the agriculturalists. It has thus upset the balance of functions on which the life of Ancient India was founded; and the only hope for the future is a restoration of the equilibrium in accordance with Indian tradition.

thoughts—is not suited to India. It is doubtless a very suitable government for Utopia.

In dealing first with the Legislative Council we have departed from the historical order of events in the constitutional development of Baroda. It is now necessary to see how the way was prepared for the introduction of a Legislative Council.

* * * * *

Some allusion has been made in Chapter X. to the manner in which His Highness set himself to restore the old Indian village community life in Baroda, sapped as it had been by the passion for centralisation. The ryotwary system, while it conferred many benefits upon the cultivators of the soil, tended to weaken the bonds which had held them together in their various villages; and the transfer of powers from the local to the *taluka* officials left the former devoid of their previous ability to oil the wheels of communal life. His Highness, gradually introducing the elective principle into the village *panchayats* and giving them wider functions, rebuilt the old communities. The village boards have now important functions in connection with sanitation, water-supply, roads, local charities, and, within certain limits, the trial of civil and criminal cases. They are provided with funds from specified items of Government revenue, and have power to raise further funds for public works. Upon them as a foundation the attempt is being made to raise up a structure of local self-government.*

But the village *panchayats*, His Highness has felt, are only the beginning, though the essential

* See *Gazetteer*, ii., 227–8.

beginning, of local self-government. On the top of them he has erected *Taluka* Boards, and on them again District Boards. The villages contribute, by election, a proportion of members to *Taluka* Boards, and the *Taluka* Boards elect members to the District Boards. The proportion of elected members on the *Taluka* Boards, as on the village *panchayats*, is two-thirds. On the District Boards it is one-half. Thus His Highness has realised his idea of a complete system of representation from the village to the *taluka*, from the *taluka* to the district, and (since the districts elect ten members to the Council) from the district to the Legislative Council of the State.

Naturally, the municipalities have not been left out of consideration in this scheme of local self-government. By an Act as long ago as 1892, Baroda City was given the privilege of electing members, one for each ward, to its Municipal Board. In 1905 another Municipal Act set up eight more self-governing municipalities; and another was added later. In these, half the members of the Municipal Board are elected, while in Baroda City the proportion is two-thirds. In the remaining municipalities of the State, which are not considered sufficiently advanced for self-government, a State official (the *vahivatdar* of the *taluka*) manages affairs with the aid of a committee.

Formerly the municipalities were in receipt of Government grants, and there was no house tax or property assessment. But with a view to making municipalities self-supporting, all grants were stopped in 1909. This sudden discontinuance, says the *Gazetteer*, "found townspeople very disinclined to tax themselves, and the result was seen in not a few empty treasuries, and a consequent breakdown of the municipal machinery. The obvious reasonableness of the new policy has been admitted; but it is not yet fully understood that privileges and responsibilities go together, and that without a realisation of this fact no true progress is possible."

"Village, Taluka, and District Boards," comments the Maharaja in one of his Huzur Orders, "have been established so as to allow the people to look after their local needs, and have been given certain powers, with due regard to local conditions. . . . These bodies should not depend wholly on Government help, but should provide for their local wants by local contributions. Officials should encourage the members to take an active interest, and should teach them the duties of citizenship."

Two points are noteworthy in this last quotation. One is that the people must learn that they have responsibilities. (The necessity for officials to teach them this is one of the reasons for the presence of officials and Government nominees on the various boards.) The other is that they must no longer look for the State to pay the piper, if they are to have a voice in calling the tune. Under an absolute autocracy they might, with some show of reason, ask that the State should provide the means for carrying out the changes which it desired to make. But the introduction of constitutionalism alters the position. If a Maharaja ceases to be a benevolent despot, his subjects cannot, with their greater freedom, escape greater liabilities.

His Highness, however, is quite justified in maintaining that in Baroda today good government is provided for the people at a very small cost to themselves. In a State where formerly they were bowed down under a heavy burden of taxation, they have but one general tax to meet: Land Revenue if they are on the land, Income Tax if they are non-agriculturalists.

Under the administration of Sir T. Madhavrao, as we have heard, a beginning was made with the reform of unjust assessment of the land and collection of revenue from the cultivators, through which they were suffering so grievously when Malharrao's reign was brought to an end. But very much remained to be done when Maharaja Sayajirao himself took over the administration of his State. It has been mentioned in Chapter IX. how he found that, through the grants made by previous Gaekwars, nearly one-tenth of the villages in Baroda practically escaped taxation. As the State depended for its revenue almost entirely on land tax, this was a serious matter. It was, moreover, an injustice to those working on State-owned land, who saw the workers on *barkhali* lands free from the burden which they had to bear. Sir T. Madhavrao's reduction of assessments and remission of arrears of Land Tax did nothing to remove this injustice.

The appointment of F. A. H. Elliot as Survey and Settlement Commissioner in 1885 marked the beginning of a serious effort to deal with the whole land question, including the alienated villages, which in many cases had passed into other hands than those of the descendants of the original grantees. Elliot completed his report on *barkhali* lands in 1889, and regulations based on his proposals came into force on May 1st of that year. The general work of his department was complicated by the scandals alluded to in Chapter XI., and in 1895 he left Baroda service, very much against the Maharaja's wishes, with his task unfinished.

The lines of survey and settlement, however, had been laid down before he left. Baroda territory being interlaced with the villages of Bombay Presidency, and land tenures being much alike in the two areas, he deemed it best to apply Bombay survey and settlement methods to Baroda. The villages were measured and mapped field by field, and on each field an assessment was laid according to its area, its soil, and the general advantages of its situation.

A start was made with the survey of one *taluka* (Padra, in 1886), and the process was extended gradually over the whole State. But, as the work went on, the need was found of some modification of plan. Old fiscal traditions had accustomed the people in many places to payments varying according to the caste of the cultivator, while in others a crop-sharing system already gave the State Treasury a part of what the land actually produced. Moreover, the capacities of cultivators of different tribes had to be considered. To demand from an ignorant and careless Koli what a skilful Kanbi could easily pay might ruin the former, while to limit the demand from the Kanbi to what the Koli could pay would be a needless sacrifice of revenue.

When the first settlements, therefore, were coming to an end in 1904, and Mr. C. N. Seddon, I.C.S., whose services were lent by the Government of India, was appointed Settlement Commissioner, he found still awaiting solution the problem of gradually equalising assessments on lands of equal value. In a series of settlement reports he examined the correctness of the old work, secured improvements in the classification of lands, and laid down the principles to be followed till the whole of the State had undergone revision. Provision was made for easy modification in assessments where lands changed in value, so as to avoid taxation of improvements by the tenant, but to secure for the State a share in increased value arising out of natural facilities.

The question of alienation of land also continued to demand attention. The fact that some of the holders had, from of old, guarantees of their tenures from the British led to much friction. This was ended at last through a suggestion by Mr. Seddon, which the Maharaja in 1907 decided to accept, that there should be a joint commission appointed by Baroda and the Government of India to examine the working of the Settlement Department. Largely owing to Mr. Seddon's own labours on this, the causes of friction were removed, and the way cleared for the efficient operation of the department. The investigation into the validity of titles to alienated land was enabled to proceed, and by judicious buying out of many holders the State has got rid of most of the anomalies affecting land tenure and the payment of taxes by agriculturalists.

In April, 1915, the situation was sufficiently open for the enactment of a Land Revenue Code, systematising the position of the cultivator, who was no longer oppressed by miscellaneous arbitrary taxes, knew exactly what he had to pay, and was allowed to pay it in two annual instalments. Further, he could take advantage of Government grants, known as *tagavis*, for the improvement of his land and the purchase of seed, stock, etc.; and in the matter of arrears of taxation he has found the Government generously minded.

In Baroda, as in India as a whole, the vast mass of the people lives on the land, and supplies the bulk of the public revenue, which gives special importance to the work of survey and settlement; but the question of taxation of the rest of the population had also to be considered. The non-agricultural population of the State once suffered, like the agriculturalists, from a multiplicity of *veros*, taxes usually small in themselves, but varying immensely both in size and in number in the different districts, so as to be in incidence entirely capricious. Sir T. Madhavrao, though he condemned them and effected some reduction in their number, had not time to abolish them. In 1892 the Survey and Settlement Commissioner reported in favour of their reformation on an uniform plan, while in the same year the Sar Subha, head of the Revenue Department, recommended a tax on income on the lines of that levied in districts under the Bombay Government adjoining Baroda.

These suggestions were both subsequent to His Highness's own initiative in 1889, when he had ordered the collection of information on the subject of *veros* with a view to their systematisation. He continued to take a great interest in the matter, and in 1896, during a visit to Padra, where the inhabitants had petitioned against the *veros* which harassed them, ordered the local Subha to submit some practical scheme of reform. The outcome was the proposal of a single tax (*ayapat vero*) on income alone, all other *veros* to be abolished.

His Highness welcomed the proposal, but as usual determined to introduce reform by instalments. He began with Padra town, then extended the change to the whole *taluka* of Padra, then to most of Baroda district (except the city), then to part of Kadi, and in 1902 to Baroda City. Two years later all the State except Amreli district had *ayapat vero*, while with the commencement of the financial year 1904-5 it was made general.

From time to time the scale of this Income Tax has been revised, notably on the occasion of His Highness's Silver Jubilee in 1907, when the minimum taxable income, originally under the "Padra Scheme" R. 100, and subsequently raised in turn to R. 300 and R. 500, was put as high as R. 750. The tendency has been all along to give relief to the possessors of small incomes, though their exemption has caused the Government loss of revenue. On the other hand, the incomes of Government servants, at first exempted from the tax, are so no longer, and the amounts demanded on the larger incomes have been progressively increased. By the appointment in 1921 of a special staff for the scrutiny of Income Tax assessment a large gain has been made.*

A certain, but not it is hoped excessive, amount of space has been devoted here to the taxation to which the inhabitants of Baroda are subject, to show how the Maharaja has carried out his idea that people who enjoy the advantages of good government should contribute towards the cost of it. If the tax-payers complain of their present burden (and it is true that the Land Tax in Baroda is higher than that in the neighbouring parts of British India), they should realise that in the past they had bad government at a much higher price than they now pay for good. There were some, no doubt, who hoped that His Highness's Golden Jubilee in 1926 would bring with it large taxation concessions. As a matter of fact, Land Revenue arrears were remitted to the extent of no less than three lakhs of rupees out of the outstanding four lakhs, and the collection of cotton Excise duty was suspended from December 1st, 1925. More could not reasonably be expected in what is not, after all, a period of great prosperity.

* In 1908-9 Income Tax realisation for the whole State was R. 98,653. In 1921–2 it had risen to R. 268,357. But in 1922–3 it was R. 332,997, in 1923–4 R. 407,639, and in 1924–5 R. 465,991.

CHAPTER XXV

GOVERNMENT AND THE PRIMITIVE TRIBES

THE last chapter has been devoted to a consideration of the manner in which Maharaja Sayajirao introduced liberal institutions into his State, and at the same time has endeavoured to inculcate into his subjects' minds that it is their duty to pay a reasonable price for the privileges which they have received, no longer looking for these benefits to be bestowed upon them as a gift from on high, entailing no duties in return.

To appreciate such a doctrine, sound as it is, however, requires the attainment of a certain standard of moral and political enlightenment; and in Baroda, as in other parts of India, there are sections of the population which are not capable of attaining that standard, and which, therefore, cannot share in the privileges and responsibilities of a partly democratic administration. Allusion is made elsewhere* to the people variously called the Forest Tribes and the *Kaliparaj*, of whom some 163,000 still remain "Animist" in faith, while another 95,000 are Hinduised to a varying extent. It is with the larger division of these people, those who retain their old religious beliefs and resist absorption by the dominant faith of Baroda, that the main problem arises—how to fit them into a modern State.

* See Chapter XX. and Appendix II.

The difficulty may be illustrated by the story of the "*Kaliparaj* Troubles" of 1922-3 in the Naosari district of Baroda State. Naosari contains the great majority of the Animistic forest people of the whole territory, over 147,000 according to the last Census. Only two of their tribes, the Chodhras and the Gamits, have any degree of education. The great curse among them has long been their heavy indulgence in alcohol. Indeed, they may be said to have been drunk for centuries past, the liquor being supplied to them in recent times by Parsi and Hindu dealers. A certain amount of temperance propaganda had been carried on among the tribes previous to 1922, actuated by genuine temperance motives on the part of *Kaliparaj* teachers and others who did not share in the vice of their fellow-tribesmen. This had provoked some counter-activity, such as picketing, on the part of the liquor-dealers, but no serious disturbance had occurred, the propaganda having, as a matter of fact, had little effect.

In November, 1922, however, the situation changed. An invasion of *gaulis*, religious mendicants, whose teaching and preaching had analogies with Welsh Revivalism, came from Baglan, in Nasik, and swept through the Songadh *taluka* of Naosari, a *Kaliparaj* stronghold. At the start there was much crude magic in their ceremonies, with brandishing of red cloth to the cry of "Here are the writings of the *Mata!*" By means of incantations the old gods and goddesses were declared to have been driven away. "There runs Sailibai," the *gauli* would shout, "there goes Devlibai"; and in place of the banished deities the goddess Bhavani, a form of the *sakti* of Siva, was installed. Her cult involved the observance of cleanly habits, abstinence from drink, and vegetarianism. In consequence, the converts sold their poultry and sheep for a song, the profiteers, mostly Musalman *Voras* or Parsis, reaping a rich harvest.

In passing, it may be mentioned that the simple villagers, in preparation for the visits of the propagandists, were in the habit of having a good carouse; but on their arrival a solemn feast was held, at which vows of abstinence were taken and all drinking vessels were destroyed.

From Songadh the wave of enthusiasm spread to Vyara and Mangrol *talukas*, and in December Mahuva was reached, in which the preachers came in contact with more educated tribes, such as the Chodhras. Here the movement took on a more secular, less religious aspect, and the original *gaulis* gave way to a number of pseudo-*gaulis*, whose language was Gujarati, not Khandeshi. Also temperance workers not belonging to the *Kaliparaj* began to take advantage of the movement to further their aims. A general conference was held at Shekpur in January, 1923, and here, or about this time, resolutions were adopted which had nothing to do with temperance, such as those in favour of the destruction of toddy-trees, the refusal to work for meat-eaters, and the boycott of all who did so.

In the four *talukas* of Songadh, Vyara, Mangrol, and Mahuva the campaign had a real, if temporary, effect on the consumption of liquor, which almost entirely ceased. The resultant loss to the Excise was heavy; but the Government, while ordering the protection of toddy-trees (which were given in trust to the tribes), took care not to hinder the temperance movement until in March its development into an agrarian agitation, with sinister elements in it, compelled intervention. By this time some violent meetings had been held in Mahuva, followed by an outbreak of intimidation and torture of people working for Parsi masters. Inflammatory language was being used against the higher classes in general, and strong measures became necessary to prevent serious trouble. A two-months' restriction of public meetings in Mahuva without a preliminary licence had a calming effect.

In June and July, however, a complication was introduced by the fact that the agitation, now mainly anti-Parsi and guided by others than temperance workers, had spread to British territory, and the Subha of Naosari had to confer with the Collector at Surat. The Collector started test prosecutions in his territory, which succeeded in checking the agrarian propaganda. Similar prosecutions in Naosari were less successful, probably through lack of proper presentation of the evidence.

Another difficulty was that the policy of the Baroda Government in prosecuting certain owners for the use of forced *Kaliparaj* labour led the forest people to think that the Government was on their side. So it was, to the extent that it desired to put down forced labour; and some important reforms were now pushed through, such as the *Kaliparaj* Land Act, the Rent Relief Act, and the setting apart of half the pasture-land as a *Kali-*

paraj preserve. But the tribesmen got the idea that the Government sympathised with them entirely, and acts of personal violence grew in number, until in August it was found necessary to arrest about twenty of the ringleaders and ask them to show cause why they should not be bound over for security against communal discord.*

A rift was opened amongst the heads of the movement, the moderates doing their best to assist the Government in the preservation of order, while the others—mostly agitators in Naosari town, aided by central organisations in Baroda and Bombay—continued a vigorous campaign against the Parsis in particular, leading to open conflict with the Government. The Subha consulted Baroda, with the result that four of the leading agitators were arrested and bound over, and public meetings were again proclaimed, this time in the whole of the *Kaliparaj* area.

By December the agitation had become furious, and a big *Kaliparaj* deputation was sent to see the Maharaja. After this the condition of affairs grew better. The principal temperance reformers gave guarantees to abstain from violence, the right of public meeting was restored, the four agitators

* To a large extent the temperance side of the movement had been obscured. As early as July, 1923, drinking in Songadh and Vyara was back at its old level, and it was said that some of the former advocates of teetotalism were themselves running liquor-shops. Gangs of *Kaliparaj* roughs, organised by the drink interest, broke up attempts to hold temperance meetings. On the other hand, the Subha closed down many toddy-shops, and in Mahuva, at any rate, the consumption of drink was about half of what it used to be.

under arrest were induced to apologise, and the cases against them were then withdrawn.

In fact, the whole trouble, which had threatened to develop into class war, thanks to the activities of people always ready to avail themselves of genuine grievances to manufacture artificial campaigns, subsided unexpectedly soon. The temperance movement among the *Kaliparaj*, though it has produced little permanent effect, is now working on safe lines. Where propagandist meetings have been held of late, there has been an absence of the racial and class bias which was imported with the original crusade.

Towards the peaceful settlement of the real grievances of the forest tribes of Naosari much has been done by the State. His Highness's interest in the backward section of his subjects has always been keen, and it did not require the deputation which waited on him at the end of 1923 to stimulate it. Co-operative Credit Societies have been formed in *Kaliparaj* areas, new boarding-schools have been opened, and further measures may be expected with a view to improving the position of the tribesmen. About the middle of 1925 a committee of investigation was appointed, which began its sittings in December, after a questionnaire had been sent out to officials in the areas concerned. One of the subjects on which His Highness invited the committee's opinion was whether, as had been represented to him by the Naib Subha of Vyara, some of the land measures in aid of the *Kaliparaj*, notably the Rent Relief Act, were premature. The result has been that, after hearing the committee's report, the Maharaja has annulled these measures as not having served the object for which they were passed.

This chapter may seem rather in the nature of a digression. It seemed necessary, however, to supplement Chapter XXIV., which dealt with Maharaja Sayajirao's constitutional policy regarding his more enlightened subjects, with a few words of explanation as to why he could not make his policy general throughout the State. It is one of the problems of Baroda how to combine the comparatively rapid advance of a large portion of the inhabitants towards the idea of citizenship with the slow and hardly perceptible movement of a smaller portion towards civilisation itself. The forest tribes are interesting people, especially to the anthropologist,* but the question of fitting them into their proper place in a progressive community is a serious one. In Appendix II.† some indication is given of the way in which one aspect of the question is being faced. Education is having some effect on a few. But it is a few—about 350 children at a time out of the 147,000 forest people in Naosari *prant*—and many years must elapse before any appreciable proportion of the *Kaliparaj* can take their part in the general life of the State.

* Very striking, for instance, and very unlike Hindu dancing, were the dances of the Bhil men and women witnessed at some of the Palace fêtes during the celebration of His Highness's Golden Jubilee.

† See pp. 300-1, and footnote.

CHAPTER XXVI

JUSTICE

MUCH might be written on the subject of the administration of justice in Baroda, and obviously the matter is one closely connected with the question of good government. But we shall confine ourselves to a brief account of the principal reform which Maharaja Sayajirao introduced into the judicial system of his State, a reform on which he may rightly claim to be far ahead of his contemporaries in India. This was the separation of the judicial and the executive powers.

Formerly, though there was a semblance of courts of law in Baroda City, in the districts the administration of justice, both civil and criminal, was in the hands of the revenue-farmer, with such bad results as might be expected. The Revenue Department, indeed, under the Gaekwars who immediately preceded His Highness, was a huge, overgrown department, whose functions extended in all directions, almost regardless of the connection with revenue. Sir T. Madhavrao, while purifying the administration of justice in Baroda, took away from the *vahivatdars*, the revenue heads of each *taluka*, their power to try civil cases, which was given to *munsiffs*, or sub-judges. The revenue officers were left, however, with powers in criminal cases. His Highness very early in his actual reign turned his attention to a state of affairs which he saw must be remedied. His travels in the districts showed him that the *vahivatdars* were overworked in their dual capacity of executive and judicial officers, and impressed him at the same time with the impropriety of one man being simultaneously prosecutor and judge.

He moved with the cautious progress which was already his mark. He took advice of his ministers, and, though he was bent on reform, only introduced it in some few *talukas* at the start, where three-quarters of the criminal work was transferred from the *vahivatdars* to *munsiffs*. He had been warned by opponents of his scheme that it would result in the revenue-collectors being unable to carry out their duties. If the British authorities refused to make such an experiment, he was asked, how could he hope for success? But he was unconvinced. In 1890 he extended the scheme to other *talukas*, appointing additional magistrates to undertake the work taken off the shoulders of the *vahivatdars*. In 1907-8 he completed his task, relieving the revenue-officers of all judicial powers, and setting up the necessary extra *munsiff* courts to exercise them instead.* At the same time care was taken that the new magistrates should be properly qualified men.

On his visits to Baroda in 1909 the Earl of Minto publicly assured the Maharaja that "his bold attempt to separate the judicial and executive functions had elicited the warm interest of the

* "All criminal and civil work is now performed by *munsiffs*, who have their courts in almost all the *talukas*, while the revenue and executive officers devote all their time to their legitimate revenue duties" (*Gazetteer*, ii., 265).

THE LAW COURTS AND SURSAGAR TANK.

Government of India." The attempt, indeed, had been and is still attended by success. The collection of revenue was not impeded, and the speedier administration of justice was secured. This latter point is one of special interest to His Highness. In an instruction concerning courts of law in Huzur Orders he writes: "They should make efforts to surpass the British Indian courts in this respect. The average time-limit, for instance, for the disposal of a case should be brought down to at most three-fourths of that in British India."

The result of the separation of functions of judicial and executive officers has been found satisfactory. Nevertheless, in order that the Revenue Department staff may not lose all experience of criminal trials, an arrangement has been made for the exchange from time to time of some of its officers with the Judicial Department's. The training of officers in the work of more than one department is characteristic of Baroda. The Maharaja insists on the necessity of an all-round training for men who are likely to rise in the service of the State.

One other item in connection with the administration of justice may be mentioned. Up to 1908 public prosecutions before magistrates were conducted by police officers, whereas in the District Courts and the High Court qualified pleaders were employed. In 1908 His Highness empowered the Legal Remembrancer (whose department was set up in 1904 to assist the Government in all matters of law) to appoint qualified prosecutors for the lower courts also.

* * * * *

We said at the beginning of this chapter that we should confine our attention to the principal reform which Maharaja Sayajirao made in the judicial system of Baroda. However, it seems convenient here to mention the very important boon which he conferred on his subjects by a codification of the laws of the State. Only a passing allusion has been made to this on an earlier page.

The matter was one which was bound to interest the Maharaja keenly, with his passion for system. He found the legal position in Baroda chaotic in the absence of codes. In 1882 he appointed a Law Committee, composed of High Court judges, to deal with legislative work. As the committee's progress was not as rapid as he desired, in 1892 he entrusted to Messrs. J. S. Gadgil and J. R. Naylor, both eminent legal experts, the tasks of drafting Civil and Criminal Codes respectively. The Law Committee, and afterwards the High Court, as such, continued the work until the creation of the Legal Remembrancer's Department, since when a separate office for framing laws has been abolished.

All through His Highness himself constantly suggested new subjects for legislation. Indeed, it may be said that most of the laws and regulations framed during his reign have been due to his initiative. He has, in many cases, worked personally on the details. On the whole, the legislation of Britain and British India has been taken as a model, but modifications have been introduced to which local conditions seem to point. In some respects, as is mentioned in Chapter XXI., Baroda has progressed beyond British India.

The total result fully entitles the *Gazetteer of Baroda** to boast that "the administration of justice has been brought to such a high state of efficiency and integrity that the decrees passed by the Baroda courts are executed in British India as if they were passed by the British courts themselves."

* ii., 260.

APPENDIX I

SOME DIFFICULTIES OF INDIAN PRINCES

At various points in this book reference has been made to what the Maharaja Gaekwar has written in his letters to friends and acquaintances, including his own officers, some of the Residents in Baroda, etc., on the subject of the difficulties with which he and other Indian Princes are confronted in their relations with the Paramount Power. I have thought it advisable to give in this Appendix further quotations from the letters, illustrative of his ideas on the question, which, owing to their length, could not be well included in the body of the book.

No apology is needed, I think, for devoting some more space to these views, for His Highness has fearlessly grappled with a very difficult problem, or collection of problems, which is of the highest importance to the Government of India, and his analytical mind has made his contributions to the discussion of real value.

I do not limit myself merely to the matter of the relationship between the Government of India and the ruling Princes, and begin, therefore, with an exposition of the elements of weakness in an Indian State, addressed to a former Governor of Bombay with whom the Maharaja was on terms of close friendship for many years:

"There is the division into innumerable castes, further multiplied by division according to race, language, sects, and territories, not to mention those that are created by individual and official likes and dislikes. There is the lack of a broad public spirit and a disinterested and abiding love of genuine progress. There is the disposition to uncharitable censoriousness which, in a small society not of a liberal mind, naturally grows from too close an intimacy with one another's failings. There is the want of awe generated by the highest authorities being too close and accessible to wrap themselves in the impressiveness of mystery and distance. There is a great desire to criticise on the part of the people like pleaders, journalists, raw young men who consider themselves educated by the degrees they may have got, but have not the tact, knowledge, and temperament to criticise justly and usefully. There is the existence of numerous immunities and privileges attached to particular castes and classes, which a broader sense of government, more or less modelled on the British, must necessarily deal with in order to equalise burdens. Then there is the power of the nobles and influential officials, whose capacity of creating troubles under the new conditions has, to say the least, not diminished. There are weaknesses attaching to our society, which the growth of Western ideas ought to have corrected, but has not. They have, on the contrary, become exaggerated; certain elements of the old order have been impaired without being replaced, and fresh weaknesses have superimposed themselves on the old. For instance, the new ideas have loosened the old reverence for authority, and have emphasised the influence of the Mohammedan system, which tended to measure the respect of the governing power by the extent of the physical force. Nowadays, therefore, our people have respect only for such orders as overawe them by a combination of great intellect and physical superiority. Of the latter, the administration of the Native States had none; and of the former, what small amount it has it cannot always utilise. The fact is, while the old ideas, which were systematically and profoundly felt, are fading, the new ideas have established themselves without being thought out, and, as is always the case with imperfectly assimilated notions, have been powerful to destroy, but not unite and reconstruct." (Letter to Lord Reay, January 20th, 1897.)

On the top of this, he continues, come the imperfections of the political system, which seems to him created more by a blind succession of historical events than by an intelligent adaptation to actual needs. "Its effect has been to weaken the old bases of power without satisfactorily replacing them. To take some details, the ease with which the Princes are made and unmade, without much enquiry, or are compelled temporarily to transfer their powers to the Political Officer, and rarely to their own servants; the small respect shown to their last wishes and dispositions; the manner in which their servants are rewarded with titles, without the least reference to the Government which employs them, so that officers really not well inclined to the State can easily, by ingratiating themselves with the Political Officer,* at once

* "Through the power of the Resident," His Highness said on another occasion, "Indian Ministers, being usually weak, are made to feel two fears, one of their own Raja, the other of the Resident."

aggrandise themselves and show the weakness of the State. It is obvious how all these are disintegrating elements, which forcibly break the continuity of rule and destroy that sense, which once existed among the people, of the certain and abiding presence of the Raja and his family. The system, in short, brings liberty to the subjects, and . . . gives them the means of using it effectually, but leaves no safeguards against their misusing it. . . . Then there is the unsympathetic attitude of some Political Officers towards attempts at progress on original lines, which leads people to think that solid progress is not zealously favoured, but that, while copies, and bad copies, of British models will be tolerated, even a slight departure from them is at times looked upon somewhat as an act of presumption to be discouraged.

"All these circumstances—our own natural weaknesses, the one-sided effect of Western ideas, and the weakening influences of the political system—are so many shackles upon the energetic and progressive ruler. They render progress uncertain, slow, and ineffective, and deprive the ruler of all power to do real good. People wonder whether the old Rajas, who did nothing, and were content, as a rule, with women and drink, were not individually better off than the new, who labour and worry themselves without, after all, being able to effect much that is worth effecting." (Same letter.)

On the difficulties created for a Prince by certain actions of the Government of India His Highness has much to say. In particular, Lord Curzon's

Circular of August 25th, 1900, on the visits of Princes to Europe, inspired him to make vigorous protests. He was in Germany when he first expressed his views on this at any length.

"It is a cruel and humiliating treatment," he writes, "we Indian Rajas are put to by the Government of India. I consider in many respects we are worse dealt with than servants and labourers. This statement may seem a startling one, but consider. A Raja, if found troublesome, may be deposed or punished without any public enquiry. A Raja is asked to produce a medical certificate if he desires to visit Europe for his health, a treatment which is inconsistent with his dignity and rights, one which lowers him in the eyes of his people, besides weakening his hold on the administration. He is asked to obtain leave of absence, and this may be granted or not, according to the wishes of the Government of India, or whoever may exercise that power on its behalf. What guarantee is there that it will not ask many irrelevant questions before it lets him go ? Again, what certainty is there that an officer will invariably be just, if not sympathetic, to a Native Raja ? . . . Even if he wants any competent medical officer to attend on him, as any private patient may do, the doctor is not allowed to approach him without the permission of the British Government, if he happens to be in its service. . . .

"Lord Curzon considers himself under the necessity of passing a strong circular on the subject, wherein he speaks of the Rajas with the scantest courtesy. He criticises the disposal of the State revenue after putting on nineteenth-century spectacles. He might as well adversely criticise the financial system of Alfred the Great, because it did not tally with our present democratic notions and principles. The ideas of public and private property in India are not the same as here. The application of these criticisms of finance has had the result of leaving the Rajas and the members of their family without any right of property whatever. . . . The result of this treatment will, in my opinion, be that the Rajas will be so disgusted as to prefer to be treated as pensioners, and to give up the fictitious, evanescent pomp of an Indian Chief." (Letter to Sir John Puleston, September 23rd, 1900.)

To another friend soon after he describes the Circular as "most mischievous and quite unnecessary." It will affect the ruling power of the chiefs, and render them still less able to administer their affairs satisfactorily. "Their interests are separated from those of the State, a fact which will hasten their silent but sure absorption into the rest of British India. . . . The Rajas must, to secure legitimate personal happiness and freedom, cringe and fawn to secure favours. Under this treatment they cannot acquire habits of independence and possess good character. The logical result . . . will be to lower self-respect and make them meanest of the mean." (Letter to Sir John Watson, November 14th, 1900.)

In the course of a very long letter to Lieutenant-Colonel M. J. Meade, the Resident at various periods between 1901 and 1909, His Highness admits that the irritation caused by compliance with the Circular may, no doubt, in time be deadened, " but this will be because it is felt to be inevitable where authority is arbitrary, and will not mean that the evil itself will have disappeared." " The provision requiring all the circumstances which bring about the journey to be stated for the consideration of the Government of India is inquisitorial in its nature, and ignores the fact that the circumstances may be of a delicate or domestic character, which the Prince would prefer to keep private. But, apart from exceptional circumstances, the restriction itself will become with every day a greater hardship, as daily the contact of ideas with Europe and the interest in it become closer and deeper." The Circular involves a serious alteration in the position and dignity of Indian Princes. (Letter of May 1st, 1903.)

The letter to the Resident was unofficial, but it was followed by a note from Shrinagar on May 30th, authorising him to forward it to the Viceroy. His Highness had long had under contemplation the idea of addressing to Lord Curzon a formal protest against the Circular. He did not find it necessary to proceed to such a step, for apparently his informal remonstrance through the Resident had its effect.

One more point may be added. His Highness on various occasions expressed his disapproval of the custom which used to prevail of attaching a Political Officer to the suite of a travelling Raja. In his fragment of diary in 1900 he writes that this officer has powers and position unknown to the person after whom he is to look, and his theory of his duties varies according to his whims. " I think it a useless item of expenditure which . . . only causes irritation and distrust in the mind of the Raja"—who has to pay it!

* * * * *

Talking to a friend in Paris in October, 1926, His Highness alluded to another difficulty of the Princes. The Government of India likes to see a State well ruled—which, of course, involves the expenditure of money upon reforms. At the same time the Government insists on the restriction of certain industries—*e.g.*, cotton, salt, etc.—which prevents the raising of revenue on what seems to the Princes perfectly legitimate lines. Consequently, the Princes are in a dilemma. If they protest, they are disloyal. If they acquiesce and adopt a *laisser-aller* policy, they are worthless.

APPENDIX II

EDUCATION IN BARODA

THROUGH the courtesy, and generally in the pleasant company of Mr. N. K. Dikshit, Commissioner of Education, I was given the opportunity in the winter of 1925-6 of visiting a large number of educational institutions in Baroda City, and some in the districts. I make here a few observations which could not well be introduced into Chapter XX. without overweighting it, and obscuring the picture of Mahajara Sayajirao himself as educationalist.

PRIMARY SCHOOLS.—It is difficult for a foreigner, even for one who has spent some part of his life in the East, to appraise the standard of education reached in the vernacular schools of Baroda. It can be seen that the children, as a whole, are happy and well cared for, and that the teachers, both male and female, do their best to cope with such difficulties as insufficient accommodation and over-large classes.* To go deeper would require a knowledge of both Gujarati and Marathi.

The latest detailed statistics (1924-5) show 2,355 vernacular schools for boys, with 129,033 pupils; and 368 for girls, with 66,093 pupils. A

* I do not mean that these difficulties are general. But they are frequent, and, seeing the heavy State expenditure on education, suggest that there is a wide field for those who are both benevolent and rich to show their philanthropy.

later summary gives the total as 2,838 schools, with 202,713 pupils, boys and girls. The cost of primary education is put at R. 668 per school.

As for "results," in 1924 the sixth standard examinations—the compulsory standard limit is the fourth—attracted 4,094 candidates (166 girls), of whom 2,766 (132 girls) passed. The attainment of the sixth standard carries with it the right to a clerkship in a Government office.

It is noteworthy that at twenty-nine primary schools English is taught to 1,405 pupils. Naturally, since all the teachers are Indians, and since the rate of pay for teachers in the vernacular schools is insufficient to draw the best to them, progress with English is not very rapid. Both reading aloud and recitation are rather singsong and expressionless. This is true also in the higher schools. Nevertheless, the spread of English-speaking in Baroda is remarkable.*

In the primary section of education, though there is no religious, caste, or class discrimination in general, the "Untouchables" have their own separate schools, as well as facilities for using the

* In his *Baroda Census Report for* 1922 Mr. Mukerjea put the number of people over five years of age who are literate in (*i.e.*, speakers and readers of) English at 8·46 per 1,000 (15 per 1,000 men, 1 per 1,000 women); but this figure conveys a false idea, for included in the Census, of course, are not only people too old to have been touched by the modern educational movement, but also the wild tribes of the forest regions, of whom very few are "literate" at all. Between the ages of fifteen and twenty 39·4 per 1,000 males and 2·4 per 1,000 females are literate in English throughout the State; for Baroda City alone the corresponding figures are 264·5 and 31·3.

There are no statistics of those who can speak, without writing, English.

others. In the village of Chhani, which I visited, lying about six miles from Baroda City, there are two *antyaja* schools, in one of which the master was an *antyaja* himself. There was no indication that the boys were inferior in intelligence to others born in more fortunate classes, and I was told that in mixed schools above the primary standard *antyajas* often show more than average brain.

In the same village of Chhani was a girls' primary school, in which the top class contained a *sudra* girl, mixed with higher caste girls, Jains, daughters of zamindars, money-lenders, etc.

A feature of all the schools which I visited, in Baroda City and elsewhere, is the allocation of part of the curriculum to "games" and drill. The games are of the Indian variety, often among the girls very graceful. The drill was usually excellent. Singing was another regular feature, both for boys and for girls.

Seven is the compulsory age at which children must be sent to school. But there are often younger children to be seen, aged five or six, for whom suitable instruction is provided, from the Kindergarten stage upwards. Kindergarten schools or classes, however, are a separate institution, and do not come under the head of primary schools. In 1925 there were ten of them in the State commanding good financial support from the people, and attracting over 1,000 children of from four to six.

SECONDARY EDUCATION.—According to the figures in the pamphlet *Education in Baroda in 1875-1925*, there are 19 High Schools for boys, 1 for girls, 47 Anglo-Vernacular Schools, and a certain number of other institutions which rank under "English" as opposed to "Vernacular" institutions. These are not all Government-supported.*

Further enquiry shows that 5,534 boys go to Government High Schools and 1,941 to aided High Schools; 3,719 to Government, 752 to aided, and 904 to unaided Anglo-Vernacular Schools. The Maharani High School, Baroda, has 330 girls.

The principal High School for boys is that of Baroda itself, the building of which was completed in 1918 at a cost of R. 280,000. Having now nearly 900 pupils, it has become somewhat straitened for accommodation. Like all the High Schools, it is affiliated to Bombay University, and if at the age of sixteen the boys pass that body's School Leaving Examination, they are entitled to enter Baroda College; otherwise they are superannuated. The headmaster, when I was in Baroda, was a Brahman, and his principal assistant a Parsi. The teaching staff is entirely Indian, but all the boys learn English, and cricket is among the games played. Drill receives much attention.

In the year 1924-5, 149 students and 6 ex-students took the School Leaving Examination, of whom 96 and 4 respectively passed.

The Petlad and Patan High Schools, two of the next largest to Baroda, in the same period sent up

* In his *Report on Public Instruction*, 1923–4, Mr. Dikshit speaks of "15 Government High Schools, 25 Government A.V. Schools, 8 aided A.V. Schools and Classes, 13 unaided A.V. Schools and Classes." There is an accidental omission here of the five aided High Schools of which he speaks later.

66 and 62 candidates, of whom 36 and 15 respectively passed.

An interesting addition to the list of High Schools is that at Mehsana, formerly a State-aided Anglo-Vernacular School. A good building was erected in 1908 at a cost of R. 38,200. Here a staff of 19 teachers instruct nearly 300 pupils, among whom are included 5 girls, there being insufficient demand for a separate girls' High School. The boys vary in age from ten to eighteen or nineteen. Teaching is conducted in English and Gujarati. A small amount of Hindustani is also taught. Among the games cricket is played.

From Mehsana in 1924-5, 14 out of 18 competitors passed the School Leaving Examination, the best percentage of any of the High Schools in the State.

Girls' High School.—There is but one at present, the Maharani G.H.S. in Baroda, under an English Principal, with an Indian staff. Before 1896 there were no facilities for the higher education of girls. English classes opened in that year received small support; but in 1907 an Anglo-Vernacular School for Girls was instituted, from which the High School developed, the present building being erected in 1917. Here 330 girls receive instruction. In his report published in 1925, Mr. Dikshit says that the school now works on a modified form of the Dalton plan.

"The chief modifications have been made in the direction of foreign-language teaching and in science teaching, in which the full number of class lessons are now given. The characteristic feature of the plan is the encouragement given to individual effort, and in the beginning of this, the third, year the results in increased responsibility on the part of the pupils may be clearly seen."

The girls are prepared for the Bombay School Leaving Examination, and also for the Women's College, Poona.

Attention is given to music, drawing, and needlework. This is the case in all the principal girls' schools in the State. Cookery classes are attached to the Baroda, Petlad, Patan, Naosari, and Amreli schools.

The advance that is being made in female education is evident from the large number of highly accomplished and intellectual Indian women to be met with in Baroda. No doubt many of them came from outside the State originally, but even then their influence must be immense. Those whose ideas of Indian womanhood are vaguely connected with the word "zenana" would be considerably astonished during a stay in Baroda, particularly if they could see such a musical and dramatic entertainment as was given by the Ladies' Club in February, 1926. The example of Her Highness the Maharani is, of course, a strong incentive towards a fuller life for women.

Baroda College.—It would be impossible to do justice to the work carried on by Baroda's chief educational institution except by devoting several chapters to it, which is outside the scope of this book. A few remarks must, therefore, suffice.

The actual College building was erected in 1887, after the design of Mr. R. Chisholm, and cost over R. 600,000. The institution, however, was founded five years earlier, with 33 students on the rolls.

20

Its growth was not very rapid at first, for in 1892 the figure had only reached 151, and in 1902 only 206. A big increase was witnessed in 1910, to 315; and another in 1914, to 550. Fluctuations then occurred until 1922, when the number rose from 526 to 625. Another 150 students were added in 1923, and another 69 in 1924, high-water mark to date.

An examination of the rolls (courteously provided for me by the Principal, Mr. S. G. Burrow, B.Sc., London) shows that the present 814 students include 13 women; 754 Hindus, 28 Parsis, 25 Mohammedans, and 7 "others"; 203 from Baroda City, 225 from the rest of the State, 58 from various Indian States, 278 from Bombay Presidency, and 40 from elsewhere in India.

Ten per cent. of the students may be admitted free, and there are half (or smaller) feeships for those who cannot afford to pay full fees. The latter are now R. 50 per term, as against R. 30 in 1922 and R. 40 in 1923. The receipts from fees in 1925 were R. 91,718. The expenditure was R. 1,486,614, so that the net cost of educating each student was R. 183.

The College course is four years long, bifurcating after the first year for the Arts and Science degrees of Bombay University. The comparative popularity of the two schools is shown by the figures of candidates (with the figures of passes in brackets) in 1925: M.A., 5 (3); B.A., 144 (58); Intermediate Arts, 242 (89); B.Sc., 34 (21); Intermediate Science, 116 (55).

The regular languages are English, Gujarati, and Marathi; the extra languages, Sanskrit, Persian, and French. The last named has but few students, owing to the lack of colloquial practice in Baroda.

Under the English Principal is an Indian staff of fifteen Professors, two Assistant-Professors, three Lecturers, two Demonstrators, and two Fellows.

The College has a good library of its own, to which the Government grants R. 1,000 a year, with a special grant of R. 500 for scientific books. An initial grant of R. 2,000 for the purchase of historical literature has also been sanctioned. The Students' Union supports a reading-room and a debating society, and provides funds for cricket, lawn tennis, football, hockey, badminton, and table tennis. Physical training is greatly encouraged, and the College possesses some remarkably fine athletes, judged by both Indian and Western standards.

The list of those who have graduated at Baroda College includes a great number of names distinguished in India—officials (some in British service), judges, magistrates, lawyers, solicitors, teachers, authors (historians, dramatists, novelists, poets), journalists, bankers, business men, chemists, etc. Many have been lost to Baroda, but the College is, as we have seen, open not only to the State, but to all Indians who choose to avail themselves of its opportunities.

As has been mentioned in Chapter XVIII., a Science Institute is now in the course of erection in the grounds of Baroda College; and it is proposed to add to the Faculties of Arts and Science, for which the College is already equipped, the Faculty of Law. Whether by this expansion, coming on the top of the past educational advances of Baroda, is foreshadowed the foundation of "the larger structure of a University for Baroda, or, for the matter of that, for the whole of Gujarat," as Sir Manubhai Mehta hinted before Lord Reading in January, 1927, remains to be seen.

TRAINING COLLEGES.—Baroda possesses two of these, one for men and the other for women. The first definite school for training male teachers was started in 1885, but closed thirteen years later, there being small demand for trained teachers for the limited number of schools then existing. In 1905 it was reopened with the status of a college, and placed under the general supervision of the Principal of the Kalabhavan. The coming of compulsory education led to a great demand for trained primary teachers, and in 1908 the Training College was separated from the Kalabhavan, put directly under the Education Department, and reorganised. Its curriculum was altered from two to three years, its staff was enlarged, accommodation was made for 250 students each year, and Mr. N. K. Dikshit, the present Commissioner of Education, who had had two years' training in pedagogy in England, was made Principal. By the end of the official year of 1911-2 there were 375 students, of whom 202 were first-year. The next step was the opening of a new building in the Kareli Bag, north-west of Baroda City.

About the same time an additional Training College was started, which in 1915 was shifted to Patan, while in 1918-9 first-year training classes were opened at Naosari and Amreli. All these three institutions were closed four years later through the need of retrenchment in educational expenditure, and the number of admissions to the original Training College was reduced. In 1925 there were 110 first-year, 44 second-year, and 34 third-year students. For these were scholarships of R. 9 for each first-year student, and twenty scholarships of R. 10 for the second-year.

An interesting feature, when I visited the Training College, was the presence of ten *antyaja* students, for whom special provision is made, though they mix with the others on terms of equality. Naturally these students, when they complete their training, are of special value as masters in the *antyaja* schools.

Another interesting feature was the two "practising schools"* attached to the Training College, in which the students get experience in the art of teaching children. In addition, juvenile classes from other schools pay periodical visits to the College to afford the students further practice.

In connection with the Training College is a hostel, housing nearly 150 boarders. The students have their Union, with a reading-room and debating society, and a Social Service League.

The total cost of the Training College for men is well over R. 46,000, in spite of the retrenchment which it was found necessary to effect.

To the Training College for Women some notice has been given in Chapter XX. Sanction has been given for the subsidising of 150 women training as teachers; but, as has been said, the number

* Practising School No. 1 is the best Gujarati school in the State. It has over 300 pupils, for whom free mid-day meals are provided by private subscription.

in training at the College is under 70. All these are Hindus, and 40 of them are widows, only 6 being unmarried women. It is evident, therefore, that the difficulty of attracting women to the teaching profession in Baroda is great. In the whole State there are at present only 340 trained women teachers.

The College is well housed, facing the Sursagar Tank, and has a good hostel attached to it, where some of the girls from the Maharani High School lodge, in addition to some 40 of the College students.

THE KALABHAVAN.—The origin of this institution has been described in Chapter XX. A number of visits paid to it in the winter of 1925-6 sufficed to show me that the work done under Mr. C. H. Vora, who has been Principal since the end of 1908, has not been in vain. The Kalabhavan has had its vicissitudes, and as a School of Art it has perhaps accomplished little, being inferior in painting of late years to the classes at Baroda High School, where painting is an extra. As a technical institute, however, it can claim successes, and when the workshops are reconstructed, should be able to claim more. Good workshops are, indeed, very important. For the safe housing of expensive machinery they are essential. The Kalabhavan building is a fine one, designed by Mr. A. H. Coyle; but it has never had workshops worthy of it.

The staff includes five foreign-trained teachers, three of whom, including the Principal, have been to Europe, two to America. The students in 1925 numbered 404 (207 from Baroda State), a drop of no less than 44 from the previous year's figure.

Of these, 124 were studying mechanical engineering, 81 civil engineering, 72 art, 59 textile manufacturing, 46 dyeing, bleaching, and calico-printing, and 22 commerce. A Government grant of R. 1,200 a year is made to provide scholarships for the first two boys in each class, and there are a number of other small scholarships which they may hold, including nine given by other States than Baroda for their own subjects studying at the Kalabhavan.

The age of admission is 16, except for the mechanical engineering course, where it is 17. The courses of instruction are either diploma (varying from 3 to 4 years), certificate (2 years), or apprentice. The diploma courses and the certificate course in commerce are conducted in English, the other courses in Gujarati. The Kalabhavan draws upon two distinct fields for its pupils. The higher-class students are engaged on work which, by tradition, is entirely unfamiliar to them. The apprentice class, on the other hand, come of artisan stock, and are enabled at the Kalabhavan to get instruction which is denied to them outside, owing to the jealous father-to-son transmission of trade secrets.

The annual tuition fees vary from R. 25 to R. 50, the latter being the charge in the School of Mechanical Engineering. From the fees and the profits of the workshops (for, in accordance with the advice given in Professor Hay's report in 1921, a sales section was organised) the Kalabhavan in 1925 had an income of R. 12,573. Against this, its expenditure was R. 114,331.

It would not be to much purpose to go into the

matter of examination results, though these are by no means unsatisfactory, and the latest achievement by the Kalabhavan was its recognition by the City and Guilds of London Institute as a centre for holding their technological examinations. Most of the work done by the Kalabhavan bears fruit after the student has left. For instance, there is at Petlad a Turkey-red dyeing industry set up by a former student. Much may be expected from the soap industry in the future. Baroda is rich in the necessary oils and fats. Ordinary soap has been manufactured for some time past, and plant for toilet soap manufacture has now been imported from Germany. What the State very properly aims at is the establishment of industries on a commercial footing as the result of the training which it gives.

THE BACKWARD CLASSES.—In a country like Baroda a very serious problem is that of the education of those of its people who may be roughly classed together as "backward." They vary widely in race and social characteristics. The main divisions, according to the usual classification, are the *antyajas*, the Moslems, and the forest tribes. Out of the total Baroda population of 2,126,522 in the 1921 Census, 176,924 were returned as *antyajas*, 162,328 as Moslems, and 258,447 as forest tribes (163,077 Animist by religion, 95,370 Hindus).

The *antyajas*, the Hindu "depressed classes," or "Untouchables," have long been objects of Maharaja Sayajirao's particular solicitude, as was shown in Chapter XX. Schools were opened for them as early as 1883, and the latest figures show

219 schools, of which 5 are exclusively for girls. Nearly 14,000 *antyaja* children, or about 8 per cent. of their whole number in the State, are in receipt of primary education, about one-third of them being in the ordinary Gujarati schools, where there is provision for small special scholarships for them. They have ten scholarships also in the secondary schools, and liberal treatment, as has been stated, at the Training College for Men. In 1925 there were four *antyaja* hostels at Baroda, Patan, Naosari, and Amreli, with an aggregate of 133 boarders, for whom all was provided free; and on December 11th of that year a second hostel was opened by the Maharaja in the Kareli Bag, Baroda, on the lines of the hostel already existing there.

It is scarcely just to class the Moslems with the backward classes. In his Census Report for 1921 Mr. S. V. Mukerjea says: "The Musalman, unlike his *confrère* in British India, is in this State better off educationally than his Hindu brother, and in this respect in both the sexes is this superiority seen. In the age period fifteen to twenty the Hindu has only 354 literate males and 100 literate females to the Musalman's 424 and 109 (per 1,000). There is no doubt that the Musalman takes greater advantage of the local educational machinery, at least in the primary stages of vernacular instruction, than the Hindu does."

The contrast here is, of course, between the comparatively small body of Moslems in Baroda and the great Hindu majority, including the "Untouchables," the Hinduised forest tribes, the Anjanas of Kadi (who have only 14 per cent. male literates), etc. When it comes to a question, however, of the utilisation of facilities for higher education, the Mohammedans themselves admit that their progess in Baroda is slow. They are inclined to attribute this in part to a lack of Government sympathy with them and a disproportionately small share in the prizes of education; but many of them confess that the general demand among their co-religionists for advanced instruction is very small, among the women almost non-existent.

The first two Government schools for Mohammedans, with the teaching conducted in Urdu, were opened in Amreli in 1892-3. There are now 124 Urdu Schools, 98 for boys and 26 for girls, the pupils numbering about 6,600 and 1,700 respectively. Some 8,300 Mohammedan children attended the Gujarati schools in 1925, and the total of Mohammedan children receiving education in the State is given as 16,693.

Private effort meets some of the small demand for further education after Moslem ideas, as at the Madresa-i-Anwarul-Ulum, in Baroda City, which is contemporaneous with the present reign; but this has no Government aid.

The forest tribes, the *Kaliparaj*, are the really backward section of the Baroda population. Over 163,000 of them still remain Animists, who, as the 1921 Census Report says, "show the most dismal results in education in spite of all that has been done for them." Their literacy rate is 2 per cent. As early as 1885 a *Kaliparaj* or, as it is generally called, *Dhanka* boarding-house for boys was opened at Songadh, Naosari, where now 100 pupils receive education, clothing, lodging, and board. Four other boarding-houses for these boys have been opened in Naosari, and one for girls at Songadh, bringing the total of *Kaliparaj* children thus being educated to about 300 boys and 50 girls.* To two of the boys' schools, Songadh and Vyara, small model farms are attached, at which practical agriculture is taught, a most useful training for members of primitive tribes capable of little else that is of service to the State. The fact, however, that a few of the pupils, both boys and girls, have been able, after leaving their boarding-houses, to gain admission to the Training Colleges for Men and for Women shows that occasionally they can assimilate a higher education.

Other backward people, such as the Vaghers of Okhamandal, the Kolis, and the Bhils, have also received educational facilities, either by the opening of boarding-houses or by the institution of special scholarships in the Government schools. Some of the Vagher boys at Dwarka, where a boarding-house was started for them in 1920, are making good progress, which confirms the impression of various officers during the British control of Okhamandal that the Vaghers are not as wild as they were painted.

* * * * *

* The 1923–4 *Administration Report* says: "The progress of the *Dhanka* students having been so far satisfactory and the change in their habits and civilisation being remarkable, it was thought advisable to keep them no longer aloof from students of higher communities; so the Vernacular Boys' Schools at Vyara and Mahura and the Girls' School at Songadh were combined with the (*Dhanka*) Boarding Schools. Similar arrangement was made in the two boarding-houses recently opened."

No discussion of education in Baroda would be complete which did not mention the Library Movement and the Boy Scouts Organisation. To deal with them—and especially with the former—adequately is out of the question. I must content myself, therefore, with a few remarks on each.

THE LIBRARY MOVEMENT.*—A Library Department was definitely established in Baroda in 1910. Previous to that, however, as early as 1906, after his first visit to the United States, Maharaja Sayajirao had provided for the setting up of circulating libraries in various parts of his realm, with reading-rooms attached. On his eighth foreign trip, when he again visited the States, he engaged the services of an expert, Mr. W. A. Borden, who spent three years organising the Baroda Library Department, including the Central Library, district libraries and reading-rooms, travelling libraries, and a library class. American system marks the work of the department to this day, and it is not a little surprising to find this in Western India.

His Highness himself furnished the nucleus of the Central Library when he handed over to it his own private library of some 20,000 volumes, down to 1910 kept in a hall at Laxmi Vilas. With the aid of the State this number has now grown to

* Early in 1926 a new edition of the *Baroda Library Handbook* was brought out by Mr. N. M. Dutt, Curator of State Libraries, of whom it is not too much to say that he has made the Central Library of Baroda known to librarians all over the world. I have availed myself freely of his account of the Library Movement.

over 100,000,* exclusive of more than 18,000 books which are issued through the Travelling Library Section to areas which have no libraries, or do not contain books asked for by particular readers. In round figures there are 51,000 English, 19,000 Gujarati, and 14,000 Marathi books, the rest being in various vernaculars, or belonging to the Sanskrit Library Section mentioned below.

The Central Library proper has a Lending Section, which in 1925 issued over 83,000 volumes to readers in the city; a Reference Section, which includes valuable works that cannot be lent out and a little museum of book curiosities; a Reading-room for newspapers and periodicals; and Ladies' and Children's Libraries, which combined lent over 10,000 volumes in 1925. All these sections are housed in the Old Sarkarwada, or Palace, except the Reading-room and the Ladies' Library, which are in buildings facing this.

The Sanskrit Library, housed near the Record Office, and opposite the Kothi or Secretariat, has nearly 6,000 printed books and over 13,000 manuscripts, some of them of great value, which make the collection one of the foremost in India. From here is published, under the editorship of that eminent young scholar Dr. Benoytosh Bhattacharyya, who is Oriental Librarian, the *Gaekwad's Oriental Series*, which was designed by Maharaja

* Mention must not be omitted of the recent enrichment of the library by the large collection of books belonging to His Highness's brother, Shrimant Sampatrao Gaekwar, who as early as 1891 made them into a free Public Library, under the name of the "Shri Sayaji Library." This collection was begun when its gatherer was at Oxford University, and contains over 8,000 English books of very wide range.

Sayajirao to preserve and render accessible to scholars of Sanskrit (and some other languages) works otherwise doomed to ultimate destruction. The series includes one volume devoted to a catalogue of Vedic MSS.

The essence of the Library Movement is to provide literature free to the inhabitants of Baroda, and where the City is concerned this plan is carried out. In the Country Department the system is one of State aid. Though readers have access to books free, their provision calls for the co-operation of the District Boards and the public with the Government. That an advance in reading is being made in the districts is shown by these figures for 1911-2 (after the Library Department opened) and for 1924-5:

	Libraries.		*Reading Rooms.*	*Readers.*
1911-2	Town, 9	Village, 265	60	6,200
1924-5	,, 43	,, 618	87	47,506*

The budget of the Library Department in 1925-6 was R. 111,500, as compared with an expenditure of R. 76,500 in 1923-4 and R. 90,000 in 1924-5.

If any adverse comment is to be made on the progress of the Library Movement in Baroda, it is that the Central Library, with its really fine collection of books, has an entirely inadequate home. The old Sarkarwada is historically interesting,

* This figure does not include 4,555 readers who had recourse to the Travelling Libraries.

but is unsuited for the accommodation of books, allows them to deteriorate through climatic conditions, and is exposed to the risk of fire. His Highness has long had the idea of a worthier building. Early in 1917 he wrote to his Chief Engineer, Mr. A. H. Coyle, to invite competitive designs, and named a site on the edge of the Sursagar Tank. At the time of the Golden Jubilee it was fully expected that the scheme would be put on foot; but the decision was taken to erect rather a Science Institute, of which, as described in Chapter XVIII., the foundation-stone was laid by Lord Reading in January, 1926.

THE BOY SCOUTS ORGANISATION.—This is, indeed, a remarkable development, which a visitor to an Indian State could scarcely be prepared to find. At almost every outdoor public ceremony in Baroda the Boy Scouts have a part to play. In the maintenance of order during great popular gatherings, such as the prize-giving at the Hind Vijaya Gymkhana in December 26th, 1925, they might truly be said to have done far more than the police. On all the Maharaja's district tours, even in distant Okhamandal, they are much in evidence. The serious spirit in which they take their work is manifest.

The movement was sanctioned in 1918, and began its activities in January, 1919. The number of boys enrolled was 820 in 1922-3, 1,125 in 1923-4, and has now reached nearly 2,000. The first troop, selected from the schoolboys in Baroda City, was reviewed by the Maharaja in the grounds of the Laxmi Vilas Palace, was presented by him with troop standards, and had conferred on it the title of "H.H. the Maharaja Gaekwar's Own Boy Scouts." Under this title now are included numerous troops in Baroda City and district, among which must be mentioned a special troop for *antyaja* boys and another for boys at the reformatory, all of whom are enrolled, and who are allowed once or twice a year to take part in a general rally there.

In 1920 the movement was extended to Naosari, where it now flourishes. The *antyajas* and the Mohammedans have their own troops. Kadi and Amreli next came under the influence, and Okhamandal has followed suit. On the occasion of the Maharaja's visit to Dwarka and Adatara in February, 1926, a troop of Vagher Boy Scouts was especially noticeable for its fine physique (as might be expected from that well-built tribe) and its excellent drill.

The Scouts organisation is too well known for it to be necessary here to go into details as to the training of the Scouts of Baroda, which is modelled on the original lines, intended above all to produce good citizens—an object which from the first induced Maharaja Sayajirao to take a keen interest in the movement. Certain modifications have been introduced, with the consent of the heads of the parent organisation. In Baroda the difficulty at the start of the movement was that not only had a general prejudice against its novelty to be overcome, but also parents of *swarajist* sympathies had to be convinced that their sons were not being imbued with contrary ideas if they became Scouts. If it were incompatible to wear a "Gandhi cap" and to be a Boy Scout, progress would be checked.

THE MAHARAJA INSPECTING THE BOY SCOUTS.

306]

But a relaxation of some rules had enabled Boy Scouting to grow rapidly into popular favour in Baroda.*

In comparison with the Boy Scouts, the Girl Guides Movement is in its infancy in Baroda; but the Women's Training College has taken up the idea, and slow progress is being made, which will doubtless become more rapid in due course. The uniform is already to be seen in some of the girls' schools in the city.

* "The public," says Mr. R. K. Nulkar, Scout Commissioner, Baroda, in a review of the organisation down to the end of 1924, "are making the movement their own by forming Scout Associations in almost every locality. . . . In a few years more it is confidently expected that . . . the public at large will take full charge of the local work and supply all other scout needs, the State providing the central guidance only."

INDEX

Aberdeen, Lord and Lady, 118
Adatara, 183-5, 231-3
Ajwa, 73
Albert Victor of Wales, Prince (Duke of Clarence), 86-7, 252
Alexandra, Queen, 172
Amreli, 67, 159, 185, 229, 235, *etc.*
Anandrao (Gaekwar), Maharaja, 81
Angre, Jaisinghrao, 96, 98

Ballantine, Serjeant, 19
Bapat, V. S., 95
Baroda City, 52-3, 73, 78, 236-7, 258, *etc.*
Baroda District, 67, 224, 226, *etc.*
Barr, J. T., 7, 12
Bhattacharyya, Benoytosh, 303
Birdwood, General Sir George, 154 *n.*
Birdwood, H. M., 31
Birkenhead, Lord, 168
Borden, W. A., 302
Burrow, S. G., 292

Chelmsford, Lord, 150, 152, 154, 157
Chimnabai I., Maharani, 40, 41, 43-4, 75, 76
Chimnabai II., Maharani, 64, 75-6, 83, 88, 98 *n.*, 104-6, 112, 118, 129, 130, 134, 143, 144, 145, 146, 148, 153, 156, 157-8, 163, 166, 176, 180, 209, 291
Connaught, Duke of, 106, 111
Cooch Behar, Jitendra, Maharaj Kumar of, 72, 144-5
Cooch Behar, Maharani of, *see* Indira Raja
Coyle, A. H., 296, 305
Cross, Lord, 84-5
Curzon, Lord, 103, 105-6, 110 *n.*, 111, 113-4, 281-4

Dabhoi, 172-3, 222
Damnaskar, R. V., 110
Davidson, Colonel C., 7
Deshpande, K. G., 138-9
Devine, General, 18, 20
Dhairyashilrao, Prince, 129, 166, 185
Dikshit, N. K., 286, 289 *n.*, 290, 294
Dufferin, Lady, 77-8
Dufferin, Lord, 77-9, 82, 85
Dutt, N. M., 302
Dutt, R. C., 115-6
Dwarka, 184-5, 229-30, 234, 306

Edward VII., King, 28-31, 79, 109, 118
Elgin, Lord, 103
Ellerman, Sir John, 233 *n.*
Elliot, F. A. H., 7-8, 31-2, 35, 37, 38, 44, 46, 57, 67, 80, 81, 82, 86, 92, 95, 97-8, 100, 108, 212, 260-1

Fatesinghrao, Prince, 75, 102, 107-8, 122, 226
Fatesinghrao (Gaekwar), Regent, 22
Fergusson, Sir James, 50-1
Fraser, Lovat, 150 *n.*
French, T. H., 102, 107, 108

Gaekwar family, the, 1-5, 22
Gaekwar, Anandrao, 2, 23, 24 *n.*, 152-3
- Dadasaheb, 5, 28
- Damaji (I.), 22
- Damajirao (II.), 1-2
- Ganpatrao, 22, 24
- Ganpatrao Trimbakrao, 60
- Ganpatrao Vithalrao, Shrimant, 84
- Jhingoji, 22
- Kashirao, 1-5, 23, 35
- Khanderao, 22, 24
- Murarrao, 22, 24
- Okhajirao, 3-4
- Prataprao, 1-2
- Sadashivrao, 22, 24

Gaekwar, Sakharam, 3
Sampatrao, Shrimant, 2, 28, 67, 83, 84, 94, 108, 118, 153, 303 *n.*
Gaekwar, *see also under* Anandrao, Fatesingrao, Ganpatrao, Khanderao, Malharrao, Sayajirao II.
Gandhi, "Mahatma," 215 *n.*
Ganpatrao (Gaekwar), Maharaja, 7, 90 *n.*, 222
George V., King, 130, 132, 146, 157, 168
Ghatge family, the, 76
Ghose, Arabindo, 140
Gokhale, G. K., 132
Gupta, B. L., 116, 144
Gupta, Sir K. G., 135

Hall, Dr. Cuthbert, 118
Hardie, Keir, 136
Hardinge, Lord (Viceroy of India), 131, 132-3
Hardinge, Viscount, 136
Hay, Professor Alfred, 204, 297
Hyderabad, Nizam of, 130, 131, 133

Indira Raja, Maharani of Cooch Behar, 72, 126, 129, 143, 144-5, 176
Indore, Maharajas of, 25, 34 *n.*, 145
Indumati, Princess, 153
Iyangar, S. R., 96, 105

Jagannath, Laxman, 83
Jaisinhrao, Prince, 85, 102, 107, 108, 111, 129, 143, 144, 156, 157-8, 163
Jamnabai, Maharani, 11-14, 19, 22-5, 27, 28, 30, 33, 36, 39, 99
Jamnagar, Jam Saheb of, 184, 231
Jayajirao, 17, 20, 21, 22

Kadi, 66-7, 174-5, 222, 228, *etc.*
Kapurthala, Maharaja of, 105, 150
Kashmir, Maharaja of, 148
Kathiawar, 183, 229 *ff.*, *etc.*
Kavlana, 1-3, 185
Khanderao (Gaekwar), Maharaja, 2, 3-4, 7, 12, 63, 72, 81, 159, 222, 223
Khanvelkar, Nana, 15, 18
Kolhapur, Maharaja of, 151 *n.*, 153
Kollengode, Maharaja of, 148

Lamington, Lord, 137, 138
Lansdowne, Lord, 88
Laxmibai, Maharani, 17, 21
Laxmi Vilas Palace, 43, *etc.*
Locke, W. W., 44
Lynam, C. C., 107
Lytton, Lord, 33, 110

Madhavrao, Sir T., 23, 30-1, 37, 39-42, 44-5, 46-7, 51, 52 *ff.*, 60, 66-7, 72, 188, 197, 223, 233, 260, 263, 273
Mahalsabai, Maharani, 17, 20, 21
Makarpura, 9, 63, 180
Malharrao (Gaekwar), Maharaja, 4, 11 *ff.*, 27 *n.*, 29 *n.*, 52, 54, 81, 197, 198, 223, 260
Manibhai Jasbhai, 92, 95, 96, 97 *n.*, 98, 199
Martelli, Colonel N. C., 90, 97
Mary, Queen, 130, 137, 146, 157
Meade, Colonel M. J., 112-3, 122, 283
Meade, Colonel (afterwards Sir) Richard, 14, 18, 20-1, 24-5, 27-8, 51, 122
Mehsana, 224, 226-8, *etc.*
Mehta, Sir Manubhai, 65, 109, 149, 183, 187, 194, 218, 254-5, 294
Melville, P. S., 19, 30, 31, 34, 35, 37, 43, 44, 51, 52, 54, 197
Middleton, Sir Thomas, 243
Minto, Lord, 120 *n.*, 123, 124-5, 127, 274
Mitra, S. M., 130
Montagu, E. S., 150, 153 *n.*
Morley, John (afterwards Lord), 119, 121, 129
Mukerjea, S. V., 208, 210 *n.*, 255, 287 *n.*, 299
Mysore, Maharaja of, 161, 230 *n.*, 283

Nabha, Maharaja of, 150
Nanavati, M. B., 238 *n.*, 239, 240
Naoroji, Dadabhai, 16
Naosari, 2, 67, 185, 229, 267 *ff.*, *etc.*
Nawanagar, *see* Jamnagar
Nevins, Dr. J. E., 88 *n.*, 96, 102
Northbrook, Lord, 15, 29, 97 *n.*, 106, 135
Nulkar, R. K., 307 *n.*

Okha, Port, *see* Adatara
Okhamandal, 159-61, 183-5, 229 *ff.*
Outram, Colonel J., 90 *n.*

Pandit, K. R., 26
Pant, Damodar, 18, 21
Patel, J. M. F., 63
Pelly, Colonel Sir Lewis, 16-8, 20
Phayre, Colonel Robert, 14, 16-8
Pratapsinghrao, Prince, 122, 172
Puleston, Sir John, 283
Purohit, D. L., 139-40

Randle, C. E., 122
Reading, Lady, 180-2
Reading, Lord, 168, 180 *ff.*, 235, 294, 305
Reay, Lord, 77, 86, 88, 97, 106, 153, 278
Rice, Stanley, 192
Ripon, Lord, 44, 71

Samarth, V. M., 66, 96, 241
Sane, C. V., 243
Sardesai, G. S., 36
Savantwadi, Raja of, 40, 99
Savantwadi, Raje Saheb of, 99
Sayajirao (Gaekwar) II., Maharaja, 6-7, 11, 81, 90 *n.*
Sayajirao III., Maharaja of Baroda (Golpalrao Gaekwar): birth, 1; family, 1; little early history, 2; his native village, 3, 185; taken to Baroda, 5; elevated to throne, 5, 25; his predecessors in Baroda, 6 *ff.*; adopted by Maharani Jamnabai, 24; his installation, 25; education begins, 26; meets Prince of Wales (Edward VII.), 28-9; receives him in Baroda, 30-1; has English tutor, 32; first Indian tour, 33; new honours, 33; his intensive schooling, 35-8; first marriage, 39-43; early termination of his minority, 44; his finishing education, 45-8; invested with full powers, 50; his lack of sympathetic advice, 57; attitude towards opposition, 58; harassed by petty details, 59-60; love of system, 60-2; too little relaxation, 62; but regular in exercise, 62-3; patron of athletics, 64-5; his visitation of his kingdom, 66 *ff.*; organisation of district tours, 68; dislike of elaborate ceremony, 70; visits Calcutta, 71; his care for Baroda's water-supply, 72-4; loses his first wife, 75; his second marriage, 75-6; purdah abandoned, 76, 145; his craving for family life, 77; visited by Lord Dufferin, 77-9; receives G.C.S.I., 80; his early progressive measures, 80; the land question, 80-1, 260-3; trip to Ceylon, 82; first foreign tour, 83-5; at Windsor Castle, 85; second foreign tour, 85; receives Prince Albert Victor of Wales, 86-7; third foreign tour, 87; fourth and fifth, 88; his method of keeping in touch with Baroda, 89; his views on travel, 91; on new and old ideals, 92; troubles in Baroda, 94; loses Elliot's services, 95-8; his grievance against the Residency, 97; two bereavements, 99; visits Egypt, 99; plague, rebellion, and famine, 100-1; his children's education, 102, 107-8; first impression of Lord Curzon, 103; sixth European tour, 104; resents the Curzon Circular, 105-6; sorrow over Queen Victoria's death, 107; views on the Coronation Durbar, 109-11; complaints on the treatment of Princes, 13, Appendix I.; views on Imperial Service, 113-4; supports the Council of Princes, 114, 150-2; continues his reforms, 115; his views on caste, 117, 214 *ff.*; on female emancipation, 117, 208; seventh European tour, 118; visits America, 118-9; his Silver Jubilee, 120-1; establishes Bank of Baroda, 122; loses his eldest son, 122; receives Lord Minto, 124-5; first signs of storm, 127-8; eighth European tour, 128-9; ninth, 129; at King George's Coronation, 130; the Delhi Durbar (1911), 130 *ff.*; accusations of disloyalty, 133-4; the

Deshpande and Purohit cases, 138-40; effect of the charges, 141; some domestic upsets, 143; his definition of his policy, 144; tenth tour, 144; founds the Picture Gallery, 145; eleventh tour, 145; surprised by the war, 146; his war gifts, 147; visits Kashmir, 148; receives G.C.I.E., 152; views on the war, 153-4; twelfth tour, 156-8; thirteenth, 162; receives Prince of Wales in Baroda, 162-3; fourteenth tour, 163; fifteenth, 165-9; his Golden Jubilee, 170 *ff.*; founds the Kirti Mandir, 176; receives Lord Reading, 180-3; opens Port Okha, 184, 232-3; starts on sixteenth tour, 187; his reforming aspirations, 188 *ff.*; not leaving the helm yet, 196; as educationalist, 197 *ff.*; makes education free and compulsory, 201; his ends in education, 203-4; his religious attitude, 211-3; his sympathy with the "Untouchables," 215-8; views on marriage laws, 219-21; as railway builder, 222 *ff.*; his aspirations in Kathiawar, 235; his work for agricultural and industrial development, 239 *ff.*; views on constitutionalism, 252 *ff.*; founds Legislative Council, 253; his restoration of community life, 257; interest in the backward tribes, 271; his judicial reforms, 273 *ff.*; his promotion of the Library Movement, 302

Sayaji Sarovar, 73

Sayaji Vihar, 179-80

Seddon, C. N., 138, 144, 162

Shahabuddin, Kazi, 46, 66, 83, 94, 95

Shakespeare, Sir Richmond, 11

Shantyanand, Shankaracharya, 185, 230

Shinde, Bhau, 13

Shivajirao, Prince, 63 *n.*, 102, 107, 108, 126, 129, 143, 148-9, 156-7

Spielmann, M. H., 137, 140

Tarabai, Princess, 12, 13, 40, 41, 99

Temple, Sir Richard, 34, 43

Thakersey, Sir Vithaldas, 231

Travancore, Maharaja of, 148

Tyabji, Mrs., 209

Victoria, Queen, 33, 79, 80 *n.*, 85, 99, 106-7

Vora, C. H., 296

Wales, Prince of, 157, 162-3

Walker, Colonel C. A., 158-9

Watson, Sir John, 94, 96, 106, 148 *n.*, 283

Willingdon, Lord, 152

Wilson, Sir Leslie, 171

Windham, Colonel C. J., 166

Wyllie, Sir Curzon, 123